THE HIGH FIRMAMENT

THE
HIGH FIRMAMENT

A Survey of Astronomy
in English Literature

A. J. MEADOWS

LEICESTER UNIVERSITY PRESS
1969

First published in 1969 by
Leicester University Press

© A. J. Meadows 1969

Distributed in North America
by Humanities Press Inc, New York

Set in Monotype Baskerville
Printed in Great Britain
by Spottiswoode, Ballantyne & Co Ltd

SBN 7185 1082 8

"When I sitting heard the astronomer where he lectured with
much applause in the lecture-room,
How soon unaccountable I became tired and sick"

WALT WHITMAN

Contents

Foreword

THERE are, perhaps, two main reasons for studying how scientific trends are reflected in non-scientific literature. In the first place, the scientific outlook has changed so vastly over the past few centuries that unless a special analysis is made many literary references to science become incomprehensible to a modern reader. On the other hand, the world view of even educated non-scientists has sometimes differed appreciably from that of their scientific contemporaries. As a result, a study of non-scientific literature can be of value in the history of science since it provides an insight into the diffusion of scientific ideas throughout society as a whole. It is hoped that this book may be of some use from both these points of view.

Astronomy, which forms the subject matter of the present survey, was the first of the sciences to attain a recognizably modern form. Partly as a result, it was held in greater public esteem than any other branch of science until the nineteenth century. Literary references to astronomy are therefore very numerous. As a further consequence, important astronomical concepts can sometimes be found appearing in quite unrelated areas, e.g. Newtonian concepts in eighteenth-century political thought. Major examples of such transference of concepts will be mentioned, but not examined in detail. Astronomical ideas have sometimes also lingered on as literary devices long after they have lost their original scientific value, e.g. the music of the spheres. Petrifications of this sort will, for the most part, be ignored.

The period covered by this book extends from roughly 1400 to 1900, although both terminal dates are rather hazy. Within these limits the discussion is restricted to literature produced in the British Isles—American literature has been excluded. For further reading in the broader field of science and literature, reference may be made to a very useful annotated bibliography by Marjorie Nicolson in *American Journal of Physics*, Vol. 33, p. 175 (1965). Two important books which do not appear in this list are: C. S. Lewis, *The Discarded Image* (1964), dealing with the medieval period, and W. P. Jones, *The Rhetoric of Science* (1966), dealing with the eighteenth century.

I am indebted to Dr G. S. Rosseau for reading Chapter VI and suggesting some improvements. I am also indebted to Macmillan & Co. Ltd. for permission to quote from *Tennyson as a Student and Poet of Nature* by Sir Norman and W. L. Lockyer.

Leicester, May 1968   A. J. MEADOWS

THE WORLD SYSTEMS

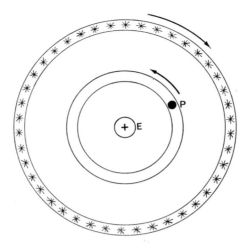

Aristotelian/Medieval system

Arrows represent motion in the indicated direction.
E—the Earth; P—a planet; ✳—a star
+— the centre of the Universe..

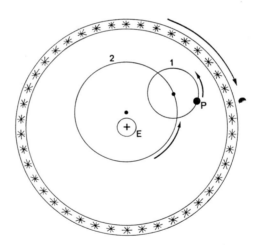

Ptolemaic system

1—epicycle, moving on 2— an eccentric deferent
(i.e. deferent whose centre is displaced from
the centre of the Earth).

The World Systems

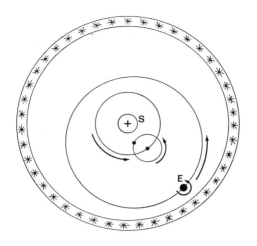

Copernican system

S — the Sun

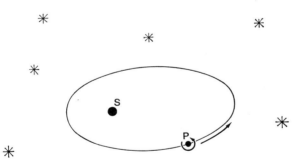

Newtonian system

The World Systems

CHAPTER I

The Medieval Universe

THE major aim of contemporary science is to reduce the apparent diversity of the universe to a unity. Yet in this respect, our present world picture lags far behind that of our predecessors five hundred years ago. It is, indeed, a central feature of the medieval universe, and its great intellectual attraction, that it bound together apparently unrelated phenomena. It was not internal tensions—although these did exist—that eventually swept away the old system of thought, but the fact that its fundamental method of approach came to be denied. Our modern concept of the universe is based ultimately on observation; the medieval picture appealed rather to authority. Thus it is impossible to read far even in, say, Chaucer, without noting the appeal, either implicit or explicit, to some earlier author. This is true of all fields of medieval thought—astronomy as much as any other. In the final analysis, the medieval world picture depended mainly on the views of the earlier, classical writers.

Medieval is a flexible term. It will be used here as a shorthand expression for that period of time during which astronomical ideas were based on a synthesis of classical authorities, and more particularly on the writings of Aristotle. The period, so defined has no determinate close. Some astronomers abandoned the medieval position in the sixteenth century, but it remained strongly entrenched amongst educated laymen until well into the seventeenth. Thus it was still used by Milton as the basis for his cosmology in *Paradise Lost*.

Not all parts of the medieval synthesis fell into disuse at the same time, but most of the astronomical ideas disappeared together: in general, the medieval world picture was so closely integrated that loss of even a single part cast doubt on a large proportion of the remainder.

It is also impossible to distinguish a precise beginning for this period. In the twelfth century, texts of various Aristotelian writings came into the hands of Christian scholars in Europe. They came from two main sources. The first, and more important, was via Arabic translations from the Greek. These had been circulating in Moslem countries for some time, and began to diffuse into Europe as parts of Spain were reconquered. The other source was in Italy; particularly Sicily, where commerce with Byzantium still continued. Here copies in the original Greek were circulating. In both cases, the first necessity was for translation into Latin, the vernacular language of the scholars. Then followed a period of assimilation during which the new, and strange, Aristotelian methods, particularly in logic, were gradually absorbed. During this period there were marked fluctuations in the fortunes of Aristotelian scholarship. His works were at times banned by the Church. Finally, there was a period of reconciliation, during which the new ideas were brought within the body of Christian dogma. This was dominated by the work of Albertus Magnus and his follower, Thomas Aquinas. Subsequently—by the end of the thirteenth century— the Aristotelian world picture quickly established itself in western Europe. Prior to this, the major classical authority in western Europe had been Plato, some of whose ideas (often highly distorted) had long been available in various Latin compendia.

The basic features of this quasi-Aristotelian universe changed only slowly between the end of the thirteenth and the middle of the sixteenth centuries. There was a considerable development in the science of mechanics, but this only gradually influenced the contemporary astronomy. More important to astronomy during this period was the Platonic influence, which, although attenuated, still continued from earlier times. There was, of course, no clear-cut division between Platonic philosophers on the one hand and Aristotelian philosophers on the other: philosophical writings of the thirteenth, and later centuries often mingle ideas from both. In astronomical thought, however, there was a fairly distinctive criterion: one, indeed which still remains with us. The Aristotelian approach emphasized the physics of the universe—why something occurred— and was less interested in mathematical formulation; the

Platonic approach emphasized mathematical description—how something occurred—and was less concerned with a consistent physical picture. It is obvious enough to us now that the advance of astronomy, and of science in general, depended on solving the simplest problems first. Such were the problems of the science of mechanics and, in astronomy, of celestial motions. The study of the nature of bodies, as distinct from their motions, is highly complicated, and can hardly be said to have developed into a science until the latter half of the eighteenth century. For this reason, it tended to be the followers of the Platonic approach who produced the major advances in astronomy until the time of Newton. The 'Aristotelian' emphasis was not important until the nineteenth century. As would be expected, an Aristotelian was more likely to emphasize the mechanistic or, at least, concrete view of nature, whereas the Platonic emphasis generally led to a spiritual, or more abstract, view.

Just as the medieval world view was not derived solely from Aristotle but contained strands from other ancient writers, so also it was a compromise with Christian ideas of the universe. In general, the Bible says very little about the ordering of the universe, so that clashes of opinion were not very frequent. Some Aristotelian concepts—his belief in the eternity of the world, for example—did disappear in the medieval synthesis. Where possible, however, the biblical narrative was interpreted so as to emphasize the agreement between Aristotelian and Christian thought. The principle of accommodation, that is, the possible metaphorical interpretation of biblical passages, was especially stressed 'It should rather be considered,' Aquinas wrote, 'that Moses was speaking to ignorant people and that out of condescension to their weakness he put before them only such things as are apparent to sense.'[1]

There was, then, beneath the apparent unity of the medieval scheme, still some slight interplay of tension—between Christian and pagan attitudes, and between different classical authorities. But these differences must not be overemphasized: to the average educated observer of those days the universe presented itself as an intelligible, explicable and interrelated whole. To some extent this makes the medieval model difficult to describe, for

2

there is no obvious starting point. However, so far as astronomy is concerned, one particular aspect of the picture does appear to be fundamental. This is the belief that the Earth was immovable, and that it lay at the centre of a finite universe. The overall nature of this universe was determined by a further Aristotelian concept: that space and matter could not exist independently of one another. The universe, being everywhere a world of space, was therefore completely filled: matter was continuous— atomic theories, where discrete packets of material moved through a void, were ruled out. It was this insistence on the continuity of matter that produced the typical Aristotelian belief in the impossibility of a vacuum. So Milton's God proclaims that he fills

Infinitude, nor vacuous the space[2]

But notice here the Christian adaptation of Aristotle: space has become the plenum of God. Again, whereas Aristotle had been vague as to what (if anything) existed beyond the sphere of the material universe, in the Christian picture the observed heavens were immediately enclosed by the empyreal heaven, which was the abode of God and his angels. (Milton, himself, preferred *empyrean* to *empyreal*.) Note too, that Milton speaks of the infinitude of space—a complete contradiction of Aristotelian thought. This reflects the fact that he was writing when the medieval synthesis was already in a state of disruption. The world picture in *Paradise Lost* represents a compromise between the Aristotelian concept of finite space and the seventeenth-century concept of infinite space. Milton envisaged a finite Aristotelian universe suspended from Heaven, and surrounded by an effectively infinite chaos.

The form of the medieval universe was determined by one of the most pervasive of classical concepts—the belief that certain shapes were of greater perfection than others. In particular it was believed that the sphere and the circle represented the ultimate limit of perfection. This idea was taken over into medieval thought. Thus Johannes de Sacrobosco, the author of the most used astronomy text of medieval times, gives three reasons why the heavens must be spherical. First, because the sphere has neither beginning nor end. Secondly, because it has the largest volume for a given size. Thirdly, because any other type of volume would leave some unfilled space. These reasons, particularly the third, are good Aristotelianism, but the first reason provides a basic insight into Greek thought. It applies, evidently, to a circle as much as to a sphere. The perfection of the circle, its symmetry and eternal sameness, made it the only suitable path for celestial bodies. This belief became deep rooted in European thought. When Vaughan at the end of the medieval period envisaged eternity, he naturally saw it as a great ring of pure and endless light.[3] Similarly John Donne was obsessed with the supernatural significance of the circle.[4]

On the Aristotelian scheme, the Earth and the heavens were naturally all of the same shape. (This was in any case required by the continuity of matter in the universe.) Although the sphericity of the Earth had been known in Europe before the medieval synthesis, it received new emphasis from the Aristotelian scheme. It had, after all, been claimed in earlier centuries that some biblical passages (e.g. *Isaiah* 40: 22) affirmed that the Earth was flat. The general acceptance of a spherical Earth in medieval times, and the associated (often erroneous) ideas of its size, played their own part in stimulating later explorations of the Earth's surface.

The sphericity of the universe was also closely linked with the observed motions of the celestial bodies. It is worth remembering, in this context, that for both classical and medieval writers the word *astronomy* had a much more restricted meaning than it has today. The beginning and end of astronomy for them was to account for the regular movements of the heavens. Until the advent of the telescope early in the seventeenth century, the number of known celestial bodies remained constant. There were two groups: the seven planets (Sun, Moon, Mercury, Venus, Mars, Jupiter and Saturn) on the one hand, and the stars on the other. Nowadays we would remove both the Sun from the category of *planet* (because we consider it to be a star) and also the Moon (because we consider it to be the satellite of a planet). This reflects the fact that our modern classification is a physical one, whereas the medieval division was based on differences of motion. Their distinction was between the stars, which moved together across the sky in a regular, repetitive manner, and the planets (or wandering stars) which moved in a rather haphazard manner relative both to the background stars and to each other.

Sometimes there may be some uncertainty as to whether a medieval writer is referring to stars or planets. This is usually because the word *stars*, then as now, was often applied generically to all celestial objects. Thus, Gower declares that astronomy can give man knowledge

> Of Sterres in the firmament,
> Figure, cercle and moevement
> Of ech of hem in sondri place,
> And what between hem is of space,
> Hou so thei moeve or stonde faste.[5]

Here the reference may be to both stars and planets: according to the Aristotelian picture both would move in circles (though the planetary circles were more complicated than the stellar). With the exception of the pole star, however, it is only the planets that can seem to stand fast, i.e. remain motionless for an instant. The space between the stars to which Gower refers could be either the angular distance apart of the stars on the celestial sphere, or, if he also had planets in mind, their different distances from the Earth. It should be added that shortly after this passage Gower does specifically distinguish the seven planets from the stars.

In order to explain the differing motions of the planets, each was assigned a spherical shell (its *sphere*) which was concentric with the Earth. Every sphere had its own peculiar rate of rotation. Because the spheres were transparent this motion could not be seen directly. It was thought, however, to be reflected in the movements of the planets since they were firmly attached to their own spheres. As all the planetary motions differed, no sphere could control more than a single planet. Each planet was therefore isolated from its fellows by the sphere which contained it. So we have the expression 'out of one's sphere,' or, as Ophelia is told concerning Hamlet, he is 'out of thy star'. (Here *star* is being used for *planet*: a practice we have noted before. Another interchange which can be found is to refer to a planet's sphere as a synonym for the planet. The word *sphere* itself, is sometimes replaced by *heaven*, or occasionally by *element.*) The fixed stars, since they moved as a unit, were assigned to a single shell.

The medieval universe was thus rather like an onion, with the central core of the Earth closely surrounded by the layers of the planetary spheres. Mephistophilis, when questioned by Faustus concerning the celestial bodies, describes them as

> Even from the moon unto the empyreal orb
> Mutually folded in each other's spheres[6]

(The Moon's sphere and the empyreal sphere were chosen by Marlowe as marking the two extremes: the former being the closest sphere to the Earth, and the latter the farthest away.)

The basic motion of all the planetary spheres agreed with that of the firmament, which was sometimes also called the *stellatum*. This was the sphere of the fixed stars (*fixed* in this case meaning at rest relative to each other). To an observer on Earth the firmament seems to revolve approximately once a day, rising in the east and setting in the west. The stars follow circular paths round an axis which is directed so that the northern end passes through a point in the firmament close to the pole star. This is the north pole of the heavens and corresponds, of course, to the north pole on Earth. Similarly, a celestial equator can be defined to mirror the terrestrial equator. If watched for a single night, the planets seem to follow the motion of the firmament (which is why Mephistophilis, in the speech quoted above, also describes them as all moving 'upon one axle-tree'). If followed for several days or weeks, however, they are found to change their positions relative to the stars; the main alteration being a slow drift towards the east. The rate of drift varies from planet to planet. So, when Faustus inquires

> Why are not conjunctions, oppositions, aspects,
> eclipses all at one time, but in some years we
> have more, in some less?[7]

Mephistophilis replies that these variations in celestial phenomena are due to the planetary bodies moving in different directions and at different speeds. (The technical terms used by Faustus all refer to positions of the planets relative to each other. As we shall see, they were particularly important in astrology.)

It had been recognized from very early times that, although the planets move at different rates, they all follow roughly similar paths across the sky. These paths always lie within a few degrees of the ecliptic—the track of the Sun relative to the background stars. The ecliptic can be imagined as a circle in the sky, tilted relative to the celestial equator, and therefore crossing it at two points; the vernal and autumnal equinoxes (so called, because the arrival of the Sun at these intersections marks the beginning of spring and autumn in the northern hemisphere). The inclination of the ecliptic circle to the celestial equator (about $23\frac{1}{2}°$) is called the obliquity of the ecliptic. The stars along the ecliptic were long ago separated into twelve groups—the signs of the Zodiac—each covering 30° of the Sun's path. As the zodiacal stars circulate endlessly westward, each planet moves slowly past them towards the east; thus returning, after a certain period of time, to more or less its original position. Values for the planetary periods had been known quite accurately since classical times. So, when Mephistophilis says that all the planets 'move from east to west in four-and-twenty hours upon the poles of the world, but differ in their motions upon the poles of the Zodiac',* Faustus replies scornfully

> Who knows not the double motion of the planets?
> That the first is finished in a natural day,
> the second thus, Saturn in thirty years:
> Jupiter in twelve; Mars in four; the Sun, Venus, and
> Mercury in a year; the Moon in twenty-eight days.
> These are freshmen's suppositions.[8]

It must be remembered that the figures given here are based on the assumption that the Earth is stationary, i.e. the geocentric hypothesis. The figures in a modern astronomy text would assume that the Sun is stationary (the heliocentric hypothesis) and would therefore, in general, be different. The periods based on the Sun as centre are essentially constant, but

---

* I.e. in their motion round the ecliptic.

those based on the Earth as centre may vary appreciably from one cycle to the next. As it happens, Marlowe misquotes the figure for Mars: the period then accepted was more like two years than four. However, determining the correct period for Mars seems to have a major problem of medieval astronomy— widely differing estimates can be found. These presumably reflect the large deviations which the Martian period can have from its mean value.

The observed motions of the planets were believed to be caused by the peculiar rotations of the planetary spheres to which they were attached. As we shall see, all such motion was supposed to derive ultimately from the rotation of the firmament. The nearer a planetary sphere was to the firmament, the greater the difficulty it had in moving in a contrary direction. Hence, the more distant a planet from the Earth, the longer its period. It was therefore deduced that the Moon occupied the first sphere, nearest to the Earth. Then came Mercury, Venus, the Sun, Mars, Jupiter and Saturn—in that order. The major uncertainty—left over from classical times—was the relative arrangement of Mercury, Venus and the Sun.

> Plato believ'd the Sun and Moon
> Below all other planets run.
> Some Mercury, some Venus, seat
> Above the Sun himself in height.[9]

(This passage—from Samuel Butler—reveals a further characteristic of the Aristotelian synthesis: since the Earth formed a fixed centre to the universe, the words *up* and *down* had a physical connotation. A planet which was below the Sun was closer to the Earth than the Sun's sphere.) The root of the problem can be observed in Mephistophilis' account of the planetary periods. The Sun, Mercury and Venus all had the same average period, and so the normal method for determining the order of their spheres broke down. The physical significance of this is that neither Mercury nor Venus are ever very far away from the Sun in the sky. Both are morning and evening stars; although that name is usually reserved for Venus alone: partly because of its greater brilliance, and partly because it can move further away from the Sun than Mercury and so be seen for a longer time.

It is presumably because Mercury, Venus and the Sun are obviously connected that Mephistophilis says

> Nor are the names of Saturn, Mars, or Jupiter,
> Feigned, but are erring stars[10]

(An alternative text of *Doctor Faustus* here reads less comprehensibly *evening stars* rather than *erring stars*.) Marlowe is presumably distinguishing these three planets as being the most evidently independent.

Despite this confusion, it was generally accepted in medieval times that the proper place for the Sun's sphere was at the centre of the planets.

> And therefore is the glorious planet Sol
> In noble eminence enthron'd and sphered
> Amidst the other[11]

That is to say, there were three planets closer to the Earth than the Sun (the Moon, Mercury and Venus) and three further away (Mars, Jupiter and Saturn). The reason for thus placing the Sun seems to have been astrological as much as astronomical, and will be taken up in Chapter III. The only problem left was then the relative positions of Mercury and Venus. It was generally assumed that Mercury was closer to the Earth, though the alternative arrangement with Venus closer was sometimes entertained.

In the simplest medieval model of the universe (there were several variants) the outermost sphere—the firmament—besides containing the stars also provided the source of motion for all the other spheres. Hence, it received the name of *primum mobile* or *first mover*—as it was generally translated.[12] (Milton also refers to it as the *first mov'd* or *first moving*.) The *primum mobile* rotated in such a way that the apparent diurnal path of the stars across the sky was reproduced. Now the Aristotelian scheme supposed that the spheres were made of aether—a transparent, crystal-like material—in which the planets and stars were embedded. Owing to the necessary continuity of matter, each sphere was in perfect contact with those on either side. The motion of the firmament was therefore communicated by friction to the next sphere down, namely Saturn's, and so on to all the others, as far as the Moon. In this way the main diurnal motion of the stars and planets, their rising and setting each day, could be explained. The second motion of the planets, counter to that of the firmament, could then be explained if each planetary sphere had a slow rotation of its own opposite to that of the *primum mobile*. For example, the peculiar motion of the Sun's sphere had to be sufficient to take the Sun once round the firmament each year. Moreover, the rotational axis of the Sun's sphere had to be so inclined to the rotational axis of the firmament that the path traced out by the Sun followed the ecliptic.

This simple picture had one major drawback: it was incapable of providing even a qualitatively correct description of the observed planetary motions. It had been known from antiquity that the planets move with a non-uniform velocity relative to the stars. In particular, the planetary motions can, from time to time, become retrograde: that is, instead of moving from west to east relative to the stars, the planets, at some points, travel from east to west. If their positions are followed at these times, it is found, in fact, that they slow down, loop back, slow down again, and then move on in their normal direction. These singularities had been well known to the classical philosophers. The system which Aristotle employed (borrowed from his friend Callippus, who derived it in turn from Eudoxus) actually provided an explanation of the loops. It postulated not one sphere for each planet, but several—each with its own peculiar motion and axis of rotation. A planet was attached to the innermost sphere of the group which served it. By adjusting the number of spheres and the resulting combination of circulatory motions about different axes, it was possible to give a fair representation of the planetary orbits—so far as they were known in Aristotle's day—including the occurrence of spasmodic retrograde motion.

This more complicated picture evidently required a considerably larger number of spheres. Aristotle, indeed, used fifty-five, although the need for many of these arose from his method of transmitting the rotational motion inwards by friction from the *primum mobile*. However, it was realized in antiquity (even, apparently, by Aristotle himself) that the observations were still not entirely explained. It was known, for example, that the brightness of Venus and Mars increased considerably when they were retrograding. It was deduced—quite correctly—that this was due to a decrease in the distance of the planet from the Earth at this time. On the Aristotelian scheme, with the planet rigidly attached to a crystalline shell, such distance variation could not occur. Moreover, later Greek observations of position increased in accuracy and it became apparent that Aristotle's system of spheres could provide no more than a very rough quantitative picture of the planetary orbits.

For these reasons, attention turned elsewhere and the final Hellenistic explanation of the orbits, given by Ptolemy, although in some ways similar to Aristotle's, did not depend on crystalline spheres. The Ptolemaic system, unlike the Aristotelian, was intended to be a purely mathematical description of the way in which celestial bodies moved. If the motions could be reproduced in detail—or as the Greeks and, following them, the medieval scholars said, if the phenomena could be saved—all was well: there was no need to question why the planets moved in the way they did. The problem evidently reduced to a search for mathematical devices which would best serve this purpose. As might be expected, such devices were always based on some form of circular motion. The phrase 'save the phenomena' or 'save the appearances' deserves a passing comment. The implication was that an astronomical theory need not be physically true so long as it explained the observations adequately. Medieval scholars recognized, at least in theory, that planetary motions might be explained by some mechanism other than the Ptolemaic-Aristotelian, but they did not regard this as important: all theories which accounted for the observations were equally acceptable. In practice, even the scholars tended to invest the medieval world picture with a physical reality: certainly the ordinary writers of the period did.

The Ptolemaic description of planetary motion started with a circular orbit centered on the Earth, just as Aristotle had done. This basic circle—called the deferent—was then subjected to various modifications until a reasonable representation of the observations was obtained. For example, the planet might be given a second circular motion round a smaller orbit, the centre of which, in turn, moved round the circumference of the deferent. An additional circle of this type was called an epicycle. By adjusting the periods of the deferent and epicyclic motions, a good first approximation to planetary behaviour was obtained. It could account not only for retrograde motion, but also for variations in planetary brightness, since the epicyclic motion altered the distance of the planet from the Earth. But it was found that this still did not produce a detailed agreement between calculated and observed positions. Further modifications were therefore made, which fell into three main groups. In the first, further epicycles were added. The planet, that is, could move in an epicyclic orbit which was itself centred on an epicycle. Next, the deferent was displaced so that the Earth was no longer exactly at the centre. This could be combined, if desired, with motion of the deferent centre round an epicyclic orbit of its own. Finally, Ptolemy introduced the concept of an equant. In this a planet, although following a circle based on the Earth as centre, did not move uniformly with respect to the Earth. Instead, it was made to move uniformly with respect to some other point within the circle. This was the equant point.

These devices could all be applied, if necessary, to determine the orbit of a planet. It is, perhaps, hardly surprising that with all these various mechanisms available Ptolemy finally achieved quite a fair approximation to the observations. The mathematical techniques he required were, however, very cumbersome.

Although medieval scholars were familiar with Ptolemy as a name, few of them ever penetrated very far into his astronomical writings. (The word *astronomical* is stressed here, for Ptolemy's fame in medieval Europe was founded more on his astrological writings. These certainly were read, and, indeed, are still apparently in demand today.) His astronomical theory was so complicated in detail that it was normally more read about than read. In fact the original Greek text of the work was not generally available until shortly before the death of Copernicus towards the middle of the sixteenth century. Prior to that it was only known in more or less corrupt translations. Thus the name by which it was, and is, generally known—the *Almagest*—came from the Arabic translation rather than from the original Greek title. There are occasional references to it scattered throughout medieval literature, e.g. by Gower.[13]

The average educated man of medieval times, needless to say, bothered very little with the details of Ptolemaic theory. Even the fully developed form of the Aristotelian picture was more than he needed. He thought instead of the very simplest geocentric universe, outlined at the beginning of this chapter, with a single sphere for each planet. This is the conception which pervades medieval literature.

It is also important to realize that medieval scholars did not think of Ptolemaic and Aristotelian ideas as different approaches to the problems of astronomy. The learning of classical antiquity presented itself to them as an integrated whole, not as a changing and evolving body of thought. The aim of these scholars, once the initial period of translation was over, was to reduce the resulting corpus of knowledge into as coherent a synthesis as possible. They kept in existence, side by side, both the Aristotelian and the Ptolemaic pictures, and sought to reconcile them. The resulting compromise had peculiarities of its own. It was supposed, for example, that the planets still occupied Aristotelian spheres, but instead of being fixed at one position in their sphere they could move through it freely in Ptolemaic orbits.* The thickness of each planetary shell could be so chosen that the nearest point to the Earth which a planet reached defined the inner radius of its shell, and, similarly, the furthest point defined the outer radius. This outer radius would then correspond to the inner limit of the next planet away from the Earth, and so on. Now Ptolemaic theory could provide a value for the relative thicknesses of these spheres. If the absolute size of any one sphere could be calculated, this approach would then provide a value for the size of the whole universe. It was relatively easy to estimate a rough distance to the Moon (which formed the innermost shell). Such an estimate had been made in antiquity—when this method of finding the size of the universe was first considered. The value for the radius of the universe derived from this calculation was known to be very large by terrestrial standards. One of the first books that Caxton published was his

---

* This device was, in fact, first suggested in classical times, when the need to reconcile Aristotle and Ptolemy was already apparent.

own translation of a French cosmography (originally written somewhere near the middle of the thirteenth century). In this, there is the following description:

> And the heven is somoche hye and ferre above us that, yf a stone were in theyer as hye as the sterres be, and were the most hevyest of alle the world, of leed or of metall, and began to falle fro an hye above, this thing is proved and knowen that it shold not come to therthe tyl thende of an hondred yere.[14]

There was a very common medieval analogy—again derived from classical times—which was used to emphasize the insignificance of the Earth relative to the heavens. The Earth was represented as the infinitesimally small centre of a circle, whilst the heavens were compared with its circumference.

> The world to the circumference of Heaven
> Is as a small point in geometry,
> Whose greatness is so little, that a less
> Cannot be made.[15]

The insignificant dimensions of the Earth compared with the universe as a whole, in medieval thought, are worth some emphasis. It is not apparent in the textbook diagrams of the period. These always grossly exaggerated the size of the Earth in order to show details of its structure. Nevertheless, the entire medieval universe was considerably smaller than the distance to even the nearest star according to modern measurements.

Medieval ideas on the size of the universe are best reflected in what might be called the 'space-fiction' of the period—the accounts of voyages through space. Cicero (the last part of the *Republic*) and Lucan had both left descriptions of ascents through the planetary spheres, and both were popular reading in medieval times. Dante's voyage springs to mind as a medieval equivalent, but the theme also appears in English works (e.g. Chaucer's *House of Fame*). The accounts often mentioned the spheres which were traversed and dwelt on the Earth's insignificance when seen from a distance. Typically, however, the writer, having described the smallness of the Earth, would then proceed to discern the finest details on its surface. Voyages of this type are still to be found in seventeenth-century literature. Donne's *Second Anniversary* is an obvious parallel, and part of *Paradise Lost* has some similarity to the genre.

Although the intermingling of Aristotelian and Ptolemaic ideas had its advantages, it also had its improbabilities. In particular, it will be recalled that the Aristotelian aether had to be extremely solid material in order to transmit the rotational forces inwards from the *primum mobile*. Here the synthesis of the middle ages ran into difficulties. If the aether was sufficiently solid for the transmission of forces, how could it be sufficiently fluid to allow the motion of the planets through it, from the inner to the outer limits of their spheres? One possibility was that the planets moved along passages drilled through the solid aether—rather like ball-bearings rolling down a tube. But the problem never did attain an entirely satisfactory solution, and later, when Aristotelianism was under attack, it was a favourite topic for ridicule. (There is a curious analogy here with nineteenth-century physics, where another conflict arose over an aether which sometimes acted like a material substance and sometimes not.)

The aether was one of Aristotle's five elements from which all the universe was made. It stood somewhat apart from the other four since it was not found on the Earth. It was therefore called the fifth essence, or quintessence. The word *element* or *essence* had some of the significance of our modern chemical element, but it had many more connotations. For example, there could be a moral overtone: as when medieval scholars called aether the purest and noblest element, since it could not occur on the fallen Earth. Similarly the four elements of the Earth could not ascend into the pure universe outside, which was therefore made only of aether. This was one of the points in which Platonic doctrine diverged from Aristotelian. Plato had agreed that the heavens were purer than the Earth, but had suggested that they were made up of some refined mixture of the four earthly elements, rather than of a separate element. This had a certain importance in the development of medieval ideas, for whereas the Aristotelian drew a sharp distinction between the sub-lunary region (the sphere of the Earth) and the remainder of the universe, this was slightly less important for the Platonist. It is the

Aristotelian view which is most often reflected in the writings of the times.

The only change which Aristotle permitted in the heavens was circular motion, since this, as we have seen, was everywhere the same and repeatable throughout eternity. Some commentators indeed believed that the motion of the spheres was necessary for the continued existence of the universe (this is another doctrine which receives a mention from Samuel Butler[16]). The circular movements of the heavens further distinguished them from the Earth, where movement was predominantly irregular and in straight lines (see, for example, the detailed explanation of motion given by Sir Francis Bacon[17]). Since terrestrial motions were limited in space and time, conditions on Earth were constantly changing, and change in the Aristotelian scheme meant decay. Eternal perfection reigned in the heavens, whereas on Earth there was only imperfect decay. This difference was emphasized by medieval Christian teaching.

The four remaining elements other than aether were, in descending order of nobility, fire, air, water and earth. (Here *nobility* means their assumed degree of similarity to the noblest element, aether.) There are innumerable references to the four elements in medieval, and later, writings. Some of these will be mentioned below: it is worth noting that the concept of four elements remained intellectually respectable long after scholars had discarded the astronomical parts of the Aristotelian world picture. One of the most important characteristics of these elements was that they each had a particular region of the Earth's sphere as their natural home. Thus fire tried to occupy a spherical shell immediately below the sphere of the Moon. Air tried to fill the subjacent sphere, then came water and, finally, earth, whose proper position was as close as possible to the centre of the universe. Descriptions of the creation of the universe—a popular seventeenth-century theme—usually included an account of the way in which the elements dispersed to their assigned places. Such accounts can be found, for example, in *Paradise Lost*, in Spenser's *Hymn of Love*, in Dryden's *Ode to St. Cecilia's Day* and in Cowley's *Davideis*.

To some extent, observation confirmed the distribution of the elements suggested by the Aristotelian scheme, but there were also obvious disagreements. Thus the earthy continents were higher than the seas; the clouds, which were known to produce water, moved in the upper air. These discrepancies were believed to result from the play of forces which continually mixed the central regions of the universe. The source of these forces was the rotating spheres—that is, ultimately, the *primum mobile*. On the one hand, the spheres were in motion, on the other, the Earth was stationary; the idea, in effect, was that the friction created between the two dissipated itself by churning up the terrestrial elements. Two types of terrestrial motion were therefore distinguished. There was either the forced motion of an element as it was driven from its proper sphere, or there was its natural motion as it returned once more to its correct position. For example, if fire was forced downwards from its sphere it might be seen as lightning striking the ground. On the other hand, when the flames of a fire leapt up towards the sky, this could be interpreted as the element returning again to its original place.

As is obvious, the Aristotelian disposition of the elements emphasized the uniqueness of the Earth. This in turn supported the theological belief in the uniqueness of man. It was an indication of man's divine essence that the empyreal heaven was centred on the Earth. Equally, it was an indication of his nature that the Earth, itself, was centred on hell. He was thus suspended between the forces of good and evil, and at the centre of their conflict. This picture is found throughout medieval literature; most obviously, of course, in Dante. This sense of being at the focus of events was one of the factors that made the large size of the universe unimportant to medieval minds.

As we have seen, the Christian form of the Aristotelian world picture added an extra sphere—the empyreal heaven—outside the *primum mobile*. No change, not even motion, was permitted there; for change necessarily implied some imperfection, and heaven was perfect. Other modifications in the system of spheres were taken over from the Moslem astronomers. (It is worth remarking that the basic assumptions and problems of medieval scholars in western Europe were similar to those of the Arab scholars before them. For example, they both assumed that the differing astronomical beliefs of antiquity could be reconciled.)

One of the important astronomical advances of antiquity was

the discovery by Hipparchus of the precession of the equinoxes. He found that the stars did not have simply a single motion of rising and setting each day. There was also a further motion, as if the celestial poles moved in slow circuits round the heavens (or, alternatively, as if the equinoxes moved slowly round the celestial equator). Due to this motion different stars lie nearest the celestial poles at different times. Our present pole star in the northern hemisphere is the brightest star in the constellation of the Little Bear. Five thousand years ago, the pole star was the brightest star in the constellation of the Dragon. Similarly, the position of the Sun in the sky at the spring and autumn equinoxes has changed. In antiquity, for example, the Sun was in the constellation Aries at the spring equinox. Nowadays it is in the constellation Pisces. To add to the confusion, it became customary to separate the astrological signs of the Zodiac from their corresponding constellations. Thus the Sun is still said to be in the zodical sign of Aries at the spring equinox but it is no longer in the constellation of Aries.

> Some say the Zodiac constellations
> Have long since chang'd their antique stations
> Above a sign, and prove the same
> In Taurus now, once in the Ram.[18]

(i.e. the zodiacal constellation of Aries now lies in the zodiacal sign of Taurus.)

In Aristotelian terms, the motion could be explained by adding an extra sphere, set at the correct angle and rotating at the appropriate rate, outside the stellar sphere. This step was taken by the Moslem astronomers, but they were uncertain of the exact rate at which the pole precessed. One school believed that the rate was variable, and introduced yet another sphere to allow for this phenomenon, which they called trepidation.

The final picture was thus of an outermost shell providing the diurnal motion, and so bearing the name of prime mover. Below it was the *coelum crystallinum*, or crystalline sphere, which contributed the trepidation. Next came the firmament, containing its embedded stars, which added the precessional motion. Since there were seven planetary spheres, the fixed stars were contained in the eighth sphere, trepidation was added

3

by the ninth sphere, and the *primum mobile* was the tenth sphere. The empyreal heaven was sometimes referred to as the eleventh sphere. Some believed that there was a further sphere below the empyreal heaven, called the *coelum igneum*, or fiery sphere, but the argument here was highly confused. It may have been suggested originally by analogy with the Earth: since the Earth was separated from the nobler heavens by a sphere of fire, so should the heavens themselves be cut off from the perfect empyreal heaven. Again, the name may have arisen through confusion with the empyreal heaven itself; for the word *empyreal* is based on the Greek word for *fire*. Sometimes the *coelum igneum* seems to be merely an alternative name for the *primum mobile*.

There were frequent references in contemporary literature to these outer spheres, which were necessarily unobservable since they contained no stars. They appear, for example, in *Paradise Lost*.

> They pass the Planets seven, and pass the fixt,
> And that Crystalline Sphear whose ballance weighs
> The Trepidation talkt, and that first mov'd[19]

Here Milton distinguishes the firmament ('the fixt'), the crystalline sphere and the *primum mobile* ('that first mov'd'). The reference to 'the Trepidation talkt' reflects the fact that the actual existence of trepidation was in dispute. At the beginning of the seventeenth century, Sir Francis Bacon dismissed it as improbable, although his contemporary, John Donne, was happily using the concept.

> Moving of th' earth brings harmes and feares,
> Men reckon what it did and meant,
> But trepidation of the spheares,
> Though greater farre, is innocent.[20]

(This quotation is interesting for its mention of 'moving of th' earth'. This might be thought to refer to some motion of the Earth, and hence be a contradiction of the medieval synthesis. In fact, it is more likely to be a reference to earthquakes.) It was during Donne's lifetime that trepidation began to disappear from the scene: mainly due to the opposition of the Danish astronomer, Tycho Brahe. As the greatest observational astronomer of the time, his opinion carried considerable weight. Thus, by the time that *Paradise Lost* appeared the idea of trepidation was already obsolete.

It has been remarked that these outer spheres of the universe were empty and unobservable. Some writers disliked this, preferring instead that each sphere should correspond to a celestial body (a feeling which seems to have been inspired predominantly by Platonic beliefs). They therefore objected to the introduction of supernumerary spheres for precession and trepidation. This attitude appears in Marlowe: when Faustus inquires

> But is there not *coelum igneum*? et *crystallinum*?
Mephistophilis replies
> No Faustus, they be but fables.[21]

The empyreal heaven was also, of course, unobservable, but it was considered to be in a different category: medieval theology distinguished between the planetary spheres which were required by astronomical theory and the empyreal heaven which was discovered by faith.

Many neo-Platonists were also opposed to the Ptolemaic explanation of the irregularities of the planetary orbits. This, too, they dismissed as being needlessly complicated. Instead of mechanical explanations, they substituted the Platonic device of celestial intelligences which actively guided the planets and stars into the paths observed by the astronomers. It therefore comes as no surprise that Mephistophilis assures Faustus that each sphere has its own 'dominion or intelligentia'. Such a concept, if pushed far enough, obviously denies not only the Aristotelian explanation of celestial motion, but also the necessity for any explanation of planetary motion at all. Nevertheless, many British astronomers regarded the idea kindly. Robert Recorde mentions it in the *Castle of Knowledge* which was published in 1556: the first English astronomy text to refer to Copernicus and his hypothesis that the Sun was at the centre of the planetary system. The idea of celestial intelligences was taken over into Christian thinking by equating them with angels. Donne favoured the concept of intelligences moving the spheres,[22] and extended it to the whole universe by visualizing Christ as, in effect, the intelligence controlling the universe.[23]

This idea was, of course, simply an extension of the concept of God as the unmoved first mover—a commonplace of medieval thought. The medieval world picture always presented the *primum mobile* as deriving its motion, either directly or indirectly, from God. One suggestion, for example, was that *primum mobile* moved at great speed because of its joy at being so close to heaven. The scholastic philosophers not only accepted the idea of angelic intelligences moving the spheres, but also traditionally named which angel, or archangel, governed each sphere. Thus Gabriel was in charge of the Moon and Raphael of the Sun (though Milton in *Paradise Lost* places Uriel on the Sun).

Another Platonic concept incorporated into the medieval model was the belief that each sphere gave out a musical note as it rotated. (This idea was actually Pythagorean in origin, but medieval scholars grouped Pythagoras and Plato together.) The notes emitted by the spheres were such that when they were combined they produced a scale.[24] According to Pliny, this scale ran C, D, E♭, E, G, A, B♭, B, D (starting at the Earth and proceeding outwards to the firmament), but there seem to have been several variants. It was often thought that the Earth was too corrupt a body to join in the celestial harmony. In that case the scale would run from D to D forming an octave. Plato believed that it was the grossness both of the Earth and of ourselves that prevented us from hearing the notes.[25] (The Pythagorean belief was rather that the notes could not be heard because they were sounding continuously and only changes in sound were distinguishable.) Many writers, including Shakespeare and Milton, were attracted by the idea of the music of the spheres. The concept that each sphere produced its own note was sometimes transmuted, however, into the more general belief that there was music in the heavens, or that the angels were singing.[26]

The medieval synthesis envisaged a close connection between mathematics, music and astronomy. In the University curriculum both music and astronomy derived from mathematics— the former being counted as applied arithmetic and the latter as applied geometry. The connection (often envisaged in mystical terms) was particularly emphasized at the beginning of the seventeenth century, as, for example, by Donne. One result of this relationship was that the motions of the spheres were often considered as a form of dance. This appears, for example, in Milton's *Comus* or *Paradise Lost* (Book III); the most extended such analogy, however, is Sir John Davies' *Orchestra*. The idea is satirized by Ben Jonson in *Love's Welcome at Bolsover* where dancing workmen receive such encouragement as

Well done, my Musicall, Arithmeticall, Geometricall Gamesters.

So far our discussion has only concerned astronomical phenomena which are periodic in character, but some celestial phenomena occur irregularly. Such are comets, meteors and aurorae. These are now clearly distinguished from each other, but no such separation was made in medieval or, indeed, much later times. As a result, it is sometimes very difficult to decide which particular phenomenon is being referred to by writers of the period. On the Aristotelian world picture these bodies, being changeable in appearance, could not occupy the unchanging region of the celestial spheres (moreover, there was no room for them there).

These burning fits but meteors bee,
Whose matter in thee is soone spent.
Thy beauty and all parts, which are thee,
Are unchangeable firmament.[27]

They were therefore all considered to be effects in the Earth's atmosphere. This led to a further confusion between astronomical and atmospheric phenomena: all were lumped together under the generic title of *meteors*. In this rather peculiar way the science of meterology acquired its name.

It was generally supposed that meteors were due to vapours exhaled from the Earth. As Dryden wrote

yet Comets rise
From Earthy Vapours ere they shine in Skies.[28]

There is an interesting passage in *Romeo and Juliet* where Juliet says that it is not the dawn she sees but

Some meteor that the sun exhales.[29]

It is not clear whether Shakespeare actually meant to imply that meteors could derive from the Sun (which would be contrary to Aristotle, although not to all classical belief), or whether he was simply saying that the exhalation was due to the action of the Sun on the Earth—a common enough conception. It was also believed that the exhalations which formed meteors were in some way connected with the origin of the winds.

> swift as a shooting Starr
> In *Autumn* thwarts the night, when vapors fir'd
> Impress the Air, and shews the Mariner
> From what point of his Compass to beware
> Impetuous winds[30]

Milton may have emphasized autumn in this passage because showers of meteors are seen in that season more than in any other. It was in the same season that James Thomson described the Northern lights, referring to them as meteors.[31]

According to medieval belief, the vapours ascending into the upper atmosphere played a further role in the economy of the universe: they fed the planets and the stars so that they might continue to shine. (Compare, for example passages by Greene[32] and Marlowe.[33]) To Fulke Greville this was simply another facet reflecting the terrestrial change and decay of which, like most Elizabethans, he was so constantly aware:

> The Ayre still moves, and by its moving cleareth,
> The fire, up ascends, and planets feedeth,
> The Water passeth on, and all lets weareth,
> The Earth stands still, yet change of changes breedeth.[34]

We are dealing here, of course, with another Platonic belief superimposed on the Aristotelian framework. It derived from the distinction remarked on previously between the aether as a fifth element, unconnected with the other four, and the aether as a refined product of the other four. The former definition produced the sub-lunary comets, meteors and vapours; the latter produced the vapours which rose to feed the stars. Milton described the process in more detail and pointed out that it was cyclical. The vapours eventually reached the Sun and gave it nourishment. The shining Sun then gave illumination which drew up vapours from the Earth and so, via the planetary spheres, back to the Sun again.[35]

In the same passage Milton explains away one of the apparent deviations from Aristotelian doctrine. We have seen that the heavens were supposed to be perfect and uniform. This included a belief that the celestial bodies were not disfigured by any blemish whatsoever. On the other hand it was obvious enough that the face of the Moon had darker patches on it (so disposed as to produce the ancient idea of a Man-in-the-Moon). The Moon's sphere was closest to that of the Earth, so it could be supposed—and this is what Milton does—that when the vapours reached the Moon, they had still not completely refined themselves. Thus they produced dark markings on the otherwise perfect Moon. The pure Aristotelian could not accept this explanation, and was driven to other expedients. For example:

> The lytil clowdes or derkenes that is seen therein,
> somme saye that it is therthe that appereth within;
> and that whiche is water appereth whyte, lyke as
> ayenst a myrrour whiche receyveth dyverse colours,
> whan she is torned therto. Other thinke otherwyse and
> saye that hit happed and byfelle whan Adam
> was deceyved by theapple that he ete, whiche
> greved all humayne lignage, and that thenne the
> mone was empesshed and his clerenesse lassed
> and mynuysshid.[36]

The first of these explanations—that the dark patches on the Moon were due to the reflection of the Earth's continents—ran into difficulties when the extensive voyages of the fifteenth and sixteenth centuries showed that the supposed reflection remained the same when seen from any part of the Earth.

The problem of providing the planets with nourishment was obviously connected with the question of whether they shone by their own light, or whether their light was merely due to illumination by the Sun. If the latter, then obviously no nourishment was necessary. There seems to have been no general consensus of opinion, and suggestions of both can be found in the literature (compare, for example, the statements by Phineas Fletcher[37] and Gower[38]).

It was generally agreed that the Moon's main source of illumination was the Sun, since it was obvious that the phases of the Moon depended on the relative positions of the Sun and Moon. Writers with neo-Platonic leanings were often possessed by a mystical admiration for the Sun (the passage from Phineas Fletcher cited in the previous paragraph refers to the Sun as 'the Heart of heaven'—a typical neo-Platonic description). They therefore tended to emphasize the part played by the Sun as the source of all light. Perhaps the commonest attitude was a compromise: most of the light from planets was reflected sunlight, but a small amount was due to the planet itself.

> By tincture or reflection they augment
> Thir small peculiar.[39]

Oddly enough, a part of the persistent belief in the intrinsic luminosity of planets was due to observations of the Moon. As Sir Francis Bacon pointed out

> The moon itself in some eclipses gives some degree of light though obscure; but in new moons and the quarters no light at all is visible except in the part which is touched by the sun's rays.[40]

The ability to discern the Moon at eclipses (as also the appearance of the old Moon in the new Moon's arms, which Bacon does not mention) is now explained in terms of illumination of the Moon by sunlight reflected, or refracted, by the Earth's atmosphere. In medieval times, however, it was often taken as an indication that the Moon had some intrinsic light of its own.

So far as the astronomical phenomena attributed to atmospheric vapours are concerned, it is probably true as a general rule that a reference to 'shooting stars' is an unambiguous indication of meteors in the modern, much more restricted sense. The name derives originally, of course, from the highly unAristotelian idea that stars could fall from their places. (See for example, Caxton[41] and Chapman.[42]) There was a popular belief that when a shooting star hit the Earth a residue of jelly was left. This is mentioned, for example, by Donne.[43] Comets were sometimes also called blazing stars (e.g. by Spenser[44]). As we shall see in a later chapter, however, a blazing star could be an essentially different type of phenomenon. Marlowe distinguished blazing stars from comets, but added that they both occupied a region just below the element of fire.[45]

There was one more celestial feature which, on the Aristotelian system, was thought to be caused by vapours in the upper atmosphere of the Earth. This was the Milky Way. The true cause of the Milky Way—that it was due to a host of faint stars—had actually been suggested in antiquity, but was not generally accepted. It was a popular belief in medieval, as in classical, times that the Milky Way was a celestial highway. As such it was often called by the names of main highways on Earth, e.g. Watling Street. Compared with comets, meteors and aurorae, however, the Milky Way was little referred to in English literature prior to the seventeenth century. It presumably excited less attention because it remained constant in appearance so that, whilst the others acquired considerable astrological significance, the Milky Way appears to have had none at all. During the replacement of the geocentric hypothesis by the heliocentric (i.e. in the seventeenth century), the Milky Way was recognized to be an extra-terrestrial phenomenon, as also were comets and 'blazing stars'. On the other hand, aurorae and meteors were correctly recognised as occurring in the upper atmosphere. Nowadays we know that, nevertheless, even these two latter are caused by an influx of material from outside the Earth. This, however, is relatively recent knowledge, and long after the medieval synthesis had been disrupted, meteors and aurorae were accepted as vapours in the atmosphere.

The account of the medieval world picture given in this chapter has naturally emphasized the astronomy. It must be constantly remembered, however, that, owing to the comprehensiveness of the synthesis, astronomical interpretations almost always had some terrestrial counterpart. We have, for example, described the idea that the elements had their proper places in the universe. By the usual scholastic method of analogical reasoning, this concept was naturally extended to human affairs (see, for example, Chaucer[46]). More generally, a universe comprehensively ordered by natural law was necessarily balanced by a human society similarly ordered by divine will. The order of the universe was essentially stable; so then should be the social order on Earth. It is therefore not surprising that in Elizabethan times, when life began to change rapidly, there should have been great emphasis on the cosmic importance of preserving order. Obvious examples of this are Ulysses' speech in *Troilus and Cressida* and the very similar account in Hooker's *Laws of Ecclesiastical Polity*.

CHAPTER II

Time and Instruments

THE enormous number of references to astronomy in medieval literature is a reflection of the importance that the subject then had in everyday life. This was partly a result of the close bond between medieval astronomy and theology; partly, however, it reflects the immediate practical benefits which derived, or were thought to derive, from a study of the stars. Firstly, there was the possibility of foretelling the future by means of astrology. This will be dealt with in the next chapter. Secondly, there was a basic need to tell the time. This was required on the one hand for agriculture—to determine times for ploughing, sowing and reaping. On the other, it was needed to determine the day, or hour, at which religious festivals and services should occur. In this chapter, we will consider medieval time determination, and the instrumentation used for this and other similar measurements.

Clocks first seem to have come into public use in this country— mounted in church towers—during the thirteenth century. Originally there were no dials: the clocks consisted simply of bells which rang the hours. By the end of the fourteenth century, dials with an hour hand, but no minute hand, began to appear. However, the normal medieval stand-by for time determination during the day continued, as in earlier centuries, to be the sundial. This might be either large and stationary, such as is still to be seen in gardens, or it might be small enough to carry in the pocket—as was Touchstone's in *As You Like It*.[1]*

A sufficiently experienced observer could make quite accurate estimates of time without a sundial by using the length of his own shadow.

* The reference might, however, be to a pocket-watch, examples of which began to appear around 1500.

Foure of the clokke it was tho, as I gesse:
For eleven foot, or litel more or lesse,
My shadwe was at thilke tyme[2]

Or he could use the length of the shadow cast by some stationary object:

Our Hoste sey wel that the brighte sonne
Th' ark of his artificial day had ronne
The fourthe part, and half an houre, and more;
And though he were not depe expert in lore,
He wiste it was the eightetethe day
Of April, that is messager to May:
And say wel that the shadwe of every tree
Was in lengthe the same quantitee
That was the body erect that caused it.
And therfor by the shadwe he took his wit
That Phebus, which that shoon so clere and brighte,
Degrees was fyve and fourty clombe on highte;
And for that day, as in that latitude,
It was ten of the clokke, he gan conclude[3]

The innkeeper, though no deep expert in astronomical lore, seems to have required a fairly agile mind. This passage was worth quoting in full because Chaucer outlines here the logical steps which are necessary to work out the time of day from the length of a shadow. A comparison of an object's height with the length of its shadow gives the altitude of the Sun in the sky. This depends on the hour of the day, but it also depends on the time of year and the latitude of the observer. Hence time can only be determined when the last two factors have been eliminated. The calculations required to do this are most unlikely to have been a common place with medieval man. He would, however, circumvent them by learning off by heart a set of shadow lengths for different times of the year. Since he probably did not often move very far from home, variation in latitude could be ignored, and only differences relating to the time of the year needed consideration.

Time at night, in a fixed location, was often judged by the appearance of a group of stars relative to a building. (This was

particularly popular at monasteries for determining the times
of services.)

> An't be not four by
> the day I'll be hang'd; Charles' Wain is over
> the new chimney and yet our horse not pack'd[4]

(Charles' Wain is an old English name for the Plough.)

It was also possible, of course, to determine the time without
reference to buildings simply by noting which constellations
were up and how they were disposed in the sky.

> 'The Dog-star and Aldebaran, pointing to the restless Pleiades,
> were half-way up to the Southern sky, and between them
> hung Orion, which gorgeous constellation never burnt more
> vividly than now, as it soared forth above the rim of the land-
> scape. Castor and Pollux with their quiet shine were almost on
> the meridian: the barren and gloomy Square of Pegasus was
> creeping round to the north west; far away through the plan-
> tation Vega sparkled like a lamp suspended amid the leafless
> trees, and Cassiopeia's chair stood daintily poised on the
> uppermost boughs. "One o'clock", said Gabriel.'[5]

This passage is taken from Thomas Hardy's *Far From the
Madding Crowd*. A similar incident also occurs later in the same
novel. Both indicate that the art of telling time from the stars
remained common amongst country people until quite recently.

The time of the year could be established by comparing the
positions of the Sun and the stars. Since the Sun moves through
the zodiacal constellations once every year, a precise determination of its position in the Zodiac indicates the date.

> the yonge sonne
> Hath in the Ram his halfe cours y-ronne[6]

In this way, Chaucer confirms at the beginning of the *Canterbury Tales* that the scene is set in April. This method of fixing the
date is common in the writings of Chaucer and his contemporaries, and persists into Elizabethan times:

> It was the month, in which the righteous Maide,
> That for disdaine of sinfull worlds upbraide,

Fled back to heaven, whence she was first conceived,
Into her silver bowre the Sunne received:
And the hot *Syrian* Dog on him awayting,
After the chafed Lyons cruell bayting[7]

Spenser is saying that the Sun has just left the constellation
Leo and is now in Virgo. In this part of the ecliptic it is at its
closest to Sirius, the Dog-star. This occurs in August, during
the hottest days of midsummer, which were therefore called the
Dog days. (It must be remembered, incidentally, that the date
corresponding to a given position of the Sun in the Zodiac
actually changes slowly with time as a result of precession.)

Once the time of the year is approximately known the particular day can be specified by reference to the position of
the Moon, since it traverses the Zodiac much more rapidly
than the Sun. (The month, of course, derives its name from the
Moon's period.)

Whan that Lucina with hir pale light
Was Joyned last with Phebus in aquarie[8]

i.e. when the Moon and the Sun were last in conjunction in
Aquarius, indicating a day around the end of February.

References to the Moon can give the day of the month, references to the Sun can give the week, or month, of the year, but a
reference to the positions of the planets can fix the year. This is
simply a result of their slower motion. A writer who describes
the planets as they appear to him therefore fixes the time of
writing. This is of interest because works of medieval and Elizabethan writers can sometimes be dated in this way. Thus there
is a passage in Chaucer's *Troilus and Criseyde* which tells us that

The bente mone with hir hornes pale,
Saturne, and Jove, in Cancro joyned were
That swich a rayn from hevene gan avale,
That every maner womman that was there
Hadde of that smoky reyn a verray fere[9]

Shortly after the First World War it was realized that this might
refer to an event which had actually been witnessed by Chaucer.
Subsequent calculations showed that a conjunction of Saturn,

Jupiter and the Moon in Cancer had indeed occurred during May, 1385. Some confirmation that Chaucer was writing with this episode in mind was provided by the further discovery that one of the greatest storms ever experienced in England took place two months after the conjunction. Prior to this astronomical interpretation of the text, no date had been known for the composition of *Troilus and Criseyde*.

Approximate estimates of time could be obtained from the general appearance of the heavens. A more accurate determination involved the use of instruments. These were normally of fairly simple construction and could be used to determine position on the Earth's surface as well as time. Often instruments of similar design had been in use for centuries. For example, the cross-staff (a crude instrument for measuring the angular distance between celestial objects) had been used by Archimedes in much the same form as in medieval times. This instrument is referred to occasionally—usually under the name of Jacob's staff.[10] George Herbert may have had it in mind when he wrote:

> Philosophers have measur'd mountains,
> Fathom'd the depths of seas, of states, and kings,
> Walk'd with a staff to heav'n[11]

The most popular medieval instrument—the astrolabe—was, however, quite complicated in construction and had undergone more recent modification at the hands of the Arabs. The astrolabe's popularity was partly due to its portability and partly to its all-round usefulness: it could be used for finding the time by day or night, for determining latitude, for measuring heights, and a good deal more. Geoffrey Chaucer was one of the leading English writers on astronomy in the fourteenth century. He has left an excellent introductory treatise on the astrolabe (written for the benefit of his son). This was illustrated in the original but, although his diagrams survive, they do not appear to have been published in standard editions of his works.

There were many different types of astrolabe; that described by Chaucer was the commonest sort called the planispheric astrolabe (because the sphere of the heavens was projected onto a plane). The basis of such an instrument was a circular metal plate called the *mother*. A ring was attached to one edge of this plate so that it could be suspended vertically. Superimposed on the mother were two more circular plates: the *tablet* and the *rete*. The latter was an openwork metal plate, so that the tablet could be seen through it. A pin passed through the centre of the tablet, holding it to the mother and the rete, and representing the North Celestial Pole. One can think of the rete as providing a chart of the brighter stars, whilst the tablet underneath supplied information on the altitude and azimuth of any point in the sky. So, if the rete was rotated over the tablet, the position of a star could be found for any given time. (Alternatively, of course, if the position of a star was known the corresponding time could be determined.) The position of the ecliptic was also included, so that measurements of the Sun's position during the day could be similarly used for finding the time. The reverse side of the mother was used for the actual observation. It had a bar, pivoted at its centre, with sights at either end. With the astrolabe hung vertically, this *alidade*, or *rule*, could be sighted on any desired star, and its altitude thus found.

Chaucer describes the whole process in the following way:

Tho wolde I wite the same night folwing the hour of the night, and wroughte in this wyse. Among an heep of sterris fixe, it lyked me for to take the altitude of the feire white sterre that is cleped Alhabor; and fond hir sitting on the west side of the line of midday, 18 degres of heighte taken by my rewle on the bak-syde. Tho sette I the centre of this Alhabor up-on 18 degrees among myn almikanteras, up-on the west side; by-cause that she was founden on the west syde. Tho leide I my label over the degree of the sonne that was descended under the weste orisonte, and rikened alle the lettres capitals fro the bordure: and fond that it was passed 8 of the clokke the space of 2 degres.[12]

In other words, Chaucer selected the star Alhabor (a medieval name for Sirius) and obtained its altitude by sighting along the rule. He then set the position of this star on the rete over the corresponding altitude circle (or almucantar) on the tablet. Finally, he moved the label (which was simply a pointer, like the hand of a clock, pivoting round the central pin) until it lay over the position of the Sun in the Zodiac for that day of the year. This position was, of course, below the horizon. He then calculated the time from the scale round the edge of the instrument. Since one degree is equivalent to four minutes, the time he found was eight minutes past eight.

As has been mentioned, geographical position was determined with the same instruments that were used to determine time. Establishing the latitude was easy enough; it simply required that the Sun, or a star, should have its elevation measured as it crossed the meridian:

> To take a latitude,
> Sun, or starres are fitliest view'd
> At their brightest.[13]

(*Brightest* here implies at their greatest elevation above the horizon.) Finding the longitude was a much more difficult problem for it involved a determination of the difference in time between two places on the Earth's surface. This can be done easily enough with an accurate clock, but there were none available in medieval times. The favourite method was to wait until there was an eclipse of the Moon (or, very rarely, of the Sun) and then to note the times at which it was seen from different places on the Earth's surface. The variation in time was a direct measure of the differences in longitude.

> to conclude
> Of longitudes, what other way have wee,
> But to marke when, and where, the darke eclipses bee?[14]

The long sea voyages which were becoming common by Elizabethan times demanded a much higher skill in navigation than had hitherto been necessary. The only methods available were based on astronomical observation.

> And wee desire to knowe the starres in Skies
> Our selves thereby to wisshed portes to bringe[15]

The requirements of navigation had a considerable influence on the development of astronomy in the seventeenth and eighteenth centuries.

Observations with the astrolabe concentrated on the Sun and

4

stars. Some much more complicated device was necessary if planetary predictions were desired, for any such instrument was required to reproduce the Ptolemaic system of epicycles, equants and so forth. A few instruments, usually referred to as equatoria, which were used for this purpose, have survived from the middle ages. (Large equatoria were sometimes associated with cathedral clocks during medieval times.) An interesting discovery of recent years is a treatise on the use of an equatorium, the authorship of which has been provisionally attributed to Chaucer.* It is possible that Chaucer also wrote on the geometry of the sphere, although no copy of such a work has yet been unearthed. It might be speculated that he mapped out, in fact, a general introduction to observational astronomy, as it was practised during the medieval period, and that the treatise on the astrolabe was one part of this. If so, it would be the first such work in English. Whether the entire treatise was intended for his little son is another matter. The boy is known to have gone up to Oxford to study when he was ten years old (which did not, of course, indicate a precocious ability in those days). This was, presumably, at least part of the reason why the astrolabe Chaucer used for his treatise was 'compowned after the latitude of Oxenford'. (Astrolabes were only designed to give accurate results at one latitude. If it was desired to use them at a radically different latitude, then the tablet had to be changed.)

There was another reason for employing Oxford, however. The university (particularly Merton College) was renowned throughout Europe at that time for its learning. Astronomy was especially studied there. Extensive astronomical tables giving the positions of the celestial bodies were constructed, and these, naturally enough, were referred to the latitude and meridian of Oxford. Makers of astrolabes based their work on these tables and therefore on the position of Oxford. It is worth noting that Merton was also renowned at this time for its physicians (as we shall see, astronomy and medicine were then intimately connected via astrology), and for its theologians, one of whom was, of course, John Wycliffe.

The joint requirements of time determination and astrology produced a demand for astronomical almanacs. After the intro-

* See: D. J. Price. *The Equatorie of the Planetis.* C.U.P. (1955).

duction of printing, these became an increasingly profitable business. The almanacs combined astronomical data and astrological predictions, with the emphasis heavily on the latter. Almanacs were highly popular among the less-educated, and generally despised by the educated. It is the rude mechanicals in *Midsummer Night's Dream* who look for an almanac.

> SNUG: Doth the moon shine that night we play our play?
> BOTTOM: A calendar, a calendar! Look in the almanac; find out moonshine, find out moonshine.[16]

The almanacs usually contained an elementary, and often distorted, introduction to current astronomical thought. Most writers, however, went to the more reputable textbooks for their knowledge. As has been mentioned, the most popular of these was the *Tractatus de sphera* of Johannes de Sacrobosco, which was written towards the middle of the thirteenth century. The author's name is sometimes anglicized to John of Holywood, or Halifax, though whether he was English in origin is uncertain. Certainly he spent most of his life teaching at the university of Paris. The book went through innumerable editions during the following centuries, and had equally innumerable commentaries attached to it. These were of two types. Either the commentator thought that the Sacrobosco had included too little astronomy, or else he thought that there was too much. In the first case, the commentary would consist of an exposition of Ptolemaic theory to add to the Aristotelian theory of the original text. In the second, the commentary would be devoted to an amplification of the astrological implications. The book remained in popular use from the time it was written until well into the seventeenth century. It was used by Milton during the early 1640s as a textbook in his academy, and John Flamsteed, the first Astronomer Royal, was inspired by it to take up the study of astronomy. Sacrobosco and the other popular medieval texts were, of course, in Latin. The first major astronomical text in English was Caxton's translation of the *Mirror of the World* (quoted in the first chapter). This had been written by a contemporary of Sacrobosco, but it was considerably larger than his *Tractatus*, mainly due to the inclusion of a large amount of geographical information.

The original writings of classical authors—insofar as they were known—were also used as textbooks in medieval times. The most popular was probably Manilius (another author used by Milton at his academy). Vives, the celebrated sixteenth-century educationalist, recommended Manilius for general study, but added that he should only be read under instruction as there was a good deal of false superstition. During the sixteenth and seventeenth centuries, a new text, called the *Zodiacus Vitae*, became very popular. Originally in Latin, it was translated into English in 1565. Its author, Marcellus Palingenius, although a Roman Catholic, strongly attacked corruption in that Church. As a result the book was placed on the Index during the sixteenth century. We may surmise that this enhanced its appreciation in Britain. One of the most used astronomy texts of the seventeenth century, the *Speculum Mundi* (or *Glasse representing the Face of the World*) similarly depended for its popularity partly on the fact that it was designed for Puritan readers.

Astronomy was taught as an integral part of the university curriculum in the middle ages. The course was supposed to introduce students to the seven so-called liberal sciences, which were sub-divided into the trivium (grammar, logic and rhetoric) and the quadrivium (arithmetic, geometry, astronomy and music). University education was intended essentially to produce clergymen, and the medieval concept of the universe was well-attuned to this task. 'The vii and laste of the vii scyences liberal is astronomye whiche is of alle clergye the ende.... By this Arte and science were first emprysed and gotten alle other sciences of decrees and of dyvinyte, by whiche alle cristiante is converted to the right faith of Our Lord God.'[17] Note that astronomy is considered here to be the most important of the seven sciences. This is confirmed by some other writings of the period.[18] The use of the word *science* deserves brief mention. In those days it was much closer in meaning to the Latin original, and implied knowledge in general. Milton's Satan, when he apostrophizes the tree of knowledge, says:

> O Sacred, Wise and Wisdom-giving Plant
> Mother of Science.[19]

The current meaning of the word was not acquired until the

eighteenth century. What we would now call science, was then called natural philosophy, or sometimes, simply, philosophy. Natural philosophers were not distinguished as *scientists* until the nineteenth century.

There was one aspect of astronomical time which was of a special interest to clergymen. This was the determination of the time elapsed since the creation of the universe. We have seen that the eternal universe of the original Aristotelian scheme had been rejected as being contrary to Scripture. The theologians believed, in fact, that it was possible to determine the age of the universe directly from a study of the various chronological statements in the Bible. The most famous such calculation was made by Archbishop Ussher in the seventeenth century, but it was only one of many. It will be remembered that he placed the creation of the universe in 4004 B.C.; this was the sort of figure generally agreed on, with only minor variations.

The deductions did not end here. The Bible tell us that

'...one day is with the Lord as a thousand years, and a thousand years as one day.'[20]

and also that

'...a thousand years in thy sight are but as yesterday'[21]

Taken together with the statement in *Genesis* that God rested on the seventh day, this led to the belief that the world would exist for six 'days' only: each 'day' being equivalent to a thousand years. Now since the date calculated for the creation of the world was 4000 B.C., this meant that the world should end in A.D. 2000 (the possibility is still with us). The Elizabethans were therefore convinced that they were living in the latter half of the last day, a fact which added considerable colour to their outlook. This is the significance behind Rosalind's remark in *As You Like It:*

The poor world is almost six thousand years old.[22]

John Donne spells it out more fully in one of his sermons.

...the two thousand yeares of Nature, before the Law given by *Moses*, And the two thousand yeares of Law, before the Gospel given by Christ, And the two thousand of Grace which are running now, (of which last houre we have heard three quarters strike, more then fifteen hundred of this last two thousand spent).[23]

This division of the six thousand years into three periods, whose ends were marked by the giving of the Mosaic laws (or, as some had it, the Flood of Noah), by the Gospel of Christ, and by the Second Coming, was common practice.

The short age of the universe was accepted by Roman Catholics and Protestants alike. Luther entertained doubts about it only because it was difficult to believe, sometimes, that the world was going to last so long. It seemed to him that the end might well come in his own lifetime. The period of six thousand years was challenged from time to time, but the order of magnitude was generally accepted.[24]

There was, in those days, another belief, connected with the past age of the world, and similarly derivable from certain biblical passages.

'Of old hast thou laid the foundation of the earth: and the heavens are the work of thy hands. They shall perish, but thou shalt endure: yea, all of them shall wax old like a garment; as a vesture shalt thou change them, and they shall be changed.'[25]

The belief, in other words, that the world was in a state of decay. Decay was an argument for the short lifetime of the universe compared with the eternity urged by Aristotle. In fact the three periods of two thousand years were sometimes represented as separate epochs, each starting well but quickly falling into decay. In past ages, men had been better: morally, physically and mentally.[26] Now the development of science does not depend on morals or physique, but it is obviously deeply concerned with man's mental stature. If man had been more intellectually able in times past, then there was little hope, or point, in trying to discover new truths about the world. The greatest ambition could not be more than to guard the fragments of knowledge that had been handed down from the giants of antiquity. The effects of this belief will be mentioned later, but it should be noted here that a certain amount of evidence for the decay of the world was derived from Ptolemaic astronomy.

First of all, the obliquity of the ecliptic was known to be decreasing. (That is, the Sun's path through the heavens was approaching more closely the celestial equator.) Spenser claimed that the angle had diminished by thirty minutes of arc since Ptolemy's day.[27] As it happens, he was exaggerating: the difference between the obliquity determined by Ptolemy and that accepted by the Elizabethans was only about twenty minutes of arc. Moreover, even this was excessive for Ptolemy had slightly mis-determined the obliquity: the true difference was only ten minutes. The obliquity is still decreasing slowly today, but the variation is now believed to be oscillatory, so that, after a long period the angle should start to increase again. It was also believed that the distance of the Sun from the Earth was decreasing and this, too, was seen as evidence for the decay of the world. According to Samuel Butler, the Sun had come about fifty thousand miles closer to the Earth over a period of twelve hundred years.[28]

Elizabethan writers—Donne, for example, and Spenser—when writing about decay, often seem to be so fascinated by it that they throw in every conceivable celestial change as another instance. Thus Spenser bemoans precession, which his forebears had regarded with equanimity.[29] He also quotes ancient records of changes in the heavens as further evidence for decay.

> And if to those Ægyptian wisards old,
> Which in Star-read were wont have best insight,
> Faith may be given, it is by them told,
> That since the time they first tooke the Sunnes hight,
> Foure times his place he shifted hath in sight,
> And twice hath risen, where he now doth West,
> And wested twice, where he ought rise aright.[30]

The same story is mentioned by Samuel Butler[31] (it derives from Herodotus).

Associated with the belief in decay, was a further belief in the previous existence of a Golden Age. This was sometimes identified with classical antiquity but, perhaps, even more frequently with the Earth before the Fall. If the latter assumption was made, then there was a tendency to see decay in the universe as being particularly pronounced at the time of the

Fall. (We have seen that the Fall was put forward as one explanation for the spots on the Moon's face.) Milton thought that the obliquity of the ecliptic (and therefore the succession of the seasons) might have been caused by the Fall.[32] Prior to that, the Sun had circled the equator and there had been perpetual spring on Earth.

The belief in decay reached its peak in the early seventeenth century, gradually declining thereafter. As we shall see in a later chapter, its disappearance seems to be clearly correlated with the growth of new scientific concepts.

Finally, in this survey of medieval ideas related to time, some mention should be made of the calendar which was in use. This was the Julian calendar, so called because it was brought into being by Julius Caesar in 45 B.C. The year in this system was taken to precisely $365\frac{1}{4}$ days, which is some eleven minutes too long. By the middle ages, this excess was becoming painfully obvious. The spring equinox was falling ten days too early in the sixteenth century, and church festivals were affected. For this reason Pope Gregory XIII promulgated a new calendar in 1582, and at the same time dropped ten days from that year. The system he instituted is the one at present in use throughout the world. However, at the time, the new calendar was widely regarded in Protestant countries as a purely papal device, which they therefore rejected. In England, the measure was actually warmly supported by leading astronomers, but parliament, led by the bishops, refused to countenance it. The Gregorian calendar was not officially introduced into Britain until 1752, and then only against strong opposition.

CHAPTER III

Astrology

FROM antiquity to the seventeenth century, the study of astronomy was always intermixed with astrology: although there was, in theory, a definite distinction between the two. Gower's definition of astronomy has been quoted in the first chapter. He immediately differentiated it from astrology.

> Assembled with Astronomy
> Is eke that ilke Astrology,
> The which in judgements accompteth
> Theffect what every sterre amounteth.
> And how they causen many a wonder
> To the climats* that stond hem under.[1]

In practice, there was considerable confusion. Faustus says:

> Come, Mephistophilis, let us dispute again,
> And reason of divine astrology.[2]

But then he goes on:

> Speak, are there many spheres above the moon?

His queries are, in fact, purely astronomical. It was, indeed, a commonplace of medieval terminology to use *astrology* as virtually equivalent to *practical astronomy*. The opposite confusion—of astronomy with astrology—is, naturally, also found. Shakespeare seems to be referring to this when he says:

> Not from the stars do I my judgement pluck:
> And yet methinks I have astronomy,
> But not to tell of good or evil luck,
> Of plagues, of dearths, or season's quality[3]

---

* 'Climats' here signifies 'climes' or 'regions'.

Similarly, *astronomer* and *astrologer* were often used interchangeably.

> O, learned indeed were that astronomer
> That knew the stars as I his characters:
> He'ld lay the future open.[4]

There was good cause for confusion. Astronomers and astrologers during this period were normally the same men, writing indiscriminately on both subjects. It is a matter of opinion whether this interdependence helped, or hindered, astronomy. There would certainly not have been so much interest in astronomy, nor so much financial support for astronomers, without the impetus provided by astrology. Kepler was one of the many astronomers who gained a livelihood in this way. He once remarked that God provided an appropriate means of sustenance for all his creatures: for astronomers He had provided astrology.

In the world of antiquity, astrology had been extremely popular. By the beginning of the Christian era it had already been shaped almost to its final form. (The description of astrology given in this chapter is therefore applicable to the entire medieval period.) The early Christian Church was generally antagonistic to astrology: both because of its pagan origin and because of its claimed ability to predict the future (which, if pushed to the logical extreme, would deny the possibility of human free will). During the early middle ages, astrology, although recognized, was not of overwhelming importance. As interest in ancient documents renewed, there arose also an increased interest in astrology. (It must be remembered that the Moslem astronomers, who transmitted most of the new astronomical knowledge, were almost all keen astrologers.) This upsurge in the study of astrology seems to have arisen first on the Continent, and then to have been transmitted to Britain, where it was widely diffused by Chaucer's time.

The study of astrology was actually divided into two fairly distinct branches. The first was Judicial Astrology which dealt with the influence of the heavens on human affairs. The second was Natural Astrology which dealt with their influence on natural phenomena such as the weather. Of these, the latter, a staple constituent of the almanacs, was uncontroversial—it was judicial astrology which excited attention and, sometimes, condemnation. References to it are very abundant in medieval and Elizabethan literature. As a rule, therefore, it is judicial astrology which we will be discussing in this chapter.

The basis of astrological belief was that the celestial bodies were able, in some way, to influence events on Earth. In particular, changes in the appearance of the heavens, due, for example, to the motion of the planets, might be used to forecast attendant changes here below. The most important datum was the position of the planets relative to the stars, that is, relative to the signs of the Zodiac. (The order in which the zodiacal signs rise above the eastern horizon—which is also the order in which the Sun passes through them during the course of a year—is still memorized by astronomers from a rhyme which was written, improbably enough, by Isaac Watts, the eighteenth-century dissenting minister.)

The zodiacal signs naturally alter their positions in the sky according to the time of the day. Astrologers also divided the region of the ecliptic into twelve sectors which always remained fixed relative to the observer. These divisions were called *houses*, or *mansions*.[5] For example, the first house covered a stretch of the ecliptic below the eastern horizon; it was called the ascendant house, since the zodiacal sign it contained would be the next to rise into view. Each house governed a particular aspect of human life: the ascendant was regarded as particularly important because it governed life and health.[6] When an astrologer was making a prediction, and searched the heavens for information, the first thing he looked for was this part of the ecliptic, which was just rising in the east. Sir Thomas Browne tells us that 'At my Nativity my Ascendant was the watery sign of Scorpius.'[7] The sign of the Zodiac lying in the ascendant was also known as the horoscope.[8] Owing to the importance of the ascendant house, the name *horoscope* came to be applied to the prediction as a whole. Whether life was to be long or short, health good or bad, depended on the planets and zodiacal sign in this house.

The different houses overlapped to some extent in the information they provided. For example, the seventh house (the ascendant house is the first) also dealt with the question of sickness. Nor were all the houses of equal power. The angular houses (which were the first, fourth, seventh and tenth) were the most powerful; then the succedent houses (which, as their name implies, came second, fifth, eight and eleventh) and, finally, the remaining four—the cadents—were the weakest. The houses were believed to be alternately masculine and feminine in character. (The ascendant and all the odd-numbered houses were masculine, the even-numbered houses were all feminine.) A similar belief was held concerning the signs of the Zodiac. Starting with Aries, all odd signs were masculine, all even signs feminine. Aries, incidentally, was the most important of the signs in astrology, because it marked the beginning of spring and the renewal of life.

There was a further division of the signs into two groups of six. The day signs, which ran from Leo to Capricornus, were under the general influence of the Sun, and the night signs— from Aquarius to Cancer—under that of the Moon. As an extra complication, each sign was itself the house of a particular planet. This meant that the planet gained an especially potent influence when it was in that sign, and must be distinguished from the previous use of the word *house*.

The Sun and Moon apart, each planet had two houses, or signs: a day house and a night house. The Sun had a day house only—in Leo—and the Moon a night house only in Cancer. As the names imply, one planetary house was taken from the six signs influenced by the Sun, and the other from the six influenced by the Moon. A planet had its maximum power if a daytime observation revealed it in its day house, or if it was in its night house for a night observation. For example, Mars has Aries as its night house and Scorpio as its day house. An observation at night that showed Mars in Aries would therefore indicate that the planet was exerting its greatest power. Curiously enough, however, the planet's influence at this time was directed not towards the sign that contained it, but to some other point on the Zodiac. Taking Mars again as an example, when it was in its night or day house the point of the heavens it influenced most strongly lay in Capricornus. This was called its exaltation. Correspondingly there was a point on the far side of the Zodiac—

in Cancer—where the planet had its least influence. This was its dejection.

A knowledge of these astrological niceties is frequently needed in reading the literature—particularly of Elizabethan writers. Thus Spenser speaks of one

> borne with ill disposed skyes,
> When oblique *Saturne* sate in the house of agonyes.[9]

The house of agonies was the twelfth house: it was normally referred to as the house of enemies, for it governed malice, envy, and imprisonment. The oblique signs were almost the same as the signs dominated by the Moon, but Capricornus was included instead of Cancer. Capricornus was the day house of Saturn, and Aquarius—also an oblique sign—was its night house. Spenser is probably implying that Saturn stood in one of its own houses and, therefore, had its power amplified. Now Saturn had the most malignant influence of all the planets. An unfortunate born in these circumstances might reasonably complain that the skies were ill-disposed.

Especial emphasis was placed on the configuration of the heavens at birth. The continually changing positions of the spheres governed life from day to day, but the basic characteristics of a person, and the main outlines of his future life, were laid down at his birth. Chapman, speaking of Mars (another unpleasant planet), remarked

> he, his second or eighth house ascends
> Of ruled nativities, and then portends
> Ill to the then-born.[10]

(The significance of this is that the second and the eighth houses dealt respectively with the wealth and death of the individual.) But, of course, you might be fortunate—as Spenser's Belphoebe was, for example.[11]

The clear distinction which was drawn between the ultimate fate of a person, laid down at birth, and the daily fluctuations of his fortune is worthy of note. On the one hand:

> But from our cradles we were marked all
> And destinate to die in Afric here.[12]

On the other:

> There's some ill planet reigns:
> I must be patient till the heavens look
> With an aspect more favourable.[13]

Of course, the distinction was not absolutely complete, since the actual celestial influence at any instant did depend to some extent on the configuration at birth.

The sign of the Zodiac in the ascendant was almost as important as any planet, for it had an influence on character, just as the planets did. Aries, for example, produced a dry, fiery nature in people born under it. (As is only to be expected from a house of Mars.) They were hot-tempered, broadset and swarthy with long faces. The zodiacal sign also indicated the best occupation for a child when it grew up. Some were obvious. If a man was born under Sagittarius he would naturally be an archer. Less obviously, he would make a good teacher, doctor, or prophet. (These would seem to be derived from the constellation figure—a centaur—which was traditionally associated with these occupations.) It has been remarked that the signs are alternately masculine and feminine. In astrology, masculine characteristics are generally fortunate and feminine generally unfortunate. Hence, it was better to be born under an odd-numbered sign.

Besides determining individual characteristics, each sign governed some portion of the human body. Aries, the first sign, governed the head, and any disease or illness that might afflict it. At the other end, Pisces, the last sign, governed the feet. This is the significance of the dialogue in *Twelfth Night*.

> SIR ANDREW: ... Shall we set about some revels?
> SIR TOBY: What shall we do else? Were we not born under Taurus?
> SIR ANDREW: Taurus! that's sides and heart.
> SIR TOBY: No, sir; it is legs and thighs.[14]

Sir Andrew and Sir Toby were, as usual, wrong. Taurus, as the second sign, actually governs the neck and throat; Sagittarius governs the legs and thighs.

The zodiacal signs and the four terrestrial elements of Aristotle were also connected. The twelve signs were divided into four groups of three, each of which was called a trigon. One trigon was reckoned earthy by nature, another watery, and so on. As Drayton remarks, they

> in their severall triplicities consent,
> Unto the nature of an Element.[15]

Or again, in *II Henry IV*, Pointz refers to the three fiery signs—Aries, Leo and Sagittarius. It is worth noting that the nature of the sign was connected with the planet that ruled it. Thus Cancer—a watery sign—was ruled by the Moon, which was the planet most associated with water.

Although both the zodiacal signs and the planets could influence human life, the latter were the more powerful. They could, for example modify, or even contradict, the indications of the stars, if they came into competition. This might occur, for example, when considering the future of certain lands, or cities, which were governed by both a planet and a sign. The exact situation could be highly complicated. Thus England was, for the most part, governed by Aries, but certain areas of the country were governed by Gemini, or Leo, and some of the cities were under the dominion of other signs again. Oxford, for example, was influenced by Capricornus (perhaps because natives of Capricornus were believed to have a rather dishevelled, goat-like appearance).

According to Gower, Saturn governed the Orient, and Jupiter, Egypt. Mars ruled the Holy Land (because there never seemed to be a permanent peace there). The Sun, which was supposed to give wisdom, governed Greece. Venus, even in those days, was seen as a guiding influence of the Italians.[16] Mercury governed France; Germany and England were jointly ruled by the Moon.[17] Mandeville, in his *Travels*, agrees that England is governed by the Moon. The reason seems to be that the Moon, owing to its changeability, governed travellers, and the English were regarded as a great nation of travellers in medieval times.

Personal characteristics were influenced as much by the planet in the ascendant, as by the zodiacal sign. A man born under Mars would be small in stature, broad-shouldered, but not fat. The influence of the planet could, however, be modified by the sign which contained it. If Mars was in a watery sign, the man would have blonde hair; in an earthy sign, he would have brown hair; and in airy, or fiery, signs, red hair. The planet could, more importantly, be modified by the influence of the other planets. The exact effect would depend on their relative positions. A man born under Mars was expected to be basically fierce. This fierceness could be combined with magnanimity, if the other planets were favourably placed, or with cruelty and treachery, if they were badly placed.[18]

The planets were generally graded according to their influence for good or evil. Saturn was the most unfortunate planet, followed by the slightly less unfortunate Mars. These were balanced by the highly fortunate Jupiter and the somewhat less fortunate Venus.[19]

'Have not starres their favourable aspects, as they have forward opposition? Is there not a *Jupiter* as there is a *Saturne*? Cannot the influence of smiling *Venus* stretch as farre as the frowning constitution of Mars?'[20]

Mercury, the Moon and the Sun were generally regarded as neutral—intrinsically neither good nor evil—although the effects of the Sun generally seem to have been beneficent. Mercury, on the other hand, seems to have been viewed more often as a bad influence than a good one. 'Whether it be that *Mercurie* is Lord of their birth, or some other peevish planet predominant in the calculation of their nativitie, I know not.'[21] The Moon was believed to be the governor of women.[22] From this point of view its effects were usually regarded with disfavour.

> And make the moone inconstant like thy selfe;
> Raigne thou at womens nuptials, and their birth;
> Let them be mutable in all their loves,
> Fantasticall, childish, and folish, in their desires,
> Demanding toyes:
> And starke madde when they cannot have their will.[23]

This quotation comes from John Lyly's *The Woman in the Moone*, the entire plot of which is based on astrology. The heroine, Pandora, changes violently as one planet after another, starting with Saturn and ending with the Moon, takes control of her character. The play is concerned with the effect of these changes on her admirers. At the end, as we see, it is decided that she is only fit to be linked with the Moon. (Writings of this sort—where the plot depends almost entirely on the succession of planetary influences—were quite popular, cf. Robert Greene's *Planetomachia*.)

When an astrologer set about casting a horoscope, it was natural therefore that he should first look to the planets. It was their disposition amongst the houses at the time of birth which established the main factors affecting the future life of the child. Next he would consider the other influences present (such as the positions of the zodiacal signs) to see how this basic picture should be modified. Of course, it was not necessary for the astrologer actually to be present at the birth of the child in order to cast the horoscope. So long as the time of birth had been accurately recorded, the corresponding configuration of the heavens could always be deduced from tables of planetary positions. Scott provides a description of the process involved in *Guy Mannering*.

'He accordingly erected his scheme, or figure of heaven, divided into its twelve houses, placed the planets therein according to the Ephemeris, and rectified their position to the hour and moment of the nativity. Without troubling our readers with the general prognostications which judicial astrology would have inferred from these circumstances, in this diagram there was one significator, which pressed remarkably upon our astrologer's attention. Mars, having dignity in the cusp of the twelfth house, threatened captivity or sudden and violent death to the native; and Mannering having recourse to those further rules by which diviners pretend to ascertain the vehemency of this evil direction, observed from the result that three periods would be particularly hazardous—his *fifth*—his *tenth*—his *twenty-first* year.'[24]

Here we see the procedure set out. First the assignment of the planets to their houses at the time of birth. Then the observation that Mars was powerful in the twelfth house (the House of Enemies). Then the modification of this threat by other influences present so that the danger focussed onto certain periods.

Although people were usually governed by one particular

5

planet, they were influenced by all the planets; in just the same way that they were born under a particular zodiacal sign, but influenced by them all. Chaucer's Wife of Bath uses this fact to help explain her moral lapses.[25] The exact nature of the planetary influence depended on the celestial configuration as a whole at the time of birth. The various possible positions of the planets relative to each other were called their aspects.[26] Let us suppose, as an example, that one planet is situated in Aries. If there is another directly opposite it—in Libra—the two are said to be in opposition.[27] Planets in Leo, or Sagittarius, are said to form a trine aspect with Aries. (That is, they form an equilateral triangle.) Planets in Cancer, Libra and Capricornus are in quartile aspect with Aries (forming a square). Planets in Gemini, Leo, Libra, Sagittarius and Aquarius are in sextile aspect with Aries. Finally, if two planets are both situated in Aries at the same time, then they are said to be in conjunction.[28]

The aspects were classified according to their astrological significance. Opposition and quartile were generally deemed unfavourable. This is the import of King Richard's words

> Lo, at their births good stars were opposite[29]

Trine and sextile, on the other hand, were thought to be favourable.[30]

> For sure the milder planets did combine
> On thy auspicious horoscope to shine,
> And ev'n the most malicious were in trine[31]

Their exact influence varied somewhat with the circumstances. Nor were all astrologers in entire agreement as to the effects of a given aspect: thus some seem to have considered quartile aspect as favourable. Conjunction might be either good, or bad, depending on the natures of the planets involved.

It was widely believed that the biblical flood took place when all the planets were in conjunction in Capricornus, and that the world would end when they all came to conjunction in Cancer. Gower noted that the world was created when the Sun was in Aries, and this is confirmed by other writers.[32] A Platonic belief, which attracted some attention, was the idea of a Great

Year, at the end of which the planets returned to the configuration they had had at the Creation (that is, they were all in conjunction in Aries). It was sometimes suggested that this return to the initial state would mark the end of the world, rather than a conjunction in Cancer. There was one difficulty: Plato had assigned a period of ten thousand ordinary years to the Great Year, and this was longer than the accepted lifetime of the universe. Other philosophers of antiquity had, however, suggested that a shorter period was possible. Milton makes use of this concept in Book V of *Paradise Lost*.

Astrology obviously provides another example of the interconnectedness of medieval thought. It was a dynamic relationship: in the sense that events in the heavens affected events on Earth. But the medieval mind also envisaged a static relationship where the structure of the heavens was reflected both in the overall development of Man's life and in the structure of Man himself. Thus an analogy was drawn between the seven planets and the seven ages of Man (which were, in turn, related to the biblical assessment of Man's lifespan as seventy years).

'Our Infancy is like the *Moon*, in which it seemeth only to grow, as Plants: in our next age we are instructed as under Mercury, always near the Sun: Our *Youth* is wanton, and given to pleasures, as Venus; our Fourth Age Strong, Vigorous and Flourishing, is like the Sun: Our Fifth Age like *Mars*, striving for Honour: our Sixth like *Jupiter*, Wise and stayed; our Seventh like *Saturn*, slow and heavy.'[33]

Shakespeare draws the same analogy in *As You Like It*. The comparison has its subtleties. The Moon, for instance, was appropriate for children because it showed rapid growth and change. But the Moon, because of its connection with the tides, also governed excessive moisture.

There was also believed to be a one-to-one correspondence between the parts of the human body and the universe at large.[34] For example, the streams and rivers that flowed over the Earth's surface were analogous to the arteries and veins of the human body. Man, the microsm, showed in himself the universe, or macrocosm. John Donne, characteristically, inverted the relationship

> She, to whom this world must itself refer
> As suburbs, or the microcosme of her[35]

The list of analogies could be very extensive—see, for example, *Microcosmus* by John Davies and *The Purple Island* by Phineas Fletcher—but few were of much astronomical interest.

Just as the heavens showed a certain astronomical symmetry, so also they were believed to possess a degree of astrological order. We have seen that the Sun was the middlemost of the planets revolving round the Earth. Correspondingly, in astrology, it had a balancing influence and was often represented as an arbitrator between the planets. Again, the sphere of the fortunate Jupiter lies between the spheres of the malignant Saturn and Mars, and so he

> cuts his way
> Through *Saturns* ice, and *Mars* his firy ball;
> Temp'ring their strife with his more kindely ray[36]

(cf. Drayton[37]).

Similarly, Venus and Mercury are so placed as to influence the Moon for the better.[38] Here, in a minor sphere, is evidence once more of the internal consistency of the medieval universe: astrology and astronomy intertwining in their explanation.

The planets, as the two last quotations show, were divided into hot and cold groups. According to Francis Bacon

> Of planets, Mars is accounted the hottest after the sun; then comes Jupiter, and then Venus. Others, again, are set down as cold; the moon, for instance, and above all Saturn.[39]

Besides their connection with human beings, planets were also linked with the inanimate material on Earth. Thus each planet was related to a different terrestrial metal.[40] (Characteristically, there were believed to be seven metals: exactly the same as the number of planets.) The assignment of the metals to the different planets seems fairly logical. Gold for the Sun, and silver for the Moon, follow from the similarity of their colours. Mars is connected with iron: the metal from which swords and armour were made, and which turned red when it rusted. Mercury is the fastest-moving planet; hence it is related

to quicksilver. In a similar way, each planet was assigned its
own colour. Some, such as the Sun (yellow) and Mars (red),
were related to the actual colour of the planet. Others such as
Saturn (black), reflected the astrological characteristics of the
planet. The zodiacal signs were also connected with particular
colours. Their relationship is often hard to see, but a few, such as
Aquarius (light blue) and Pisces (a silvery colour) may have
been drawn from the constellation name.

Through the planets, astrology was connected with time-
reckoning. In medieval times, two sorts of hours were in use. The
day could be divided into twenty-four equal portions, as it is
today, thus producing what were called the hours equal. Otherwise, the period from sunrise to sunset could be divided into
twelve equal portions, and the night, from sunset to sunrise,
into another twelve. This produced the hours inequal, since,
except at the equinoxes, night and day differ in duration.
(The two kinds of hours were also referred to as 'hours of the
clock' and 'hours of the planets'.) Time-reckoning in astrology
was in terms of the hours inequal—each hour being governed
by one of the planets. An astrological day started at sunrise and
was named after the planet that governed its first hour. If the
first hour after sunrise was ruled by Saturn, then that day was
Saturday. The second hour would then be ruled by Jupiter,
the third by Mars, and so on through the planets in the reverse
order of their accepted distances from the Earth. The eighth
hour would again be ruled by Saturn, as would the fifteenth
and twenty-second hours. The twenty-third hour would be
governed by Jupiter, the twenty-fourth by Mars and the twenty-
fifth by the Sun. But the twenty-fifth hour was, of course, the
first hour of the next day, which was therefore called Sunday.
Following the cycle through in this way, each day of the week
could be equated to a corresponding planet. The relationship
is somewhat obscured in English, since the Norse gods have been
used in naming the days, rather than their Mediterranean
equivalents. (The basic system can be recovered by equating
Mars with Tew, Mercury with Woden, Jupiter with Thor, and
Venus with Freya.) The existence of a seven-day week was thus
intimately related to the existence of the seven planets in the sky.
Similarly, the twelve months of the year were connected with the

twelve zodiacal signs. (Each month was, of course, governed by the sign which contained the Sun.)

The most propitious time for a planet to influence the Earth was, naturally enough, during one of the hours that it ruled. Sir Thomas Browne noted that 'I was born in the Planetary hour of Saturn and I think I have a piece of that Leaden Planet in me.'[41] ('Leaden' here can be interpreted in two senses. In the first place, lead was the metal associated with Saturn; in the second, Saturn is the slowest-moving planet and, hence, its motion might reasonably be described as leaden.) A more extended reflection of this same belief occurs in *The Knight's Tale*, where we read

> The thridde hour inequal that Palamon
> Bigan to Venus temple for to goon,
> Up roos the sonne, and up roos Emelye,
> And to the temple of Diana gan hye.[42]

It is known from the context that the sunrise Chaucer refers to ushered in the first hour of Monday. Emily therefore chose this hour to go and pray to Diana, the Moon goddess. This was the third hour inequal after Palamon had gone to the temple of Venus which, on reckoning back, shows that he went in the hour governed by Venus.

Besides the general influence of the zodiacal constellations, individual stars also had some affect on the Earth. Gower mentions fifteen particular stars, each of which ruled a specific stone and a specific plant.[43] Individual stars could also have a more general effect for good or evil. Algol is the name of a bright star in the constellation Perseus. It marks the position of the Gorgon's head which Perseus is carrying, and was early considered to be a most unfortunate and dangerous star. This probably derives from the Perseus myth; though there has been occasional controversy on this point, for Algol actually varies in brightness, and it has been suggested that its adverse reputation might have been based on this. Another star with a bad name was Sirius. This was because the Sun approached it most closely (and was therefore most influenced by it) during the hot days of summer, when the insanitary conditions of medieval towns made life distinctly unpleasant.[44]

The Pleiades, one of the few clusters* of stars visible to the naked eye, were also assigned an especial influence. They often seem to be linked in action with the Moon

> we that take purses go by the moon and the seven stars.[45]

Milton, on the other hand, obviously thought of them more favourably.

> and the *Pleiades* before him danc'd
> Shedding sweet influence[46]

Any sudden change in the heavens was naturally of great astrological import. Hence, references to the possible terrestrial effects of meteors (in the medieval sense of the word) are common. The most significant of these unexpected omens were the comets. They were normally regarded with dread as foreboding some great evil. Thus Milton, when he wished to describe Satan, compared him with a comet

> That fires the length of *Ophiucus* huge
> In th' Artick Sky, and from his horrid hair
> Shakes Pestilence and Warr.[47]

This is an interesting passage, for the constellation Ophiucus (the Serpent-Bearer) is not one of the most northerly; indeed, it stands astride the celestial equator. Ophiucus is usually represented as a man holding a snake (the neighbouring constellation of Serpens). Perhaps there was a confusion here because there is another snake in the heavens—Draco—which actually does encircle the north celestial pole. Moreover, in Milton's time, there was some confusion between Ophiucus and Serpens, for the former was often then referred to by its alternative name of Serpentarius. However that may be, the implied reference to a serpent is sufficiently obvious.

Comets generally forewarned of a coming change in the governance of a state.[48] This was often expected to be the death

* A star cluster is a group of stars which are physically connected: in other words, they would appear to be together in the sky whatever the viewpoint of the observer. This distinguishes them from constellations, where the grouping is only an optical effect: an observer from some vantage point other than our solar system would not see the same constellation figures that we do.

of the king or, sometimes, of another leading noble.[49] Many a tyrant died happy in the knowledge that his greatness had received its rightful accolade. On the other hand, the death foretold was not normally a peaceful one.

> O thou soft naturall death, that art joint-twin
> To sweetest slumber: no rough-bearded Comet,
> Stares on thy milde departure.[50]

Problems of interpretation occasionally arose when two great men died during the appearance of a single comet. The comet seen in England in 1066 (which later came to be called Halley's comet) was generally thought to have presaged the death of Harold. There was some dispute, however, when news arrived from the east that the same comet had also presided over the death of the emperor in Constantinople.

The astrologers assigned different influences to a comet depending on its shape, position and proximity to any of the planets. (It was generally accepted that comets were generated by or, at least, connected with certain planets—particularly Mars.) Thus a sword-shaped comet was believed to presage war. Very rarely, certain types of comets could actually have a beneficial influence.[51]

Meteors and aurorae were confused with comets astrologically, just as they were astronomically. Meteors, being commoner, were generally treated less seriously. The rapidly changing forms that aurorae could produce were often transformed by imagination into the most fearsome spectacles. A favourite interpretation was of armies fighting.[52] (This was, perhaps, the origin of the Valkyries.)

Eclipses of the Sun were equivalent in astrological effect to comets. Indeed, their prognosis seems to have been even gloomier. Like comets, they betokened change to the inhabitants of the world. Milton remarked on this in a passage comparing Satan with the eclipsed Sun (just as elsewhere he compared him with a comet).[53] Milton also suggested in *Lycidas* that the ship in which his friend perished was built during an eclipse.[54] This is, perhaps, a reference to the custom of finding an astrologically propitious day for the launching of a ship (or, indeed, for the beginning of any other important business).

A detailed account of the astrological effects of eclipses may be found in *King Lear*.

> These late eclipses in the sun and moon portend no good to us: though the wisdom of nature can reason it thus and thus, yet nature finds itself scourged by the sequent effects: love cools, friendship falls off, brothers divide: in cities, mutinies; in countries, discord; in palaces, treason; and the bond crack'd 'twixt son and father.[55]

Elsewhere, Shakespeare suggested that the correlation between evil on Earth and signs in the heavens worked both ways: an atrocious event on Earth (in this case, the murder of Desdemona) should be reflected by eclipses in the heavens.[56]

It must be remembered that the celestial bodies, as well as affecting human life, were also supposed simultaneously to be influencing natural phenomena. Comets, for example, could have evil effects on the weather as well as on human beings.[57] Such an influence was counted a part of meteorological astrology—one of the major sub-divisions of natural astrology. Meteorological astrology was not, however, the most important part of natural astrology: that honour was generally reserved for medical astrology. A knowledge of certain parts of astrology was regarded as an essential prerequisite for medieval doctors because the remedies they applied, and the times of application, depended on the configuration of the heavens.

> With us ther was a DOCTOUR of PHISYK
> In all this world ne was ther noon him lyk
> To speke of phisik and of surgerye;
> For he was grounded in astronomye.
> He kepte his pacient a ful greet del
> In houres, by his magik naturel.
> Wel coude he fortunen the ascendent
> Of his images for his pacient.
> He knew the cause of everich maladye,
> Were it of hoot or cold, or moiste, or drye,
> And where engendred, and of what humour;
> He was a verrey parfit practisour.[58]

There are two words of interest in this passage—'images' and 'humour'.

Images were one of the major stock in trade of the medieval doctor. They were usually small, inscribed, metal medallions which were worn as charms against disease. The doctor made, or inscribed, them at a particularly favourable time for the patient (especial reference being made therefore to his ascendant). Donne seems to have had a considerable interest in such images.[59] He mentions the loss of the art as an example of decay in the *First Anniversary*.[60] The use of images, however, smacked more of judicial astrology than of natural astrology and, as such, came in for a certain amount of opprobrium.[61]

It was a basic tenet of medieval medical theory that the human constitution was governed by the relative proportions of the four humours which the body was supposed to contain. Illness occurred when their equilibrium was disturbed. These humours—blood, phlegm, choler and melancholy—were themselves derived from the four elements which we encountered in Chapter I. These elements, in turn, were thought to be a product of the four contraries—hot, cold, moist and dry.[62] Hence the humours and the elements had certain properties in common: for example, phlegm was reckoned to be cold and moist, as also was water. Since both the planets and the Zodiac had close ties with the elements, they were therefore also related to the bodily humours. This was, indeed, the basic reason for the importance of astrology in medieval medicine.[63] Greene cites the humours as another example of the reciprocal relationship between the Earth and the heavens.

> The starres from earthly humours gaine their light
> Our humours by their light possesse their power[64]

For example, the Moon was considered to be cold and moist. It was therefore the governor of both water and phlegm, which had a like nature.

An excess of any one of the humours produced a particular type of character: mirrored to some extent in the way we use the names today—sanguinary, phlegmatic, choleric and melancholy. The Elizabethan comedy of humours, such as was written, for example, by Ben Jonson, concerned itself with people having an excess of one or other of the humours. However, the balance of the humours had a more general influence; it determined not only the variation in character from one individual to the next, but also the psychological differences between the sexes.[65] Obviously the concept of a balance presupposes that the effects of one humour can counteract those of another. In fact the humours (as also the elements) were formed into opposing pairs; thus choler was opposed to phlegm, blood to melancholy.[66]

It was in good part because of this connection between medicine and astrology that the medical profession throughout the medieval period had a continuing reputation for irreligion. We are told of Chaucer's doctor that

His studie was but litel on the bible.[67]

Some two hundred and fifty years later Sir Thomas Browne in the introductory paragraphs of *Religio Medico* complained that the general scandal of his profession might persuade the world that he had no religion at all.[68]

The medieval Church was generally opposed to any wholehearted commitment to astrology. This dislike was mainly based on a theological distrust of judicial astrology—especially the limitation it imposed upon free will. In its most extreme form astrology imposed complete determinism not only on man, but even on God. The greatest astrologer (and physician) of the sixteenth century, Jerome Cardan, traced the whole of Christ's life on Earth as a consequence of the aspect of the heavens at His birth. British astrologers, in general were loath to go so far, but they found it difficult to deny that this was the ultimate conclusion of their work.

In every age, opinions on the inevitability of celestial influences varied. Thus Chaucer sometimes seems to favour astrological predestination,[69] when Gower is more moderate.[70] Similarly, in Elizabethan times there is the contrast between

> Our remedies oft in ourselves do lie,
> Which we ascribe to heaven: the fated sky
> Gives us free scope; only doth backward pull
> Our slow designs when we ourselves are dull.[71]

and, on the other hand,

> the strange difference 'twixt us and the stars;
> They work with inclinations strong and fatal,
> And nothing know; and we know all their working
> And nought can do, or nothing can prevent![72]

Too much significance should not be assigned to the views of any single writer. Robert Greene, for example, sometimes speaks as if he was a firm believer in celestial predestination, and at others as if he allowed reasonable scope for free will.[73] In the same way, Chaucer sometimes accepts and sometimes opposes.[74] On the whole, pessimistic views were the commoner

> We are meerely the Starres tennys-balls
> (Strooke, and banded
> Which way please them)[75]

It was very frequently thought that stellar influence could be mitigated—given sufficient effort—but not completely averted.[76] In Lyly's *Gallathea*, the father suggests that: 'to avoide therfore desteny (for wisedome ruleth the stars) I thinke it better to use an unlawful means... and to prevent (if it be possible) thy constellation by my craft.' But his daughter replies: 'Destenie may be deferred, not prevented'.[77]

It must be emphasized that early attacks on astrology were not usually denials of celestial influence: only of the possibility of predicting its exact nature. The moderate, reasonable attitude towards astrology was thought to be that followed by Sir Francis Bacon,[78] Sir Walter Raleigh,[79] or Sir Thomas Browne

> 'Nor do we hereby reject or condemn a sober and regulated Astrology: we hold there is more truth therein then in Astrologers: in some more then many allow, yet in none so much as some pretend. We deny not the influence of the Stars, but often suspect the due application thereof; for though we should affirm that all things were in all things; that heaven were but earth celestified, and earth but heaven terrestrified, or that each part above had an influence upon its divided affinity below; yet how to single out these relations, and duly to

apply their actions, is a work oft times to be effected by some revelation, and Cabala from above, rather then any Philosophy, or speculation here below. What power soever they have upon our bodies, it is not requisite they should destroy our reasons... There is in wise men a power beyond the Stars; and Ptolomy encourageth us, that by foreknowledge, we may evade their actions; for, being but universal causes, they are determined by particular agents.'[80]

The neo-Platonist approach to celestial motions, using separate intelligences to move the spheres, did provide a possible avenue of escape from predestination; for it could always be argued that the intelligences introduced an element of free will into the system. (This could hardly be done on the Aristotelian model, where all motions were mechanically derived from that of the prime mover.) Whether or not this approach was regarded as generally valid, it is certainly true that several of the leading scientists in Elizabethan England supported both neo-Platonic ideas and astrology. Such a one was John Dee,* an important Elizabethan mathematician and scientist, who was also astrologer to Queen Elizabeth. His notoriety in the black arts was remembered long after his death. We are told of Sidrophel in *Hudibras* that

> He'd read Dee's prefaces before,
> The Devil, and Euclid, o'er and o'er;
> And all th' intrigues 'twixt him and Kelly,
> Lescus and th' emperor, would tell thee:
> But with the Moon was more familiar
> Than e'er was almanac well-willer.[81]

Dee, Kelly and Lasky (or Lescus) had together investigated alchemy, and various other magical and occult practices (including raising the dead). The emperor was Rudolph II at Prague, on whose behalf Dee worked for a time. (Rudolph certainly showed some skill in choosing his astrologers: at a later date he employed two of the greatest astronomers of the era— Tycho Brahe and Johannes Kepler.)

* John Aubrey was distantly related to Dee. Aubrey records that John Dee's son, Arthur Dee, was an intimate friend of Sir Thomas Browne.

Theologians followed two main lines of argument in their attempts to discredit the excessive claims of astrology. The first was the quotation of condemnatory passages from the Bible, such as *Jeremiah* 10: 2, or *Isaiah* 47: 13. (The astrologers reacted to this by quoting, somewhat more feebly, passages such as *Genesis* 1: 14.) These were supported by citations from extra-biblical Church authorities. Here the theologians were at an over-whelming advantage; it often seems, indeed, as if the astrologers could find no one to fall back on as a defender except the Lutheran theologian, Melancthon.

The second method used by theologians to disprove the claims of astrologers was the obvious one of comparing their predictions with results. Cardan, for example, was called over to England as medical adviser to Edward VI. Before leaving on the return trip, he used his astrological knowledge to predict a long life for the king. Edward died almost immediately. Again, there were innumerable stories of astrologers whose children died early when their fathers had predicted the opposite. (One of these, too, concerned the inevitable Cardan, whose eldest son was hanged for murder despite a most propitious horoscope.) This approach had its drawbacks, for the astrologers had at least two replies to hand. They could, in the first place, point out instances in which astrological predictions had been sig-nally fulfilled. For example, according to the Danish astronomer, Tycho Brahe, the great comet of 1577 forewarned of a prince who would be born somewhere in northern Europe, would overrun the German states, and would finally die in 1632. This prescription later seemed to have been accurately fulfilled by Gustavus Adolphus of Sweden.[82] (It is interesting to remem-ber that the measurements of this same comet of 1577 were used by Tycho Brahe to cast doubt upon the Aristotelian theory of comets: he found no difficulty in reconciling the astrological and astronomical significances.)

The last great English astrologer, William Lilly (from whom some of the characteristics of Sidrophel in Samuel Butler's *Hudibras* may have derived) was generally credited with the prediction of both the great plague in 1665 and the fire of London a year later. He had published some drawings in 1651 which, allegedly, illustrated major events of the future. One of these showed two men digging graves. On the ground around them lay three corpses and two coffins, indicating, it was said, that more people had died than there was time to bury. This was the prediction of the plague year. Another illustration showed two children falling headlong into a fire which bystanders were trying, ineffectually, to put out. Since London was governed by the zodiacal sign of the Gemini—and the two children could, presumably, be taken for twins—this picture was believed to predict the fire. Lilly was called before a committee of the House of Commons, who were trying to find the cause of the double catastrophe. He told them modestly, that although he had foreseen the plague and fire, he had not known the exact times at which they would occur, nor the reason for them. (One suggestion which was canvassed at the time was that they were a judgement on the country for harbouring that terrible atheist, Thomas Hobbes.)

A second argument which astrologers advanced in defence of their art was that, although their predictions were completely accurate, the influence of the stars was distorted in reaching men. It was generally accepted that celestial influence acted indirectly on human beings, via the Earth's atmosphere and the humours of the body, either of which, it was argued, could in some subtle way alter the original effect. A further element of confusion was added by the astrologers themselves. Some based their calculations on the time of birth of the child, others on the time of conception. Use of the latter method obviously allowed considerable scope for error. Astrologers were often so confident of their work that, if their predictions did not appear to fit the life as it actually developed, they would alter the time of conception, or even of birth, until agreement was reached. A Protestant astrologer found that the heavens at Luther's birth were insufficiently impressive. He therefore changed the birth date by more than a month, until a horoscope of sufficient excellence was obtained. (In *Tristram Shandy*, Sterne has the papal astrologers casting Luther's horoscope, and thence concluding that he was unavoidably damned from birth.)

Finally, both sides advanced physical arguments for, and against, the truth of astrology. The astrologers could, of course, always argue that there were at any rate two celestial bodies—

the Sun and the Moon—which manifestly influenced the Earth.
The generally accepted, but highly mysterious, influence of the
Moon on the tides often received a mention.[84] In Thomas
Heywood's *The Silver Age*, Prosperine (the Moon) has been
captured by Pluto, and Jupiter, giving judgement, describes the
powers attributed to the Moon. All are considered to be on an
equal footing.

> Nor rob the heavens the Planet of the Moone,
> By whom the seas are sway'd; Be she confin'd
> Below the earth, where be the ebbes and tides?
> Where is her power infus'd in hearbes and plants?
> In trees for buildings? simples phisical?
> Or minerall mines?[85]

(The Sun and Moon were supposed to play a great part in
geology by forming minerals and precious stones below the
Earth's surface.[86])

At the beginning of the seventeenth century, John Chamber, a
canon of Windsor, developed an interesting argument against
the possibility of judicial astrology, based on physical grounds.
(As a result he became involved in a controversy with Sir
Christopher Heydon, who defended judicial astrology. The
ensuing argument is referred to by Sir Walter Scott.[87]) Chamber
noted that a particular configuration of the heavens only
returned once every 36,000 years (this being the period he
took for the Great Year). Since the influence of a given stellar
arrangement could only be determined from observations of
its effects, astrologers in his time had insufficient data to make a
correct prediction. The astrologers rejoined that their work was
based on the astrological records of the Chaldeans, which went
back for 407,000 years; but they were crushed when Chamber
pointed out that the Earth was only 6,000 years old.

It should, perhaps, be added that the theologians could, in
any case, win this type of argument whether the astrological
predictions proved to be right or wrong. If they were wrong, this
proved the inaccuracy of astrology. If, on the other hand, the
predictions were right, then it was held that the astrologers had
obtained their knowledge by consorting with the devil, and
deserved condemnation for that.[88]

In concluding this chapter, it is worth repeating that astrology is simply one particular example—albeit the most important—of the medieval belief in an overall relationship between man and the universe. Other beliefs—such as the microcosm–macrocosm analogy—are evidently related to it. In general, these other correspondences were of little astronomical importance, but one—the idea of a chain of being—played a small, yet interesting, part in subsequent astronomical history. The basis of the chain of being was the belief that a continuous series of creatures existed, which varied in size and importance from nothing up to God (who corresponded, in effect, to infinity). This idea remained intellectually respectable for some time after astrology and most other medieval analogies had been abandoned. Indeed, its most interesting astronomical applications appeared in the seventeenth and eighteenth centuries and consideration of them will therefore be deferred until later.

Chapter IV

The Copernican Revolution

IT frequently occurs in the history of science that the founder of a new school of thought seems, on examination, to hold ideas which more nearly resemble those of his predecessors than those of his successors. Copernicus is a good example of this. Although his introduction of the heliocentric hypothesis subsequently led to revolutionary changes in astronomy, he himself was firmly imbued with a classical outlook.

A major factor in the development of his system was, indeed, his strict acceptance of the classical belief that only circular motions could occur in the heavens. Thus he could use the concept of epicycles quite happily, but he objected strongly to the Ptolemaic device of the equant. This, he felt, was a betrayal of the basic ideals of the classical astronomers. His calculations seemed to show that he could rid the system of the equant—leaving only a combination of genuinely circular motions—if he placed the Sun at the centre of the universe rather than the Earth. This major change apart, he was quite willing to accept other features of the classical world picture such as, for example, the sharp distinction between the sub-lunar and supra-lunar regions. Nevertheless, in one respect Copernicus clearly distinguishes himself as a forerunner of the scientific revolution: his writings reveal strong traces of a neo-Platonic influence. Thus he emphasizes the uniformity of nature and the mathematical basis of the universe, and proclaims a significant belief in the supreme importance of the Sun. This neo-Platonic tendency became a characteristic feature of Copernicanism, and was of considerable importance in the development of astronomy during the sixteenth and seventeenth centuries.

Copernicus' major contribution to the advancement of astronomy was not so much in suggesting a heliocentric universe (which had, after all, also been proposed in antiquity) but rather in showing that such a universe was mathematically feasible. It came to be believed that the Copernican methods of calculating planetary positions were somewhat easier to handle than the Ptolemaic. As a result, they were introduced into the computation of planetary tables. The widespread use of these tables meant that Copernican ideas gradually became known to most astronomers. Their serious consideration was further aided by the prestige accorded to Copernicus in contemporary discussions of calendar reform. Nevertheless, his views won little immediate acceptance. The majority of astronomers were prepared to take the heliocentric hypothesis as a basis to aid their calculations, but they were not prepared to adopt it as a physically realistic model. In taking this attitude they could, indeed, claim that they were only following Copernicus himself, for the preface to *De Revolutionibus Orbium Caelestium*—the book in which Copernicus set out his ideas—specifically advocated such an approach. When Robert Burton came to discuss the possibility of the Earth's motion, he remarked: 'Or to omit all smaller controversies, as matters of less moment, and examine that main paradox, of the earth's motion, now so much in question: Aristarchus Samius, Pythagoras maintained it of old, Democritus and many of their scholars... Howsoever, it is revived since by Copernicus, not as a truth, but a supposition, as he himself confesseth in the preface to Pope Nicholas'.[1] However, it gradually became known that the preface had not been written by Copernicus at all, but was inserted without his authority by Andreas Osiander, the Protestant theologian who saw the book through the press.

Although Copernican methods were used for computations in preference to Ptolemaic methods, the results were not greatly more accurate: the determination of planetary positions remained a problem throughout the sixteenth century. As has been mentioned in Chapter I, Mars was the planet that most defied accurate calculation. (Mercury, which might be expected to present a greater problem, was less well observed at that time.)

> Mars his true moving, even as in the heavens
> So in the earth, to this day is not known.[2]

Spenser noted three planets for which orbits were difficult to predict. First of all, Mercury

> he his course doth altar every yeare
> And is of late far out of order gone.[3]

Then Mars and Saturn

> But most is *Mars* amisse of all the rest,
> And next to him old *Saturne*, that was wont be best[4].

Spenser's main interest in these deviations lay in their use as arguments for the general decay of the universe, but the three planets—Mercury, Mars and Saturn—which he selects as having unpredictable courses are, in fact, the three which follow the most evidently non-circular orbits round the Sun and are, therefore, the ones most difficult to explain on Ptolemaic (or Copernican) theory. Good agreement with observation for these planets was not reached until the beginning of the seventeenth century, when Kepler used Tycho Brahe's observations to show that the planets follow elliptical orbits, and not orbits made up of some combination of circles.

The Copernican hypothesis was not commonly mentioned in English writings until the seventeenth century (when it was popularized as we shall see, mainly by Galileo's observations), but then it became the subject of quite frequent reference.

> I conclude therefore, and say, there is no happiness under (or, as Copernicus will have it, above) the Sun.[5]

(Notice here how the old Aristotelian concept of an absolute *up* and *down* in space continues.) Even Shakespeare, perhaps, permitted himself an oblique reference to heliocentric ideas:

> Doubt thou the stars are fire
> Doubt that the sun doth move.[6]

The best-known reference to Copernicanism in early seventeenth-century literature is, of course, John Donne's extended discussion of the 'new philosophy' in *An Anatomy of the World*. Donne seems to have been more interested in the heliocentric hypothesis than most of his contemporaries and refers to it frequently. One of his pleasantest uses of the concept is in the *Devotions*, when he is describing one stage of his recovery from an illness. 'I am up, and I seeme to stand, and I goe round; and I am a new Argument of the new Philosophie, That the

Earth moves round; why may I not beleeve, that the whole earth moves in a round motion, though that seeme to mee to stand, when as I seeme to stand to my Company, and yet am carried, in a giddy, and circular motion, as I stand?'[7]

Astronomers apart, the Copernican thesis won little general support until over a century after its first appearance in print. The main difficulty was its apparent contradiction of commonsense conclusions. Thus a French poem (du Bartas' *The Week*), which enjoyed great popularity in an English translation, referred scathingly to the heliocentric hypothesis as an absurd jest. For the most part, however, references to the idea were relatively gentle: it was generally treated as interesting, if improbable.

> Only the earth doth stand for ever still,
> Her rocks remove not nor her mountains meet;
> (Although some wits enricht with learning's skill
> Say heav'n stands firm and that the earth doth fleet
> And swiftly turneth underneath their feet):
> Yet, though the earth is ever stedfast seen,
> On her broad breast hath dancing ever been.[8]

(The concept of the heavenly round as a dance was not, of course, necessarily linked to the Aristotelian world picture.[9] Nevertheless, it gradually became less popular as the seventeenth century developed.)

A typical commonsense objection to Copernicanism was that, as the Earth rotated, anything not attached to its surface would be left behind. This could be expressed in several forms; one way, for example, was to argue that an arrow shot straight up in the air should fall slightly behind the archer, if the Earth moved. The most delightful expression of this viewpoint was recorded by Sir Thomas Browne. 'It... is no small disparagement unto baldness, if it be true what is related by Ælian concerning Æschilus, whose bald-plate was mistaken for a rock, and so was brained by a Tortoise which an Æagle let fall upon it. Certainly it was a very great mistake in the perspicacity of that Animal. Some men critically disposed, would from hence confute the opinion of Copernicus: never conceiving how the motion of the earth below, should not wave him from a knock perpendicularly directed from a body in the air above.'[10]

This, and related objections, were really questions of mechanics. The major astronomical problem was that the heliocentric hypothesis required the stars to be an immense distance away from the Earth. It was argued that, if the Earth moved round the Sun in a circle, this should be reflected in a corresponding apparent oscillation in the positions of the stars. The amplitude of the oscillation would be smaller, the further away the stars. Tycho Brahe's measurements at the end of the sixteenth century were sufficiently accurate to show that, on a heliocentric theory, the stars must be many times further away from the Sun than Saturn. This led to the unsatisfactory picture (for a medieval mind) of a large waste of empty space between the sphere of Saturn and the sphere of the stars: 'but then between the sphere of Saturn and the firmament, there is such an incredible and vast space or distance (7,000,000 semidiameters of the earth, as Tycho calculates) void of stars'.[11]

Tycho, moreover, thought that he could measure the angular diameters of the stars. At the distance required by Copernican theory, his measurements would have made the stars far larger bodies that the Sun, which also seemed improbable.

Again, on the Copernican scheme, although all the planets revolved round the Sun, the Moon revolved round the Earth. There seemed to be no reasonable explanation for this single exception. (It should be noted in passing that objections to Copernican ideas fell into two categories. The first opposed rotation of the Earth about its axis; the second opposed revolution of the Earth about the Sun. In fact only the latter motion was peculiar to the Copernican hypothesis; a geocentric system might also possess a rotating Earth. But contemporary objections to Copernicanism, as also contemporary support, tended to confuse the two issues.)

The criticisms of the Earth's revolution, so far mentioned, would have been applicable to any heliocentric theory. There was one additional criticism which applied specifically to the Copernican system. Copernicus, it will be remembered, based his ideas of the universe on much the same foundations as the astronomers of antiquity. He therefore accepted the physical existence of planetary spheres, and conceived the Earth as being permanently fixed to its own sphere. If this were so, then, as the Earth revolved round the Sun, its axis of rotation should point to different parts of the sky. In other words, the north celestial pole ought to describe a circle each year through the stars. To cancel out this unobserved effect, Copernicus gave the Earth a small motion in the opposite direction, so that the celestial pole remained stationary. This was referred to as his third motion (the first two being the diurnal rotation of the Earth round its axis and the annual revolution of the Earth round the Sun), and receives occasional mention in seventeenth-century writings.[12] The introduction of this arbitrary additional motion not unreasonably provoked opposition. As soon as the concept of planetary spheres was discarded, it became much more reasonable to assume that the direction of the Earth's axis remained fixed in space. The third motion therefore disappeared from the scene in the seventeenth century. To be fair to Copernicus, it should be added that there was a physical basis in his system for this third motion, since, by a slight modification, he could use it to explain trepidation. The idea of trepidation was itself soon dropped, however, so this hardly appeared a great recommendation to his successors. It should be noted that the term *Copernicanism* was often used—as it is in the present chapter—not just for the strict Copernican theory, but for heliocentric ideas in general.

A concise summary of contemporary objections to the Copernican theory was drawn up by Sir Francis Bacon in the early years of the seventeenth century: 'in the system of Copernicus there are found many and great inconveniences; for both the loading of the earth with a triple motion is very incommodious, and the separation of the sun from the company of the planets, with which it has so many passions in common is likewise a difficulty, and the introduction of so much immobility into nature, by representing the sun and stars as immovable, especially being of all bodies the highest and most radiant, and making the moon revolve about the earth in an epicycle, and some other assumptions of his, are the speculations of one who cares not what fictions he introduces into nature, provided his calculations answer.'[13]

It should be noticed that the Copernican hypothesis, in effect, introduced a new system of mechanics. Aristotle had explained the motions of the universe by attributing circular motions to celestial bodies, and linear motions to terrestrial bodies. But Copernicus was now denying the existence of a single natural motion which differed in different parts of the universe. A body on the earth, for example, really had four motions in the Copernican system: the three defined above, plus what could be called gravitational motion—a tendency to fall towards the Earth's surface. The idea of natural motions was, as we have seen, a fundamental Aristotelian tenet. Many of the attacks on Copernicanism, particularly by non-astronomers, revolved round this point. Thus in a seventeenth-century controversy between the pro-Aristotelian, Alexander Rosse, and the pro-Copernican, John Wilkins, Rosse objected that rotation was not the natural motion of artificial creations, such as houses, which would therefore fall to pieces if the Earth rotated. Wilkin's answer was rather summary:

> 'But supposing (saith Rosse) that this Motion were natural to the Earth, yet it is not natural to Towns and Buildings, for these are Artificial. To which I answer: Ha, ha, ha.'[14]

It was, nevertheless, an obvious difficulty of the Copernican hypothesis, that it struck directly at the roots of the Aristotelian world picture. In so doing, it threatened the whole of the medieval synthesis, and, instead of remaining a subject for academic discussion amongst astronomers, became a matter for more general concern. As we have seen, Aristotelian doctrines had become closely associated with Christian beliefs in the preceding centuries. Alterations in the former were therefore bound to produce repercussions in the latter. In one sense, of course, the Copernican hypothesis appeared at a favourable time: Copernicus, himself, lived through the first period of the Reformation, and his theory made its way into a world which no longer knew an absolute authority in teaching matters. On the other hand, the controversy between the Roman Catholic and Protestant Churches led to a tighter discipline in each. In the Roman Catholic Church, this led to an emphasis on the Church's role as sole interpreter. In the Protestant Churches, it led to an emphasis on the literal truth of the Bible. The latter view clearly appears in a saying about Copernicus attributed to Martin

Luther: 'This fool wishes to reverse the entire science of astronomy; but sacred Scripture tells us that Joshua commanded the sun to stand still, and not the earth'.[15] (The reference is to *Joshua* 10: 12–13.)

Some early Protestants even thought that there was a biblical stricture against all science, for Paul had said:

> 'Beware lest any man spoil you through philosophy and vain deceit, after the tradition of men, after the rudiments of the world, and not after Christ.'[16]

Nevertheless, the early reformers were not necessarily antagnostic to science. Luther really seems to have been little interested in the subject (although he employed astronomical ideas in his *Commentary on Genesis*). Science, he felt, could be ignored, since it had no direct bearing on salvation. Calvin, on the other hand, although he too disagreed with Copernicus, thought that science could be of definite religious value.[17]

It was evident, of course, that an acceptance of Copernicanism required certain biblical passages to be interpreted in a non-literal sense. In principle, there was no objection to this; we have seen that the idea of accommodation had been applied before to biblical statements which could not be taken literally. It was, indeed, used again in Copernicus' time to explain what was meant in *Genesis* by 'the waters above the firmament'.

> 'And God made the firmament, and divided the waters which were under the firmament from the waters which were above the firmament.'[18]

The passage had been taken literally to imply that there were waters above the heavens. (Some had seen in these waters a mechanism for removing the frictional heat generated by the fast-moving *primum mobile*.[19]) This concept raised so many philosophical difficulties, however, that by the sixteenth century a consensus of opinion had developed that 'waters above the firmament' was simply a circumlocution for clouds.[20]

In easier times, perhaps, a heliocentric theory might have been similarly absorbed. As it was, the degree of acceptance varied from country to country. Copernicanism actually advanced most rapidly in seventeenth-century England. Here, the position of the Church—partially reformed and partially unreformed—may have resulted in a somewhat less dogmatic attitude. More importantly, all the leading English astronomers either supported, or did not actively oppose, the new Copernican ideas. England had long possessed a tradition of Aristotelian criticism. In the fourteenth century the Merton school had re-examined Aristotelian mechanics; in the sixteenth century, the criticisms which Pierre Ramus of Paris directed against Aristotelian logic were very well received in this country. A part of the background to this criticism was the continuing neo-Platonic bias amongst English mathematicians. This was important for the acceptance of Copernican ideas, for neo-Platonists usually grouped Plato and the Pythagoreans together. Since the Pythagoreans were then believed to have been the originators of the heliocentric hypothesis in antiquity, there was a natural tendency for neo-Platonists to be prejudiced in favour of the concept.

Copernican doctrine received a brief, rather ambiguous mention in the mid-sixteenth century by the English mathematician, Robert Recorde, but the first important support in Britain came some years later, when both John Dee and Thomas Digges strongly upheld the heliocentric hypothesis. John Dee we have met before; amongst his other accomplishments he was a defender of neo-Platonism. Thomas Digges was the leading English mathematician of his time. His father, Leonard Digges, was a friend of John Dee (both had an equal interest in astronomy and astrology) and he, himself, had been Dee's pupil. Thomas' younger son, also called Leonard, was a friend of Shakespeare, and wrote one of prefatory verses to the first folio. When Shakespeare was in London he lived close to the Digges' house, and may have been acquainted with Thomas Digges. Certainly this would explain a reference in Hamlet, where the names, Rosencratz and Guildenstern, happen to be the names of two ancestors of the Danish astronomer, Tycho Brahe. Shakespeare could have learnt of this from Digges, who was the leading English correspondent of Tycho Brahe, and would therefore probably have been acquainted with his ancestry (of which Tycho was proud).

In 1576 Digges published a book with the illuminating title: *A Perfit Description of the Caelestiall Orbes according to the most aunciente doctrine of the Pythagoreans lately revived by Copernicus and by Geometricall Demonstrations approved*. This was not only a description of Copernicus' work: it also contained an important advance of its own. Copernicus, as we have seen, retained most of the basic features of the Aristotelian universe. In particular, he continued to conceive of the firmament as a finite shell, outside the sphere of Saturn, which contained all the stars. Digges now denied this, and asserted instead that the universe was infinite in extent. Although he seems to have been the first Copernican to have made this suggestion, the possibility was implicit in the assumption that the Earth rotated. When the stars were believed to move round the Earth, the fact that they all required the same length of time was accepted as evidence that they were all more or less the same distance away. As soon as the stellar sphere became stationary, this argument no longer applied. It became simpler to assume that all stars had the same brightness: the stars which appeared fainter were actually further away. The necessity on the heliocentric hypothesis for a large gap between Saturn's sphere and the stars also led Copernicans to doubt the existence of a stellar sphere.

Digges' innovation gave rise to two major difficulties, both of theological importance. The first—which he recognized—was that he had effectively abolished the empyreal heaven. If the stars extended to infinity, where then was the throne of God? Digges' answer, that it was among the stars but too far away to be seen, although obviously possible was not altogether satisfactory. This became particularly evident after the invention of the telescope, when it became feasible to peer further and further into space. The second problem was that an infinite expanse cannot be said to have a centre. Therefore, not only was the Earth demoted from a significant position in the solar system, but the solar system as a whole was denied a significant place in the universe.

Unlike some of their continental brethren, the English clergy raised singularly few objections to the advancement of Copernicanism. Perhaps one factor here was their above average interest in natural theology. Certainly several of the leading figures in seventeenth-century science in this country were clergymen. It is also significant that there was more scientific literature published in the vernacular in sixteenth- and early seventeenth-century England than anywhere on the Continent. In general, the clergy were prepared to condone scientific thought so long as it appeared to serve and glorify God. This provided little hindrance to the scientists, since they virtually always saw their task in precisely the same light: seventeenth-century scientific treatises constantly stress the religious utility of science. There was, perhaps, a slight distinction in outlook between clergy and astronomers, in that the former were usually imbued with Aristotelian ideas, whereas the latter were often neo-Platonists. The major practical effect of this, however, seems to have been that the clergy were more downright in their condemnation of judicial astrology.

Astronomy did, in fact, come in for its share of criticism, but this was mostly against the subject as a whole—and, indeed, against natural philosophy, in general—rather than specific opposition to Copernicanism. (It must be remembered in this connection that attacks on mathematics were also attacks on astronomy, since the seventeenth century still regarded astronomy as applied geometry.) A fairly mild criticism of mathematics was that excessive concentration on it left a person unsuited for other occupations.[21] More dangerous was the accusation that scientific study wasted time which might better be spent in seeking salvation, for the clergy were particularly sensitive to this suggestion (especially if it was hinted further that the knowledge gained only led to irreligion). 'They say miracles are past, and we have our philosophical persons, to make modern and familiar, things supernatural and causeless. Hence is it that we make trifles of errors; ensconcing ourselves into seeming knowledge, when we should submit ourselves to an unknown fear.'[22] George Herbert, in particular, liked to stress that the pursuit of astronomy hindered the vital need to concentrate on personal salvation.

The fleet Astronomer can bore,
 And thred the spheres with his quick-piercing minde
  ... Poore man, thou searchest round
 To finde out *death*, but *missest* life at hand

It is evident, however, that his opposition, too, was to all astronomy, and not just to the new astronomy. Thus he commands elsewhere

> Then burn thy Epicycles, foolish man;
> Break all thy spheres[24]

This is evidently as much a denigration of classical astronomy. Later in the century, Milton wrote in a similar vein. By that time, astronomers in this country firmly believed in the heliocentric hypothesis, although the general educated public still had its doubts. In *Paradise Lost*, however, Adam is instructed by Raphael that

> whether Heav'n move or Earth,
> Imports not, if thou reck'n right[25]

The natural philosophers, of course, tried to answer these accusations of wasting time, or of implied impiety. With some effort, scriptural justification could be found for their work; the neo-Platonists, for example, defended the importance of mathematics by citing a relevant passage in the Book of Wisdom.[26] Bacon provided a very ingenious biblical argument for the study of natural philosophy. As we have seen, there was a general belief in the decay and near end of the world in his day. Bacon suggested that the Bible actually foretold the increase of science under such circumstances. 'Nor should the prophecy of Daniel be foregotten, touching the last ages of the world: "Many shall go to and fro, and knowledge shall be increased;" clearly intimating that the thorough passage of the world (which now by so many distant voyages seems to be accomplished, or in course of accomplishment) and the advancement of the sciences, are destined by fate that is, by Divine Providence, to meet the same age.'[27]

In general, actual accusations of atheism were levelled against individual astronomers, but not against the profession as a whole (though Thomas Nashe, at the end of the sixteenth century, said that all mathematicians were atheists). An obvious individual target for such attacks was John Dee who seems to have borne a charmed life against both physical, and oral opposition. Perhaps it was due to the protection he received in high quarters. One of his supporters was Sir Walter Raleigh, who was himself highly suspect of atheism amongst his contemporaries.

Raleigh's immediate group of retainers contained in Thomas Harriot a more significant figure than Dee. Harriot, the greatest English astronomer of his generation, was described by Chapman (another of Raleigh's group) as the master of all essential and true knowledge. (For a similar opinion by someone not in the immediate Raleigh circle, see Corbett.[28]) He seems to have been on very close terms with his patron: when Raleigh was in prison, Harriot probably acted as his business agent. Harriot was caught up in the accusation of atheism with other members of the group (especially Christopher Marlowe). Later in the century, John Aubrey recorded that Harriot 'did not like (or valued not) the old storie of the Creation of the World. He could not beleeve the old position; he would say *ex nihilo nihil fit*. But a *nihilum* killed him at last: for in the top of his Nose came a little red speck (exceedingly small) which grew bigger, and at last killed him. He made a Philosophical Theologie, wherein he cast-off the Old Testament, and then the New one would (consequently) have no Foundation. He was a Deist. His Doctrine he taught to Sir Walter Raleigh, Henry Earle of Northumberland, and some others.'[29] There does not seem to have been any strong basis for these accusations, except that Harriot and other members of the group were more given to religious speculation than was common at the time. It is usually assumed that Harriot helped Raleigh when he was writing his *History of the World*, and yet the preface to that book contains a specific censure of the doctrine of *ex nihilo nihil fit*.

Presumably owing to Harriot's influence, the group round Raleigh had a continuing interest in astronomy. Harriot, himself, was a firm supporter of the heliocentric hypothesis and corresponded extensively with Kepler, one of its leading Continental proponents. It is significant in this connection that Raleigh possessed one of the few copies of *De Revolutionibus* in England at that time.

Raleigh's circle has sometimes been called the 'School of Night' from a possible reference to it by Shakespeare in *Love's Labour's Lost*. Shakespeare was, perhaps, writing in this play on

behalf of his patron, the Earl of Essex—Raleigh's chief rival
for the Queen's favour. In 1593, just before the play was written,
Raleigh had angered the Queen, for she then heard of his
clandestine marriage to Elizabeth Throckmorton. If this interpretation of the 'School of Night' is correct, we can even find a
criticism of the astronomical interests of Raleigh's group in the
play.[30]

The period around the end of the sixteenth century saw the
first realization of what results might follow from a full acceptance of the heliocentric hypothesis. This was due, at least in
part, to the writings and debates of the Italian priest, Giordano
Bruno, who spent some years in England during the latter part
of the century. Bruno, presumably influenced by the ideas of
Thomas Digges, vigorously defended the existence of an infinite number of stars scattered throughout infinite space. His
argument, like that of Digges before him and of William Gilbert
later, was theological: a God of infinite power would necessarily
create an infinite universe. He went further than most others,
however, in proposing that the stars were all similar to the Sun,
that each of them possessed a planetary system, and that these
planets were inhabited like the Earth. In other words, he
deprived the solar system of all its unique characteristics.
'If our world be small in respect, why may we not suppose a
plurality of worlds, those infinite stars visible in the firmament
to be so many suns, with particular fixed centres; to have likewise their subordinate planets, as the sun hath his dancing
still round him? which Cardinal Cusanus, Walkarinus, Brunus,
and some others have held, and some still maintain.... Though
they seem close to us, they are infinitely distant, and so *per
consequens*, they are infinite habitable worlds: what hinders?
Why should not an infinite cause (as God is) produce infinite
effects?'[31] These suggestions were evidently pure speculation:
Bruno's inspiration came mainly from neo-Platonic sources
(particularly the philosophical insights of Nicholas de Cusa—
the Cusanus of the previous quotation) and relatively little
from scientific observations. Although he was an ardent supporter of Copernicus, this seems to have meant, in practice,
only that he supported the concept of a heliocentric planetary
system. In this he differed very little from other Copernicans,

few of whom by 1600 accepted the Copernican system *in toto*. As Bacon pointed out 'if it be granted that the earth moves, it would seem more natural to suppose that there is no system at all, but scattered globes, according to the opinion of those I have already mentioned, than to constitute a system in which the sun is a centre. And this the consent of ages and of antiquity has rather embraced and approved. For the opinion concerning the motion of the earth is not new, but revived from the ancients, as I said: whereas the opinion that the sun is the centre of the world and immovable is altogether new (except one verse, wrongly translated) and was first introduced by Copernicus.'[32] (The verse that Bacon refers to—it is also mentioned by Burton in the *Anatomy of Melancholy*—is *Job* 9: 6).

The suggested existence of a plurality of inhabited worlds raised a whole range of theological problems. 'But who shall dwell in these vast bodies, earths, worlds, "if they be inhabited? rational creatures?" as Kepler demands, "or have they souls to be saved? or do they inhabit a better part of the world than we do? Are we or they lords of the world? And how are all things made for man?"'[33] Hardly surprisingly, many devout Christians refused to accept the idea.[34]

The argument, as it developed during the seventeenth century, was primarily based on the concept of the plenitude of God. So far as cosmology was concerned, this led to a belief that, if conditions were suitable for some specific thing to exist, then that thing necessarily would exist. To take a particular instance: if God created another star like the Sun, then that star would partake of the same nature as the Sun. In particular, it would possess a planetary system. By a similar argument, it was deduced that life must exist on at least some of the postulated planets. This concept has an obvious similarity—at least in its consequences—to more recent ideas on the uniformity of the universe. (In fact, Bruno actually did assume that the universe would appear to be the same wherever an observer might be situated.)

The possibility of life on other worlds fascinated many writers during the seventeenth and eighteenth centuries (an early mention of the idea occurs in Spenser[35]). After the invention of the telescope at the beginning of the seventeenth century, the

7

possibility came to be considered a near certainty by some writers. Milton was highly attracted to the concept in *Paradise Lost*, even though the cosmology of the poem was geocentric.[36]

It is difficult to assess the extent of Bruno's influence in England. Although he had plenty of opportunity—he arrived in England with letters of recommendation from the King of France and could move in any circle of society—he does not seem to have left any great immediate impression. On the other hand, his death in 1600, when he was burnt at the stake for heresy by the Roman Inquisition, may have stimulated some interest in his ideas in this country. Certainly, the themes he discussed became matters of common interest during the seventeenth century.

A more influential cosmologist than Bruno, in England, was William Gilbert, physician to Queen Elizabeth. Gilbert is mainly remembered now for his experiments on magnetism, but his contemporaries were more impressed by his cosmological speculations. In discussing these, we must remember what has been said before: that it is often difficult to distinguish, when English writers of the period attack, or defend, Copernicus, whether diurnal, or annual, motion is being discussed. Many writers were more interested in the former than in the latter; Bacon, for example, and Milton in *Paradise Lost*. The reasons for assuming that the Earth rotated on its axis were a good deal more compelling than those demanding revolution of the Earth round the Sun. At least, Tycho Brahe seems to have thought so. Tycho developed a rival model of the solar system, which had the Sun and Moon revolving round the Earth, and all the other planets revolving round the Sun. Apart from the indistinguishably small motion of the stars, this was mathematically equivalent to the Copernican model. As such, it gained a fair amount of support during the early seventeenth century: John Donne may have been one of those who considered it favourably. On the other hand, the Tychonic system could act as a stepping-stone from the Aristotelian system to the Copernican viewpoint—as was pointed out by Bacon.[37]

Owing to the confusion which existed in many minds between the diurnal and annual motions of the Earth, a belief that the Earth moved in any way at all was often sufficient to label a man as a Copernican. William Gilbert is a good example of this. He was undoubtedly a staunch advocate of diurnal rotation (we are told by Burton that Gilbert supported terrestrial rotation because he found it difficult to conceive how the firmament could move as rapidly as the Aristotelian model required[38]), but there is little firm evidence that he believed in an annual motion of the Earth. Nevertheless, he was an important figure in the advancement of heliocentric ideas in this country. His major achievement was to provide a physical basis for rotation. We have seen that one of the main arguments of the Aristotelians was that the massive Earth must naturally remain stationary, since there was no reason why it should move. Gilbert, however, suggested that the interaction of magnetic fields in the solar system would necessarily produce rotation. His explanations of the effect are distinctly obscure and seem to be virtually Aristotelian in concept (though he, himself, tended towards neo-Platonism). Despite this, his idea was taken over eagerly both by Kepler and by Galileo. Kepler used magnetic fields to explain the motion of the planets round the Sun. He suggested that a magnetic force emanating from the Sun could pull the planets along as the Sun rotated. This notion of a constant force acting to produce a constant velocity is, of course, also Aristotelian, and disappeared during the seventeenth century. The concept of magnetism as a way of transmitting forces throughout the solar system remained, however, until it was replaced by gravitation towards the end of the century.

Mainly as a result of Gilbert's work, magnetism became a matter of general interest from the early years of the seventeenth century onwards (see, e.g. Ben Jonson's *The Magnetic Lady*). Sir Thomas Browne devoted an extended discussion to Gilbert's concept of the Earth as a magnetic body.[39] Occasional references to Kepler's idea of a solar magnetic field as a source of motion can also be found.[40]

It is evident that disproving Aristotelian concepts does not of itself prove the truth of the heliocentric hypothesis. However, owing to the great degree of integration achieved in the medieval synthesis, rejection of one aspect of Aristotelian teaching was likely to cast doubt on the rest, including the geocentricity of the universe. This could, indeed, work both ways; a defence of Copernicus might simply be one way of attacking the *status quo*. Thus radical thinkers, who were not astronomers, were likely to support Copernicus as a part of their attack on Aristotle. This, in turn, naturally led to an increased suspicion of Copernican doctrines on the part of established authority.

In actual fact, the growing opinion among astronomers that some, at least, of Aristotle's ideas were wrong was probably due less to the spread of heliocentric speculation, than to the appearance of a variety of new phenomena in the heavens.[41] In 1572, a bright, new star appeared in Cassiopeia, where it continued to shine until the spring of 1574. Since, according to Aristotle, the heavens were perfect and unchangeable, the star was assumed to be situated below the Moon. Extensive measurements of its position were made by astronomers throughout Europe. In England it was observed by both Digges and Dee. The overall result was to show definitely that the new star was further away from the Earth than the Moon, and that it might even be a part of the firmament. Five years later, in 1577, one of the brightest comets of the century appeared. Tycho Brahe, whose interest in astronomy was inflamed by the star of 1572, had by this time collected together the best set of astronomical instruments of his day. With these, he made a series of accurate measurements of the comet's position, and was able to show that it, too, must lie outside the Moon's sphere.

By a curious concidence, the new star of 1572 was followed by another in 1604, this time in the constellation of Ophiucus. (The coincidence is that this type of star—a supernova*—is only seen from the Earth about once every three hundred years, on the average.) The second star, too, was visible over a prolonged period of time, not disappearing until 1606. Again the star showed no parallax,† indicating that it was further away than the Moon from the Earth. Besides these new stars—which

---

* A supernova is a rare type of exploding star which becomes extremely luminous at maximum brightness.

† Parallax is the name given to the apparent displacement of an object against its background when it is observed from two different positions. The amount of this apparent displacement depends on the distance of the object from the observer and, hence, can be used as a measure of this.

were, in effect, gratuitous pieces of evidence—two other stars were observed at the end of the sixteenth century which emitted variable amounts of light—demonstrating again the existence of change in the firmament. Their discovery was at least partly a result of the new interest in mapping the sky that Tycho Brahe had stimulated. The first was noticed by Fabricius—a friend of Kepler—in 1596. It was in the constellation Cetus, and acquired the name—which it still bears—of Mira Ceti (i.e. the wonderful star in the constellation of the Whale). The second star—now called P Cygni—was found in the constellation of the Swan in 1600. It is an irregular variable which showed major fluctuations in light during the seventeenth century.

The new stars excited attention and discussion throughout most of the seventeenth century. References to them are very common.[42] John Donne, in particular, seems to have been fascinated by them and mentions them on several occasions.[43] There was an old belief (Platonic in inspiration) that souls, after death, inhabited the stars. The blaze of a new star might therefore indicate that the soul of a great man, or woman, had reached its destination. This idea was used by Dryden later in the century when he wrote on the death of Lord Hastings.[44] Ben Jonson mentions the same belief, though not, apparently, in connection with the new stars.[45]

After 1577, measurements to determine the parallax of comets became a matter of considerable importance. We have been left a graphic account of the excitement engendered by the appearance of a bright comet towards the end of 1618.

And though wee read noe Gospell in the Signes,
Yet all Professions are turn'd Divines.
All weapons from the *Bodkin* to the *Pike*,
The Masons *Rule*, the Taylors *Yard* alike
Take *Altitudes*; and th' early Fidling Knaves
Of Fluites, and Hoe-Boyes, make them Iacobs-staves.

O tell us what to trust to; ere wee waxe
All stiffe and stupid with this Paralax.
Say, shall the old Philosophy be true,
Or doth He ride above the Moone, thinke you?[46]

The significant thing is that the Aristotelian doctrine of celestial perfection was being overthrown by means of new observational material. The intellectual questioning which characterized the latter half of the sixteenth century now extended to the astronomical measurements of antiquity, which had hitherto been considered infallible. It was during this period that Tycho Brahe rejected the concept of trepidation, which had arisen in the first place from an exaggerated regard for ancient results. In a similar vein, Kepler denied the possibility of a sphere of fire beneath the Moon for, he said, the refractive effect of the region would alter the apparent positions of the stars in a way which was not observed. John Donne referred to this in both *The First Anniversarie* ('The Element of fire is quite put out') and the *Second Anniversarie* ('For th' element of fire, shee doth not know').

The new star of 1572, and the comet following hard after, gave rise to a considerable popular literature, nearly all of it concerned with their astrological significance.[47] Both Digges and Dee were consulted by Lord Burghley to find out what portents the comet held for England. John Aubrey tells us of Thomas Allen—one of the leading astrologers of the day—that 'Queen Elizabeth sent for him to have his advice about the new star that appeared in the Swan or Cassiopeia (but I think the Swan) to which he gave his Judgement very learnedly.'[48]

In considering the astrological interpretations given to these phenomena it is often quite hard to distinguish between the star and the comet since both are frequently referred to as *blazing stars*.[49] (This is probably not too important since the suggested interpretations varied very widely in any case.) One popular suggestion for the star was that it foretold the second coming of Christ: just as the first star had foretold the birth. This fitted in with the common contemporary expectation of the final destruction of the world: predictions of the end were more or less an everyday affair. In *The Duchess of Malfi*, for example, we are told of an astrologer who, having foretold the end of the world, went mad when it failed to occur on the day he had specified. Later in the century Samuel Butler could parody the innumerable Elizabethan prognostications of final dissolution.[50] Even at the time, however, opposition was by no means absent. Thus Thomas Nashe wrote a biting pamphlet against Richard Harvey, brother to Spenser's mentor, Gabriel Harvey.[51] Harvey had published an *Astrological Discourse upon the Conjunction of Saturne and Jupiter* in 1583, in which he sought to show that the conjunction forewarned the end of the world. (It must be admitted that Nashe was probably inspired to this attack as much by dislike of the Harvey family as by dislike of the prediction.)

Astrologers professed to be undisturbed by the increasing popularity of the new Copernican ideas, and some of the leading British astrologers were, indeed, strong defenders of the theory. (Perhaps they benefited from the somewhat simpler calculations of planetary positions.) Nevertheless, the parallax measurements of the new stars and comets could create difficulties. Sir Thomas Browne wondered whether it was 'not wrong to attribute terrible astrological effects to comets and blazing stars, now that it was known that they were above the Moon.'[52] Later in the century doubts of this sort became a good deal more positive:

> we need not be appall'd by *Blazing Stars*, and a *Comet* is no more ground for *Astrological presages* then a *flaming* Chimney[53]

CHAPTER V

Bacon and Galileo

THE most important single influence on the development of
seventeenth-century science in England was the writings
of Sir Francis Bacon. Bacon was not a scientist; nevertheless, he outlined a programme for the organization of
scientific research which came to be regarded as a model by
subsequent natural philosophers in this country. His first
great step forward was the denial that all the great questions of
philosophy had been solved in antiquity.[1] He was followed in
this by every seventeenth-century writer who favoured the
new philosophy[2]; even Samuel Butler, who had very little
affection for natural philosophers, was forced to agree that

> 'Tis not antiquity, nor author,
> That makes truth Truth.[3]

Bacon objected to scholastic methods because they were
sterile.[4] Without denying the supremacy of thinkers in antiquity,
he gave two reasons why contemporary philosophers might make
further progress. In the first place, he said, not all that was known
to the ancients had been passed on.[5] Secondly, he argued that
the generally accepted decline in human intelligence since the
Golden Age did not of itself vitiate the study of natural philosophy. For information on natural phenomena need only be
gathered together purely mechanically, and then simple inspec-
tion of the results—once there were sufficient of them—would
reveal any regularities present, and this required little, or no,
intelligence.

Having decided that scientific observations were worth
making after all, Bacon next turned to the question of what sorts
of observation should be made. The duty of philosophy, he
said, was to number, weigh, measure and define.[6] Although
Bacon was not the first to stress the importance of quantitative
measurement, yet his emphasis provided a welcome opposition
to the prevailing Aristotelian use of qualitative description. In

this, he was somewhat inconsistent. Quantification of science necessarily implied the introduction of mathematics; but this was a subject which Bacon tended to despise. Indeed, he thought that far too much attention was paid to mathematics by astronomers. 'There is scarce any one who has made inquiries into the physical causes... but all the labour is spent in mathematical observations and demonstrations.'[7]

Bacon's concept of mechanics remained Aristotelian, and he much preferred mechanical explanations of phenomena to mathematical ones. This appears strongly in his discussion of the Copernican doctrine which, as might be expected, he found unsatisfactory.[8] He was, however, also dissatisfied with Tycho Brahe's system (and, indeed, with any other system that included diurnal rotation of the Earth). He propounded instead a system of his own in which the planets moved round the Earth in spirals, remarking scornfully: 'And most certain it is, if one may but play the plain man for a moment (dismissing the fancies of astronomers and schoolmen, whose way it is to overrule the senses, often without reason, and to prefer what is obscure), that this motion does actually appear to the sense such as I have described; for I once had a machine made with iron wheels to represent it.'[9] This provides an effective illustration of the limitations of Bacon's scientific thought. The possibility of spiral orbits had, in fact, been considered by mathematicians before Bacon. They had rejected it because, although it might provide some sort of qualitative picture of planetary motions, it failed to give a quantitative explanation.

Bacon suggested in *Novum Organum* that cosmological ideas were invented purely in order to explain celestial motions by perfect circles.[10] This is a fair description of Ptolemy and of Copernicus, but not of Kepler, whose concept of elliptical orbits for the planets had appeared before Bacon's comment was made. Bacon had the opportunity for acquainting himself with Kepler's work, if he wished to take it, via the agency of Sir Henry Wotton (who actually conveyed a copy of one of Bacon's books to Kepler).

Bacon's dislike of mathematics did not affect the development of British astronomy (perhaps it was partly offset by the neo-Platonism of the astronomers). His influence on the advancement of science in this country was, therefore, almost entirely for the good. He helped in two ways. In a negative sense by opposing the predominantly literary education of the well-to-do; by opposing the system of scholastic logic taught in the universities; and by opposing the prevalent pseudo-sciences (though he was willing to admit some truth in astrology). His main positive aid to the progress of science (apart from an invaluable publicity) was the installation of a spirit of optimism. He believed that, once science was organized on the lines he had suggested, the investigation of nature would only be the work of a few years.[11]

Bacon's belief in science gained little immediate acceptance. General praise for his stand is not found until towards the middle of the seventeenth century. In fact, the rise in importance of Baconian philosophy in England followed the same time-sequence as the rise in importance of Puritanism. This does not necessarily mean that the two were related; one can, however, see some obvious reasons why the Baconian approach appealed to Puritans. Thus his exposition of science was democratic: in the sense that he believed knowledge could be gathered as easily by a tradesman as by an aristocrat. This appealed to the predominantly middle-class Puritan intelligentsia. They also liked the aspect of Bacon's work which presented itself as a reformation of Aristotle—whose influence on theology they generally detested. Again, they were interested in nature as a way of approach to God; and they approved of the consignment of miracles to biblical times, in opposition to the claims of the Roman Catholic Church. More materialistically, they liked the emphasis that Bacon laid on the utility of science.

The first major observational advance in astronomy since antiquity was made during Bacon's lifetime. This was the use of the telescope for astronomical purposes by Galileo Galilei in Italy. Needless to say, it pleased Bacon: here was something concrete. 'I have to congratulate both the industry of mechanics, and the zeal and energy of certain learned men, that now of late by the help of optical instruments, as by skiffs and barks, they have opened a new commerce with the phenomena of the heavens; an undertaking which I regard as being both in the end and in the endeavour a thing noble and worthy of the human race.'[12] The advance was so radical, however, that, like many of his contemporaries, he counselled that the results should be accepted with caution.[13]

One of the 'learned men' in this quotation may have been Harriot, who was using telescopes of his own invention for astronomical observation at about the same time as Galileo. Unfortunately, Harriot published no description of his work, so little was known of it either in this country or abroad. Galileo, on the other hand, published his results as rapidly as possible. The book summarizing his observations—the *Sidereus Nuncius*—appeared in 1610 and immediately caught the public imagination. Sir Henry Wotton, writing from Italy to the Earl of Salisbury, reported excitedly

> 'I send herewith unto his Majesty the strangest piece of news (as I may justly call it) that he hath ever yet received from any part of the world; which is the annexed book (come abroad this very day) of the Mathematical Professor at Padua, who by the help of an optical instrument (which both enlargeth and approximateth the object) invented first in Flanders, and bettered by himself, hath discovered four new planets rolling about the sphere of Jupiter besides many other unknown fixed stars; likewise, the true cause of the *Via Lactae*, so long searched; and lastly, that the moon is not spherical, but endued with many prominences, and, which is of all the strangest, illuminated with the solar light by reflection from the body of the earth, as he seemeth to say. So, as upon the whole subject he hath first overthrown all former astronomy—for we must have a new sphere to save the appearances—and next all astrology. For the virtue of these new planets must vary the judicial part, and why may there not yet be more?'[14]

The circumstances surrounding the invention of the telescope are rather obscure. It is known to have been used for terrestrial observation in the Netherlands at the turn of the sixteenth century; it was the astronomical application, however, which fascinated writers. The telescope appears in seventeenth-century literature under the guise of innumerable names. *Perspective glass* was common. This was sometimes abbreviated to *perspective*[15] and sometimes to *glass*.[16] Another name which appears frequently is *optic tube*[17] or *trunk*.[18] A seventeenth-century writer might use any, or all, of these names indiscriminately. Thus Joseph Glanvill called it a *telescope, a tube* and a *perspicil*, all in the course of one paragraph of *Scepsis Scientifica*, whilst Samuel Butler referred to it as a *tube*, an *optic glass*, an *optic engine*, a *telescope* and a *trunk* in his poem *The Elephant in the Moon*. In the latter half of the century, *telescope* began to emerge as the commonest name.*

In those days telescopes were usually characterized by their focal lengths.† (Nowadays, the diameter of the main lens, or mirror, of the telescope is preferred as a datum.) Thus, when Samuel Pepys was considering buying a telescope, the instrument-maker provided him with two—one of twelve-foot and the other of six-foot focal length—so that he could compare their properties. 'I find Reeves there, it being a mighty fine bright night, and so upon my leads, though very sleepy, till one in the morning, looking on the moon and Jupiter, with this twelve-foote glasse and another of six foote, that he hath brought with him tonight, and the sights mighty pleasant, and one of the glasses I will buy, it being very usefull.'[19]

During his first few years of telescopic observation Galileo made five major discoveries, each of which contradicted some Aristotelian concept.[20] He found that Jupiter possessed four moons, that there were spots on the face of the Sun, that the Milky Way was composed of innumerable faint stars, that Venus showed phases like the Moon, and that the surface of the Moon bore a surprising resemblance to the surface of the Earth.

We have seen that it was a prime Aristotelian belief that the Earth was the centre of all celestial motions. It had been pressed as a strong objection to the Copernican doctrine that it required two centres of motion—the Sun for the planets, and the Earth for the Moon. Galileo's observations now showed that the

* 'Perspective glass' was still used occasionally as late as the nineteenth century.
† If a distant source of light is focused by means of a lens, then the distance from the lens to the point where the light comes to a focus is called the focal length of that lens. Many of the characteristics of a telescope depend on this quantity. (A similar definition holds if a mirror is used as the main focusing element rather than a lens.)

Earth was not unique in this respect: Jupiter also acted as a centre of motion.[21] A few years later, this evidence appeared to be strengthened when Galileo announced that Saturn, too, had moons. 'There are just 7 Planets or errant Stars in the lower orbs of Heaven, but it is now demonstrable unto sense, that there are many more; as Galileo hath declared, that is, two more in the orb of Saturn, and no less then four more in the sphere of Jupiter.'[22] Unfortunately, Galileo was mistaken; what he had actually seen was Saturn's ring. The odd appearances and disappearances of his supposed new satellites was a matter of considerable concern to him, for it seemed to support the claims of his opponents that his observations were really optical illusions. The true nature of the ring was not, however, elucidated until later in the century, when it was explained by the Dutch astronomer, Christian Huyghens. (Huyghens also discovered the first genuine moon of Saturn.)

The observation of spots on the Sun's surface contradicted another Aristotelian belief: that of the perfection of the celestial bodies. Moreover, the motion of the spots indicated that the Sun was rotating on its axis, whereas, according to Aristotelian ideas, it should have been rigidly attached to its planetary sphere.[23] The Jesuit astronomer, Scheiner, tried to surmount these difficulties by suggesting that the dark patches were not actually attached to the Sun but were really opaque bodies revolving round it. This possibility was soon disproved by observation, but Bacon seems to have had it in mind when he wrote: 'in the neighbourhood of the sun (it may be) where the heaven seems to become starry, and to begin to pass into the nature of the starry heaven. For it may be that those spots which have been discovered in the sun, certainly by faithful and diligent observation, are a kind of rudiments of starry matter.'[24]

Again, the Milky Way, according to Aristotelian doctrine, was some nebulous phenomenon in the sub-lunar sphere. Galileo now showed that it consisted of stars, too faint for the eye to see, but otherwise like the visible stars. The new interest in the Milky Way which, this observation excited is reflected by the increased number of references to the 'Milky Way' or 'Galaxy' in seventeenth-century literature.[25] (John Donne, as might be expected, made early mention of it.[26]) A closely related observation was Galileo's investigation of the Pleiades. To the astonishment of his contemporaries he found that he could discern there at least forty stars through his telescope as compared with the traditional tally of seven.[27]

The phases of Venus, like the spots on the Sun, contradicted the Aristotelian belief in its perfection. Moreover, the sequence in which the phases were seen showed that Venus was definitely revolving round the Sun. Although this did not constitute a proof of the Copernican system—the same result followed from Tycho Brahe's model—it did constitute a disproof of the Aristotelian scheme.

It will be noted, in fact, that none of these telescopic observations can be claimed as proof of Copernicanism; they can only be claimed as disproof of Aristotelianism. But they could, and did, make Copernicanism more credible. In one apparently minor, but actually quite important, respect the telescopic observations did strengthen the hand of the Copernicans as against followers of Tycho Brahe's system. It will be remembered that the apparent diameters of the stars (as estimated by Tycho Brahe with the naked eye) led to excessively large sizes for the stars on the Copernican hypothesis. It was now found that whereas the apparent diameters of planets increased when seen through a telescope, the size of the stellar discs remained the same.[28] This was correctly interpreted as meaning that stars could not be assigned a size—they were effectively points of light to a terrestrial observer. The apparent stellar diameters which Tycho Brahe had measured were not intrinsic, but were due to fluctuations of the Earth's atmosphere acting on the starlight as it passed through. It is, perhaps, needless to say that this result was not accepted by the supporters of a geocentric system without some argument.[29]

The observation by Galileo which created most excitement and discussion was, however, his discovery of the marked resemblance between the surfaces of the Moon and the Earth. This similarity was seized on as the first definite piece of evidence for the belief in a plurality of worlds. Writers in the early seventeenth century thought it no great step to go from the observation of valleys and mountains on the Moon to the existence of lunar inhabitants.

2 HERALD: Certain and sure news.
1 HERALD: Of a new world.
2 HERALD: And new creatures in that world.
1 HERALD: In the orb of the moon.
2 HERALD: Which is now found to be an earth inhabited.
1 HERALD: With navigable seas and rivers.
2 HERALD: Variety of nations, polities, laws.[30]

It is interesting that, when later in the century Sidrophel in Butler's *Hudibras* is defending 'astrology', and claims not only that mountains have been observed on the Moon, but even cattle grazing on them, Hudibras' immediate reaction is not to deny the latter claim, but rather to argue that the hills on the Moon had been known long before, in classical times, by Anaxagoras.[31]

However many prior guesses there may have been that the Moon was similar to the Earth, Galileo's observations were necessary before the idea could gain respectability. John Wilkins confessed that he had often wondered whether the Moon was a world like the Earth but had never dared to discuss it for fear of appearing ridiculous until observations demonstrated the resemblance.[32]

Wilkins is an outstanding example of the type of seventeenth-century clergyman-scientist who eased the transition from the medieval to the modern outlook in this country. He was a moderate Puritan, and a strong supporter of Baconian ideas. Although he obtained preferment during the Puritan ascendancy, and was married to Cromwell's sister, he was held in sufficiently high regard by Charles II to be made Bishop of Chester. His book, *A Discovery of a New World in the Moon*, may be considered as one of the first English treatises on space travel.

The early observations of the Moon showed that mountains and craters were seen in those parts of the Moon that appeared bright to the naked eye. These were thought to be the land masses of the Moon. The darker regions were found to be smooth, and were therefore considered to be the seas (which name they still have). Before the telescopic results were generally known, it actually seemed more natural to make the opposite assumption— that water would appear brighter than land. Wilkins records that both he and Kepler did so. However, John Evelyn noted in his diary that, given the correct circumstances, even terrestrial observations could show the land brighter than the water. He had climbed a tower 'the better to take a Vieu of the adjacent Country, which hapning on a day when the Sunn shoone very bright, and darted his beames without any interruption; afforded so glorious a reflection to us who were above... that I was much Confirm'd in my Opinion of the *Mones* being of such substance as this Earthly Globe, perceiving all the subjacent Country... to repercusse such a light as I could hardly look against save where the River and other large Waters, appear'd of a more darke and even surface, exceedingly resembling the Spots in the Mone according to that of Hevelius*: and as they appear in our late Telescops.'33

The existence of large areas of water on the Moon's surface was widely accepted during the seventeenth century. At the same time, some astronomers urged caution. One of these was Galileo himself, who felt that there was insufficient evidence to assert that any water was visible on the lunar surface. This was a long step towards saying that the Moon was different from the Earth, and might not, in fact, be inhabited. (Galileo was, nevertheless, prepared to believe that other planets could be inhabited.) In general, Galileo's concept of an arid Moon, although respected, was not accepted during most of the seventeenth century.

It was also obvious that there were far more craters on the Moon, than on the Earth. If the similarity between Earth and Moon was to be maintained, this difference had to be explained. Wilkins observed 'Keplar shall jest you out an answer. Supposing (saith he) that those Inhabitants are bigger than any of us in the same proportion, as their days are longer than ours, *viz.* by Fifteen times it may be, for want of Stones to erect vast Houses as were requisite for their Bodies, they are fain to dig great and round hollows in the Earth, where they may both procure water for their Thirst, & turning about with the shade, may avoid those great Heats which otherwise they would be liable unto.'24

* A Danzig astronomer noted especially for his *Selenographia*, or description of the Moon.

8

These ideas are to be found in one of the first space-fiction novels ever written: Kepler's *Somnium*, the description of a dream which Kepler has, where he follows the adventures of a young man (obviously modelled on himself) who visits the Moon with the assistance of lunar demons. Until the hero arrives on the Moon the fictional element predominates, but at this point, Kepler turns to describing the lunar surface in such scientific detail as he can. The Moon, he says, is divided into two regions: the side turned towards the Earth and the far side, which he calls Subvolva and Privolva, respectively. The two sides enjoy different climates (though neither is particularly attractive from a terrestrial viewpoint). Kepler describes the lunar surface features in considerable detail, stressing the great heights of the mountains (which Wilkins disbelieved). In a similar manner, he supposes that the creatures which live on the Moon—the Subvolvans and the Privolvans—are also built on a large scale.

This story of Kepler's attracted some interest among English writers of the seventeenth century. The neo-Platonic philosopher Henry More based one of his poems—the *Insomnium Philosophicum*—on the same sort of dream sequence. Samuel Butler used the idea when poking fun at the Royal Society. In his satire, the learned scientists look at the Moon through a telescope and see two armies fighting on the lunar surface: they deduce that these are the Subvolvans and the Privolvans engaged in a bloody conflict.[35] (Later on, when they open the telescope, they find that they have been watching a cloud of flies and gnats.)

One of the first persons influenced by Kepler's story was John Donne who, very shortly after the publication of Galileo's initial discoveries, wrote a satire entitled *Ignatius his Conclave*. (It was originally published in Latin, but soon appeared in English translation.) This fantasy also took the form of a dream and, although primarily concerned with poking fun at the Jesuits, contained several references to the new astronomy. It is evident from it that Donne had some acquaintance with the works of both Galileo and Gilbert, as well as Kepler. The most interesting incident in the story occurs when Copernicus appears at the gates of hell and demands entry. He is refused permission by

Ignatius Loyola—the founder of the Jesuit Order and, in Donne's representation, the chief spokesman for hell—on the grounds that his ideas might be true. In a flash of foresight (Donne was writing in 1610) the Jesuit leader is made to add, however, that Copernicus and his followers may be allowed to enter hell after all, if the Jesuits can persuade the Pope to define as a matter of faith that the Earth is stationary. Copernicus is surpassed as a candidate for entry by the Jesuit astronomer, Clavius, who did not support the heliocentric hypothesis. (Donne, incidentally, in his Roman Catholic youth, had probably studied astronomy in the text of Sacrobosco, as revised by Clavius.)

Donne's satire throws some light on the current reactions to Galileo's observations in Roman Catholic circles. The year after the publication of the *Sidereus Nuncius*, the leading Jesuit astronomers reported confirmation of Galileo's work. This did not mean an acceptance of his deductions, however; they tried instead to interpret the observations in terms of Aristotelian concepts. The argument now turned on whether his results provided evidence for a heliocentric system, or not. Galileo thought he could find direct proof of the Earth's motion in the tides, but not many people, even amongst the supporters of Copernicus, were convinced.[36]

During this early period, Galileo was accorded considerable personal honour for his accomplishments, but within a few years the situation changed radically. The Roman Catholic Church became badly alarmed by the continuing controversy over the heliocentric hypothesis, which expanded so rapidly as to involve theology as well as astronomy. Determined to uphold their supreme authority in matters of doctrine, the Roman Catholic leaders in 1616 admonished Galileo neither to hold that the Earth had annual and diurnal motion, nor to teach it. Galileo in succeeding years tried to have this ban lifted. Meanwhile, he turned his attention to criticism of Aristotelian physics, which had not been forbidden him. In 1632 he returned to the attack with a *Dialogue on the Two Main World Systems*. This was basically a dialogue between a protagonist of the Aristotelian-Ptolemaic system on the one hand, and a protagonist of the Copernican-Galilean system on the other. It was written in such a way that Aristotle was upheld at the end, but all the more convincing arguments came from the opposing side. The Jesuits were mortally offended by this book, which they considered as an assault on themselves. They persuaded the Pope that the work actually satirized him. Thomas Hobbes, who was a great admirer of Galileo* (he met him in Pisa in 1630), was unable to buy a copy of the book in 1634, and remarked that they said in Italy that it 'will do more hurt to their religion than all the books have done of Luther and Calvin'.[37] A year later Galileo was brought before the Inquisition and made to foreswear finally the heliocentric hypothesis. From then on, until his death, he was kept under house arrest at Arcetri, not far from Florence. He was allowed occasional visitors, one of whom was the young John Milton. In later years, when Milton was himself fighting against censorship, he recalled this meeting in a famous sentence.

> There it was that I found and visited the famous Galileo grown old, a prisoner to the Inquisition, for thinking in astronomy otherwise than the Franciscan and Dominican licensers thought.[38]

The works of Galileo were placed on the Index, together with those of Copernicus and Kepler, and remained there until well into the nineteenth century.

The acceptance of Galilean ideas in Britain was presumably aided by his persecution, but there were, nevertheless, voices raised against the new philosophy both amongst clergy and amongst laymen. One particularly indefatigable opponent was Alexander Rosse, who holds the remarkable record of having opposed almost all the major writers on natural philosophy in Britain during the first half of the seventeenth century. The major point of contention was whether or not the Bible had to be interpreted absolutely literally. The Church of England—like other reformed churches—turned to the Bible as the sole ultimate authority, and tended to emphasize a straightforward interpretation of its contents.[39] Copernicans, on the other hand, had necessarily to believe that a less direct interpretation was sometimes required. Many defenders of the literal interpretation

---

* John Aubrey says that Hobbes and Galileo pretty well resembled each other.

of the Bible were also, like Rosse, ardent Aristotelians. An example of Rosse's extreme Aristotelianism—taken from his controversy with Wilkins—has been cited in the previous chapter.

To return to the seventeenth-century interest in the Moon; the possibility that the Moon was inhabited often led on to a discussion of possible methods of getting there. Ben Jonson, for example, suggested three not very serious methods derived from antiquity.

There are in all but three ways of going thither: one is Endymion's way, by rapture in sleep, or a dream. The other Menippus's way, by wing, which the poet took. The third, old Empedocle's way, who, when he leapt into Ætna, having a dry sear body, and light, the smoke took him and whift him up into the moon.[40]

John Wilkins went one better; he suggested four ways (based on more practical considerations). Frequently, however, it was simply assumed (as science-fiction authors do nowadays) that ways of accomplishing the journey would eventually be worked out. From this optimistic viewpoint, it was not a long step to considering the Moon as a possible place for territorial expansion. Wilkins noted that 'Tis the opinion of *Keplar*, that as soon as the art of Flying is Found out, some of their Nation will make one of the first Colonies, that shall Transplant into that other World.'[41] Similar ambitions for our own country were expressed throughout the seventeenth century. Samuel Butler's learned society decided to survey the Moon in order to prepare for settling new plantations there.[42] Dryden probably had a similar idea in mind when he wrote

Then we upon our globe's last verge shall go,
And view the ocean leaning on the sky:
From thence our rolling neighbours we shall know,
And on the lunar world securely pry.[43]

(It is, however, characteristic of Dryden that he should link the concept of lunar exploration in the last line, with the very old idea that the terrestrial and celestial spheres joined at the horizon in the first line.) Hopes of conquering the Moon died down considerably in the eighteenth century when it became evident that conditions on the Moon were not very suitable for life.

John Wilkins' was not the only book about the Moon to appear in England during the first half of the seventeenth century. *The Man in the Moone*, a description of a fictitious visit to the Moon, came out at about the same time. This had been written earlier in the century by Francis Godwin, but it was not published until after his death. Godwin, who became Bishop of Hereford, provides yet another example of the interest English clergy had in new astronomical ideas. He seems to have been inspired in this direction by listening to a disputation undertaken by Bruno at Oxford during the years he spent in England. The hero (and supposed author) of the book, a Spaniard called Domingo Gonsales, has trained a flight of birds, rather like geese—they are, in fact, called *gansas*—to carry him up, when they fly, by means of cords which he attaches to them. (Some indication that Godwin's story was quite well known is provided by the occasional references to these birds in seventeenth-century literature.[44]) On one of his trips, Gonsales finds that the birds, instead of bearing him along the surface of the Earth, are flying vertically upwards. He soon realizes that they are taking him to the Moon. (This was not such a far-fetched idea in the seventeenth century as it would be today. There was then a common belief, which persisted into the eighteenth century, that some migratory birds spent part of the year on the Moon.[45])

Gonsales remarks a good deal of astronomical interest during his flight. Godwin, like Gilbert, believed in the Earth's diurnal rotation but not, apparently, in its annual revolution. His hero, therefore, when suspended in space between the Earth and the Moon, sees the former rotating, and is therefore constrained to believe that Copernicus is right in this respect. On the other hand, he is not prepared to assert that the Earth is moving round the Sun. As the flight to the Moon proceeds, a point is eventually reached where the magnetic attraction of the Moon becomes important (the magnetic attraction of the Earth having been left behind—it was thought not to extend more than a few miles above the Earth's surface). At this juncture, Gonsales finds that his position in space is suddenly reversed, so that he falls down feet first towards the Moon. It is interesting that this reversal remained a standard feature in descriptions of lunar voyages right up until the present century, even though ideas on the forces acting between the Earth and the Moon had changed greatly in the interim.

The great upsurge of interest in the Moon during the seventeenth century led to the preparation of the first maps of the lunar surface. In this the Danzig astronomer, Hevelius, took the lead just before the mid-century. He also provided the first systematic nomenclature for the lunar surface features, naming them after terrestrial analogues.

And therefore the learned Hevelius in his accurate Selenography, or description of the Moon, hath well translated the known appelations of Regions, Seas and Mountains, unto the parts of that Luminary: and rather then use invented names or humane denominations, with witty congruity hath placed Mount Sinai, Taurus, Maeotis Palus, the Mediterranean Sea, Mauritania, Sicily and Asia Minor in the Moon.[46]

These names did not survive very long (though they were used longer in Britain than elsewhere). Except for the lunar mountain ranges, they were all replaced by a new system of nomenclature, devised by the Jesuit Riccioli. In this system—which is still used today—the craters are called after famous mathematicians and astronomers, and the seas are assigned somewhat fanciful names, such as the Sea of Dreams. Riccioli, incidentally, devised the world picture which was officially accepted by the Roman Catholic Church during the seventeenth century, when it became evident that the Aristotelian model was no longer admissible. It was, in essence, a rather cumbersome modification of Tycho Brahe's geocentric system.

The rise of Baconian experimental science during the seventeenth century was complemented by a gradual dying away of belief in the decay of the world. Indeed, the concept of decay probably reached its peak of acceptance during Bacon's lifetime, though it still retained sufficient strength to engender fierce debate right to the end of the century. Its decline did not alter the seventeenth-century belief in the imminent end of the world. 'I believe the World grows near its end, yet is neither old nor decayed, nor shall ever perish upon the ruines of its own Principles.'[47] It seems reasonably certain that the growth of science was an important factor in the disappearance of the belief in decay. It became increasingly obvious (as, for example, in Galileo's work) that contemporary scientists were making discoveries which had been completely unknown to the philosophers of antiquity. It is not surprising, therefore, that the natural philosophers should have been opponents of the decay concept; it must not be supposed, however, that theirs was the only influence at work. Thus the contemporary Puritan ethic, too, was not strictly compatible with belief in a decaying world. (Milton, it may be noted, was early opposed to it.) The disputes that arose were therefore seldom straight-forward arguments between opposing groups of natural philosophers and of others. Indeed, the first major conflict in the seventeenth century was actually between two members of the clergy—Godfrey Goodman, Bishop of Gloucester, and George Hakewill, Archdeacon of Surrey—with Goodman supporting the concept of decay and Hakewill opposing it.

The argument over decay continued throughout the seventeenth century and extended into the eighteenth, gradually concerning itself less with arguments from nature, than with the human evidence. In particular, the debate hinged on whether the philosophers, writers, sculptors and architects of antiquity (the Ancients) were abler than their seventeenth-century equivalents (the Moderns), or not. There was by no means a clear-cut division of opinion. The defenders of the Moderns were often prepared to agree that the sculptors, the architects and, even, the writers of antiquity were greater, but they insisted that contemporary natural philosophers must be better, because they were building on the foundations of knowledge laid down by the Ancients. This is, of course, a Baconian argument, and it is perfectly valid, for science is cumulative in a way that most other modes of thinking, or expression, are not. One simile which was used during the seventeenth century to express this difference was to compare the modern natural philosophers to

dwarfs standing on the shoulders of giants (the Ancients)—
although the dwarf was so much smaller yet in this way he
could see further. This simile is mentioned (with disapproval)
by Goodman at the beginning of the century; at the end, it
achieved its most famous expression by Newton: 'If I have seen
farther than most men, it is because I have stood on the shoulders
of the giants.'[48]

The new astronomy played a noticeable part in discussions
of decay, particularly in the early seventeenth century. Surprisingly, perhaps, it was sometimes invoked as support for the
decay concept: the best-known example being, of course, John
Donne's *First Anniversary*. This poem seems at first sight to
present us with a mind considerably troubled by the recent
innovations in astronomy; it is not immediately obvious, however, how seriously we should take this. After all, Donne had
been handling the same topics humorously only the year
before, and, in subsequent years, again mentioned them with
equanimity. We must suppose that any dismay at the new ideas
was only temporary. In fact, since Donne also drags in older,
Ptolemaic ideas as well, we can assume that he was more interested in the concept of decay than in the observations he cited
for it. (This is also true of some other writers of the period, e.g.
Spenser.) Nevertheless, it is interesting to see which points
Donne considers as worth mentioning. He refers particularly
to the new things in the firmament, meaning by this, presumably,
not only the new stars and the comets, but also the new observations by Galileo. Then he mentions the odd courses of the
planets—their 'eccentrique parts'—described as much by
Ptolemy as by Copernicus. Similarly, the division of the celestial
sphere into forty-eight constellations, which he also cites, had
first occurred in antiquity. In Donne's time, however, there was
an increased interest in the constellations, for the long voyages
southward in the preceding centuries had revealed the existence
of many hitherto unknown stars. In 1603 Johann Bayer produced
the first important star chart (with a system of nomenclature
which is still in use). This included not only the forty-eight
ancient northern constellations, but also a few new ones which
he had constructed for the southern hemisphere.

Donne's further comment: 'then arise new starres, and olde

do vanish from our eyes' may be another reference to star charts (although it could also refer back to the exploding and other variable stars that had been discovered); the significance being that, when Tycho Brahe mapped the constellations at the end of the sixteenth century, he actually marked in fewer stars than had been noted by Ptolemy in antiquity. On the other hand, Bayer, a few years later, noted the positions of more stars than Ptolemy had done. These differences seem to have arisen through confusion over the definition of a constellation. Until relatively recently, the constellations did not include all visible stars, but consisted rather of the groupings of the major stars— the faint stars in between were ignored. Since it was rather a matter of choice which stars were included as part of a constellation and which were excluded, variations in the number catalogued could easily occur.

Subsequent references to the Zodiac and the Tropics show again that Donne's mind was not simply running on the new astronomy. But the remark that the Sun is 'now falne nearer us' does concern the more recent idea that the Sun and the Earth were drawing closer together. Throughout the poem this alternation of old and new suggests that for Donne, as for several of his contemporaries, the major significance of the new astronomy was that it raised the level of his interest in astronomy as a whole.

In the latter half of the seventeenth century the development of astronomical thought in Britain came to be linked with the new-born Royal Society. Of course, all types of science were discussed by the Society, but during its early years astronomy was of major importance. John Wallis, one of the founder members of the Royal Society, when recalling earlier scientific discussions mentioned particularly the Copernican hypothesis, Galileo's observations and the construction of telescopes, as subjects of debate. Discussions of the type he describes took place at Gresham College in London and also at Wadham College, Oxford, when John Wilkins—a leading spirit of the Royal Society—was warden there.

During its first years of existence the Royal Society was often referred to interchangeably as Gresham College because of the close connection between the two. Gresham College, a private foundation, played an important role in the diffusion of scientific knowledge in seventeenth-century England. Whereas Oxford and Cambridge remained obdurately Aristotelian throughout the century, most members of Gresham College favoured the new philosophy. Some dissemination of the new ideas must have occurred at the two universities, even if only because former professors of Gresham College took up teaching posts there. But, for example, at Oxford the professor of astronomy was enjoined by the statutes to teach Ptolemaic theory (though he was permitted to mention Copernicus).

The reactionary outlook of Oxford and Cambridge in matters affecting the curriculum led to much discussion of possible educational reforms during the seventeenth century— particularly by the Puritans. Authors as different as Milton and Defoe wrote on the subject. The latter was prepared to drop Latin and Greek, if room could be found for natural philosophy, mathematics, astronomy and navigation. Some of the other suggestions may look a little odd to modern eyes—one enthusiast advocated a course in fireworks—but there is no mistaking the general tendency away from classical studies and towards scientific. This Puritan emphasis on useful knowledge was continued among eighteenth-century dissenters, and presumably contributed largely towards the number of prominent scientists who came from nonconformist backgrounds.

Although there was a distinct, if slight, Puritan bias to the seventeenth-century interest in natural philosophy both Royalists and Puritans participated in the formation of the Royal Society. We find, for example, that when the Society decided in 1663 to improve current knowledge of the heavens by charting all the stars along the ecliptic zone, the study of the constellation Sagittarius was assigned jointly to Sir Robert Moray, one of Charles II's leading administrators, and to Lord Brouncker, who became a commissioner to the Navy Board when Pepys was its secretary. Thus interest in the new philosophy continued to grow after the restoration and even received occasional signs of mild official recognition, such as the Royal Society charter in 1662 and the foundation of the Greenwich Observatory a decade later.

The Greenwich Observatory was, indeed, founded by Charles

II (in the hope that it would provide practical assistance with navigational problems). He appointed John Flamsteed as the first Astronomer Royal (although he was not referred to by that title initially). 'There dined with me Mr. *Flamested* the learned Astrologer and *Mathematician*, whom now his Majestie had established in the new *Observatorie* in *Greenewich* Park, and furnish'd with the choicest instruments: an honest, sincere man.'[49] Evelyn's diary, from which this extract is taken, is in error at one point here. The instruments were actually provided by Flamsteed out of his own resources, for Charles (typically) ran short of money. The result, incidentally, was that when Halley took over as Astronomer Royal in 1720, he found that all the instruments had been removed by Flamsteed's executors, and he had to re-equip the Observatory again himself.

In its early years the Royal Society avowedly tried to model itself on the principles laid down previously by Sir Francis Bacon.[50] Cowley, an early Fellow of the Royal Society, compared Bacon's role with that of Moses; Bacon had led the natural philosophers out of the barren wastes and had guided them to the promised land.[51] This emphasis on Baconian thought radically distinguished the scientific community in this country from that on the Continent, where the philosophy of Descartes was the main formative influence. Descartes had his defenders in England, and, in the early years of the Royal Society, an increased interest in his work was stimulated by Royalist exiles returning from the Continent. However, most of this interest was concentrated outside the membership of the Royal Society. Indeed, it seems in some cases as if joining the Royal Society corresponded to a change from Cartesian to Baconian philosophy. Joseph Glanvill, for example, was originally a strong supporter of Descartes, but modified his position on becoming a Fellow of the Royal Society. The Society's allegiance to Bacon was buttressed by a shrewd suspicion that the Cartesian system of philosophy led toward materialism. It was for this reason that the Cambridge neo-Platonist philosopher, Henry More, changed from supporting Descartes to opposing him. (More also became a Fellow of the Royal Society.)

From our point of view, it is Descartes' cosmology which is of most interest. The Cartesian picture of the universe was of a continuous, transparent fluid in an incessant, whirling, vortex motion. The Sun and each planet was borne round on its own vortex, in such a way that the observed planetary motions were traced out. Descartes thus managed to evade the Roman Catholic edict against a moving Earth, for the Earth was stationary relative to the fluid in the vortex: it was the vortex as a whole that moved. This distinction was too subtle for Descartes' contemporaries. Joseph Glanvill summed up the common impression when he lumped Descartes together with all the other supporters of the heliocentric theory.[52] It should be added that Henry More, while he was still a supporter of Descartes, also combined Copernican and Cartesian ideas (in *Psychathanasia*).

Descartes differed radically from British scientists in advocating that the universe consisted of a continuous medium. By the latter half of the seventeenth century, it was generally agreed in Britain that, on the contrary, matter was atomic in structure. This was mainly important in the advancement of chemistry and physics, but it had another, wider significance. The atomistic theory of the seventeenth century was derived from the speculations of Epicurus, Democritus and Lucretius in antiquity. Most Christians, including natural philosophers, abhorred all three of these writers for their emphasis on the materialistic. Popular accounts of astronomy in the seventeenth and early eighteenth centuries often contain a rebuttal of the Epicurean belief in a solar system formed by the accidental confluence of atoms. (See, for example, the fourth book of Blackmore's long-winded poem *The Creation*, published in 1712.) Nevertheless, there was undoubtedly felt to be a connection between the new astronomy and the old atomic theory of matter. Democritus and Aristotle were often thought to be advocates of precisely opposite philosophies. In particular, Democritus was counted the proponent of an infinite universe of atomic matter, and Aristotle of a finite universe of continuous matter. Interest in an infinite universe was therefore naturally linked with an interest in the atomic theory. This connection made it possible for the critics of science (there were plenty of these in the later seventeenth century) to attack the Royal Society for Epicureanism with some plausibility. To make matters worse,

Thomas Hobbes—whose name was anathema to any decent Christian—was a supporter of Epicurus; an interest which he combined with the study of mathematics—as did the Royal Society. Aubrey noted that Hobbes 'had a high esteeme for the Royall Societie, having sayd that Naturall Philosophy was removed from the Universities to Gresham Colledge, meaning the Royal Societie that meetes there; and the Royall Societie (generally) had the like for him: and he would long since have been ascribed a Member there, but for the sake of one or two persons, whom he tooke to be his enemies: viz. Dr. Wallis (surely their Merciuries are in opposition) and Mr. Boyle. I might add Sir Paul Neile, who disobliges everybody.'[53] It was a fortunate thing for the scientists that Hobbes supported Descartes in the belief that matter was continuous: he could therefore not be quoted by their enemies as a friend of atomic theory. As it was, they could argue—following the Cambridge Platonist, Ralph Cudworth—that an atomic theory was not atheistic in itself: it had simply been used for atheistic purposes by the ancients. In a more positive vein, they could insist that natural philosophy actually afforded some of the best proofs for the immortality of the soul: for they believed that their discoveries of order in nature provided the basis for a natural theology pointing directly to God. The great advances in science, particularly in astronomy, during the late seventeenth century led to a very considerable emphasis on this aspect of theology during the eighteenth century.

Joseph Glanvill, incidentally, asserted that it was really the Aristotelian system which led to Epicureanism, not the new philosophy. 'What a *Romance* is the story of those impossible *concamerations*, *Intersections*, *Involutions* and feign'd Rotations of *solid Orbs?* All substituted to salve the credit of a broken ill-contrived *Systeme*. The belief of such disorders *above*, were an advantage to the *oblique Atheism* of *Epicurus*.'[54] But this was not a normal viewpoint.

Some of the early members, or supporters, of the Royal Society were, however, undoubtedly interested in Epicurean ideas. Abraham Cowley, for example, managed to combine the Epicurean with the Christian in his thinking, and Edmund Waller wrote appreciative prefatory verses for John Evelyn's

Essay on Lucretius. Cowley we have already met as a Fellow of the Royal Society, but so were Waller and Evelyn.

For long after its formation the Royal Society did not restrict its membership only to active scientists. John Dryden was another early Fellow and, although he left fairly quickly—apparently for failing to pay his dues—he remained on amicable terms with the Society, often praising its work.[55] Dryden's writings provide interesting evidence of the confused ideas concerning the system of the world which circulated in England during the latter half of the seventeenth century. Thus, apart from references to the new philosophy, he also mentions indiscriminately Ptolemaic and Cartesian concepts.

Besides writers, the Royal Society also numbered amongst its ranks many clergymen and nobles. For a time, it was a fashionable thing to attend Royal Society meetings, to hear the discussions, and to watch the demonstration experiments provided by Robert Hooke. Samuel Pepys, later president of the Royal Society, recorded his apprehension when the highly eccentric Duchess of Newcastle managed to secure an invitation to a meeting—the Royal Society was exclusively male until 1945. (The Duchess wrote considerably, though not profoundly, on natural philosophy, and was one of the English adherents of Descartes.) Pepys was worried by fear of the ridicule which this visit might bring on the Royal Society. During the first few years of the Society's life, it had, indeed, to contend with two main problems. The first was criticism and contempt; the second, lack of money. Many of the early members were dilettantes both in science and in payment of dues, and the Society was soon in considerable financial straits. These problems diminished at the end of the century, mainly due to the great popular esteem for Sir Isaac Newton, who then became President.

The growth of the new philosophy only gradually affected seventeenth-century belief in astrology, even amongst educated people. Indeed, during the Civil War, astrology became very popular and was used by both sides to buttress their cause.[56] The disturbed times certainly gave plenty of scope to the astrologers. Two bright comets appeared in 1664 and 1666, closely followed by the plague and the fire of London. The connection seemed too obvious to be ignored, and was the subject of much contemporary comment (e.g. by Dryden in *Annus Mirabilis* and by Defoe in *A Journal of the Plague Year*).

Several of the early members of the Royal Society believed in astrology. One, Elias Ashmole, was indeed a leading astrologer of the day. It is said that Flamsteed, the first Astronomer Royal, chose the date for the laying of the foundation stone at Greenwich Observatory by casting a horoscope. John Dryden, who could also cast a horoscope, certainly seems to have taken astrology seriously: there are numerous astrological references in his writings (see, for example, his play *An Evening's Love*, which is subtitled *The Mock Astrologer*). Astrological references are also to be found in other writers who were members of the Royal Society. For example, it was regarded as of great astrological significance that Venus was visible throughout the day when Charles II was born. We find the fact mentioned by Waller, by Dryden (twice—in *Astrea Redux* and in *Annus Mirabilis*) and by Cowley.

> No Star amongst ye all did, I believe,
> Such vigorous assistance give,
> As that which thirty years ago,
> At Charls his Birth, did, in despight
> Of the proud Sun's Meridian Light,
> His future Glories, and this Year foreshow.[57]

Outside the Royal Society, we find that even Thomas Hobbes thought of astrology as a science.

Of course, the fact that a writer refers to astrology does not of itself necessarily imply any great belief in the validity of astrological predictions. A closer idea of much educated reaction to astrology can, perhaps, be obtained from John Evelyn's diary. Here we find, on the one hand, scorn for the astrologers. 'Was that celebrated Eclipse of the Sun, so much threatned by the *Astrologers*, & had so exceedingly alarm'd the whole Nation, so as hardly any would worke, none stir out of their houses; so ridiculously were they abused by knavish and ignorant star-gazers.'[58] On the other hand, Evelyn was far from despising signs in the heavens; he felt that they might bear a general significance even if their specific connotation could not be known.

This Evening looking out of my Chamber Window towards the West, I first saw a Meteor, (or what ever other Phoenomenon it was) of an obscure bright Colour... resembling the brightnesse of the *Moone* when under a thin Clow'd, very much in shape like the blade of a sword... What this may Portend (for it was very extraordinarie) God onely knows; but such another *Phoenomenon* I remember I saw... about the Triall of the greate Earle of Strafford, proceeeding our bloudy Rebellion: I pray God avert his Judgements; we have had of late severall *Comets*, which though I believe appeare from natural Causes, & of themselves operate not, yet I cannot despise them; They may be warnings from God, as they commonly are for-runners of his Annimadversions.[59]

In the following century, Samuel Johnson looked back in conscious superiority on the seventeenth-century attitude to astrology, and remarked 'It had in that time a very extensive dominion. Its predictions raised hopes and fears in minds which ought to have rejected it with contempt.' He gives as an example that, when Charles I was a prisoner in Carisbrook Castle, an astrologer was consulted to find out what hour would be most favourable for his escape. He notes however, that towards the end of the century 'the credit of planetary intelligence wore fast away; though some men of knowledge, and Dryden among them, continued to believe that conjunctions and oppositions had a great part in the distribution of good or evil, and in the government of sublunary things.'[60]

CHAPTER VI

Newton

O N 5 July 1686 Samuel Pepys, in his capacity as President
of the Royal Society, gave the imprimatur to a treatise
by Isaac Newton entitled *Philosophiae Naturalis Principia
Mathematica*. The publication of the *Principia* in the following
year marks the culmination of the seventeenth-century gropings
after a new, comprehensive world system. More than that, it
marks the introduction of a different and more rigorous approach
to science. Despite its extreme complexity, Newton's work was
rapidly recognised to be of major importance. Indeed, it acquired such a high reputation that Newtonian methodology
(or some supposed approximation to it) soon spilled over into
other spheres of thought, such as the social or the moral. Newton himself was regarded with extreme admiration, and the
writings of the day ring with his praises.[1]

> Newton, *pure Intelligence*, whom God
> To mortals lent, to trace his boundless works
> From laws sublimely simple[2]

This adulation was particularly noticeable at his death in
1727. The poems commemorating this event frequently contain
descriptions of Newton's soul leaving the Earth and voyaging
out through the solar system into infinite space. As he goes he
surveys with approval the various celestial bodies, each obeying
the universal laws he has discovered.

> Mark where he halts on Saturn, tipt with snow,
> And pleas'd surveys his theory below;
> Sees the five moons alternate round him shine,
> Rise by his laws, and by his laws decline,
> Then thro' the void takes his immortal race,
> Amidst the vast infinity of space.[3]

This provides an interesting link with the general theme of souls
viewing the heavens after death which can be found both earlier

(e.g. in Donne), and later, extending on into the nineteenth century.

Some writers were a little more restrained in their enthusiasm. Pope, for example, although recognizing the pre-eminence of Newton, reminded his readers that he was, after all, only a man, however great a scientist he may have been.

> Could he, whose rules the rapid comet bind,
> Describe or fix one movement of his mind!
> Who saw its fires here rise and there descend,
> Explain his own beginning or his end?[4]

Note that Pope has used here as his prime example of Newton's greatness the explanation given in the *Principia* of the orbits of comets. In this he was following popular opinion: it was regarded as particularly remarkable that the erratic comets, which had hitherto defied inclusion in any world system, should have found an ordered position in the Newtonian system. A few lines earlier Pope had mentioned Newton's derivation of the planetary orbits and his work on tides. He also refers somewhat more obscurely to Newton's ideas on time as explained in the *Principia*.

Pope was not, apparently, opposed to Newton. On the contrary, his famous adulatory epitaph on Newton probably sums up his opinion quite accurately. We have the further evidence that he gladly helped in the composition of a suitable dedication to a posthumous work by Newton on biblical chronology. Pope did, on occasion, attack science,[5] but it was the apparent concentration on the trivial that irritated him— cosmology he regarded with some interest. We may note that the first epistle of the *Essay on Man* originally had attached to it the subtitle *Of the Nature and State of Man, with Respect to the Universe*. As such, it belonged to a very popular eighteenth-century genre. Where Pope differed from most of his contemporaries was in his insistence that we should only try to trace God in our own world and not in others. This was a slightly unusual viewpoint, and Pope was, indeed, taken to task for it. *An Essay on the Universe* (published anonymously in 1733) expressed admiration for the *Essay on Man*, but emphasized the possibility of tracing God in the universe at large. In *Truth: a Counterpart to Mr Pope's Essay on Man,* William Ayre, however, felt it necessary to go further and to defend Newton from the limitations implicit in Pope.

Newton's main achievement in the *Principia* was his explanation of planetary motions—the fundamental problem of astronomy since antiquity—on the basis of a few simple laws of mechanics plus the postulate of a universal gravitational attraction. He showed, in fact, that so long as the planets were projected with the correct initial velocities their present orbits would follow as a necessary consequence. This dependence of his system only on the initial rate of projection and the subsequent gravitational attraction of the Sun accounts for the frequent juxtaposition of these two properties in contemporary accounts.

> he by the blended power
> Of *gravitation* and *projection* saw
> The whole in silent harmony revolve.[6]

Newton was not alone in thinking his way towards this new system: several of his contemporaries were slowly groping in the same direction. Robert Hooke even claimed to have reached it before Newton. Both the laws of mechanics and the idea of a solar gravitational attraction were being freely discussed by others at the same time. (Newton's emphasis on the universality of gravitation—inside and outside the solar system—was, however, important.) What distinguished Newton from the rest was his unique ability to deduce the results rigorously from the initial assumptions.

Newton's work can be seen, in one light, as the logical culmination of the neo-Platonist strand in British science. It was commonly accepted by contemporary writers that the concept of universal gravitation was of ancient origin, having been propounded by the Pythagoreans in antiquity,[7] and the existence of a continuous line of development from Pythagoras to Newton seemed obvious.[8] But, equally, Newton was considered to be the direct successor to Bacon in terms of scientific methodology. Thus we find that when James Thomson describes the rise of science in the *Seasons*, the names he emphasizes especially are those of Bacon and Newton. (It is significant that in the original version he also mentioned the neo-Platonist Henry More.)

Newton's system of the world was utterly different from the system of Descartes, then widely accepted on the Continent. Indeed, Newton devoted a considerable part of the *Principia* to showing that the Cartesian vortices were incapable of explaining the observed motions of the planets. Supporters of Newton were therefore necessarily opponents of Descartes, and tended, in fact, to regard his work with considerable scorn. We are told by Thomson that Newton had restored the heavens

> from the wild rule
> Of whirling *vortices*, and circling spheres.[9]

In the original version of this, however, Thomson spoke much more strongly of

> the great Acquests
> By NEWTON made: Who from the wild Domain
> Of the *French Dreamer* rescu'd Heaven and Earth.

Although Newton rejected virtually all of the Cartesian world system, and was followed in this by nearly all British philosophers, Descartes' ideas on the evolution of celestial bodies—suns turning into comets, and comets turning into planets—stimulated, towards the end of the seventeenth century, a new interest in the possibility of changes during the lifetime of the solar system. The traditional picture of the universe was that it had been created by God and would be destroyed by God (neither event being describable in scientific terms): the period between these two events was not thought to have been long enough for any other significant changes to have occurred. Such a view was still held to be generally valid at the end of the seventeenth century, but the creation and destruction processes, in particular, now came to be thought of as amenable to scientific description.

The new emphasis that God's actions in the physical world were capable of minute analysis derived from the growing belief that God always chose to operate by secondary causes.[10] This belief, in turn, depended partly on the increasing success of science in explaining the operations of nature by means of scientific laws. Newtonianism, as it developed, came to put an increasing stress on secondary causes. This tendency was fortified initially by the Puritan dislike of post-biblical miracles, and by the strong strain of rationalism (usually Cartesian in origin) brought back from the Continent by returning Royalist exiles. Moreover, potential opposition was now muted, for there was a noticeable decline in the prestige of the Anglican clergy at the end of the seventeenth century. Most of this was attributed by contemporary writers to a reaction against the passions of the Civil War, but some also speak of the rise of science as a contributing factor.

The most important of the new attempts to study the history of the solar system (in the sense that it aroused the most interest and controversy) was that made by Thomas Burnet in the 1680s. Burnet was originally physician to Charles II (who encouraged him to publish his ideas), later becoming chaplain to William III. His work appeared first in Latin, and then in an English version entitled *The Theory of the Earth*. It ran rapidly through several editions; the fifth (in 1722) contained an ode to the author by Addison, and the book was praised by both Addison and Steele. (*The Spectator* was always interested in discussing natural theology.)

Burnet's ideas were formulated before the publication of the *Principia*, and he seems to have been considerably influenced by Descartes, although he was also an adherent of the Cambridge Platonists. Like virtually all other writers on the subject, his duty, as he saw it, was to reconcile the ways of God in Creation with current scientific knowledge. He finally evolved a most comprehensive scheme. The Earth, he thought, had been formed as a slightly prolate spheroid (i.e. looking something like a rugby ball). Earth and water had separated from each other, so that the water formed the inner part of the spheroid and the earth its surface layers. (That is, the central regions of the Earth were of lower density that the outer shell.) According to Burnet, the Earth originally had its axis perpendicular to the ecliptic, so that the Sun was always overhead at the equator— producing, he believed, perpetual spring. This primaeval Earth represented, he said, the Golden Age. (The concept of a perfect Earth, destroyed by Man's sin, was, of course, a commonplace of the seventeenth century, and was related to the belief in decay. *Paradise Lost* presents a very similar picture of the

Earth before the Fall.) The Golden Age ended with the Flood, which was itself a direct consequence of the Fall. The Flood was caused by the sudden collapse of the heavier, outer sphere of earth into the inner sphere of water. At the same instant, the Earth's axis was tilted from the perpendicular to its present position. (As a corollary, the Earth's surface represented the broken remains of former perfection. Wild scenery—mountains and valleys—was regarded with some contempt by Burnet and his contemporaries.)

A good deal of Burnet's writing was derivative: his main originality appearing in the description of the Flood. The separation of the Earth into an inner region of low density, and an outer of higher density had been suggested by Descartes (and was one of the points for which Newton attacked him). The belief that the Earth had a prolate shape was, again, mainly due to French scientists who, during the later seventeenth century, made measurements in France of the length of one degree of latitude on the Earth's surface. Their results for slightly different latitudes indicated that the Earth was prolate. Newton, on the other hand, had demonstrated in the *Principia* that the Earth should be appreciably oblate (i.e. flattened instead of pointed) on gravitational theory. (This disagreement is one of the suggested reasons for the slow acceptance of Newtonian theory on the Continent. It should be remarked, however, that Huyghens, on the basis of Cartesian mechanics, also determined that the Earth should be slightly flattened, though not to the extent required by Newton.)

The question was finally settled in the 1730s when two French expeditions were dispatched overseas to make further measurements at widely different latitudes. One under Bouguer went to South America; the other under Maupertuis went to Lapland. Their measures not only confirmed that the Earth was oblate, but also showed that the degree of flattening conformed to Newton's predictions. Maupertuis wrote an account of his journey—*The Figure of the Earth*—which excited considerable interest. His description of the brilliant arctic aurorae which he saw was found particularly fascinating, and was subsequently referred to either obliquely or directly by various writers in this country.[11]

Burnet's theory evoked much controversy in the succeeding decades. He was attacked from both a theological and a scientific standpoint. His contemporaries were still unaccustomed, or in some cases were actively opposed, to any attempt to explain the miraculous in terms of the natural. Distaste for mixing religion and science was evinced by both clergy and natural philosophers. Clergymen disliked Burnet for his insistence that some parts of the Mosaic account of Creation were allegorical. (All attempts to explain the formation of the Earth in terms of natural phenomena found six days too short for their purpose, and therefore followed Burnet in reinterpreting the appropriate passages. At the same time, there was very little objection to a total lifetime for the universe of six thousand years.) On the ohter hand, Burnet was criticized by natural philosophers for his belief that the Flood involved a descent from perfection—this being another aspect of the scientific battle against the principle of decay. Bacon had laid it down that science was a search for order and regularity in the world. If the Fall of Man had involved a similar fall of nature such a search would be called in doubt. The argument that science supported theology by providing evidence for God's design of the universe would likewise be groundless. John Wilkins, and many of his contemporary natural philosophers, therefore stressed that all things continued as they had from the beginning of Creation. The decline in importance of the decay concept was thus connected with the rise in importance of the argument from design.

An early criticism of Burnet's theory actually came from Isaac Newton. Burnet sent him a copy of the first edition of his book in 1681. Newton, in replying, wrote that he could not believe that the Earth's surface had ever suffered a violent change of the type which Burnet postulated. Subsequently, the naturalist, John Ray, criticized Burnet for trying to explain the miraculous: which was, he felt, something intrinsically inexplicable (though he later attempted to do the same himself). As befitted an eminent biologist, he believed that evidence for God was better obtained from the design of plants and animals than from the design of the universe (a view which Robert Boyle also held but which did not gain general currency until a century later).

In 1694 Edmund Halley suggested that the real cause of the

Flood had been the close approximation of a passing comet to the Earth. Newton was the first to show that comets probably followed orbits that were elongated ellipses[12], and that the same comet might therefore appear more than once in the vicinity of the Sun. Halley, however, was the first man to provide observational proof of this, and to predict the return of a comet. He therefore had something of a proprietary interest in them. It may be noted in passing that there are occasional unconfirmed hints that others preceded Halley in the prediction of comets. Thus John Aubrey records that the enigmatic Thomas Harriot claimed to have predicted the arrival of comets. 'Sir Francis Stuart had heard Mr Hariot say that he had seen nine Cometes, and had predicted Seaven of them, but did not tell how.'[13] And Pepys attended a lecture at Gresham College in 1665 when Robert Hooke discussed a comet which had recently appeared. 'Among other things proving very probably that this is the same Comet, that appeared before in the year 1618, and that in such a time probably it will appear again, which is a very new opinion.'[14]

Halley's ideas on the Flood were more radical that Burnet's for whereas the latter thought that the initiation of the Flood was due to an explicit act of God, Halley thought that the whole process could be described in terms of God acting through natural agents. Halley, it should be added, had a reputation as a free-thinker, and was, apparently, refused the Chair of Astronomy at Oxford in 1691 on these grounds. However, the rumours cannot have been very influential, for he was subsequently appointed to the Chair of Geometry and later became Astronomer Royal in succession to Flamsteed. There are, indeed, flattering contemporary references to his religious virtue.[15]

Halley's speculations on cometary effects were taken over by William Whiston, Newton's successor at Cambridge. He suggested that all the major physical changes mentioned in the Bible could be explained in terms of cometary collisions. (According to Whiston, the Earth itself had initially been a comet. Burnet thought it was initially a star. Both were obviously influenced by the Cartesian theory.) Whiston made an ingenious attempt to get round the time problem presented by the Genesis account of Creation. He suggested that in its original state the Earth always turned the same face to the Sun during its annual revolution (just as the Moon always presents the same face to the Earth). The biblical day of creation could then be interpreted as a year of our present time. Whiston otherwise had a picture, similar to Burnet's, of a perfect, primaeval Earth revolving in a perfectly circular orbit round the Sun. The physical structure of his Earth differed somewhat from Burnet's. It had, for example, a central core which rotated independently of the surface layers. (This had been suggested previously by Halley as a way of explaining the variation of the Earth's magnetic field.) According to Whiston, the descent from perfection was accomplished by a comet, which not only produced the diurnal rotation and the elliptical orbit of the Earth, but also accounted for its oblateness. A later comet induced the Flood, and yet another would produce the final conflagration.

Whiston's excessive utilization of comets was partly due to the very great current interest in these bodies. Newton, himself, had suggested that comets played an important role in the economy of the universe. He thought that stars might be refuelled, and planetary atmospheres replenished, by the infalling of cometary material.[16]

Various other attempts at a scientific explanation of Scripture were made during this period (late seventeenth and early eighteenth century) but they are generally of lesser astronomical interest. One slight exception must be made for the geologist, John Woodward. He provided what seemed to be the first definite scientific evidence that the Flood had, in fact, occurred. A careful study of fossils had convinced him that they were the remains of animals which had been left behind when the Flood receded. This was undoubtedly an advance over the view, previously held by many, that fossils were artefacts. On the other hand, mention was already being made of the possible greater antiquity of the Earth indicated by fossils. (There was a considerable interest in fossils at this time: as is suggested by the frequency with which they are mentioned.[17]) The age of the world was obviously of much astronomical significance. If geologists could show that the Earth, and therefore the solar system, was much older than the accepted six thousand years, this would have a considerable effect on cosmological theories. For the moment, however, fossil placement by the Flood permitted the short time-scale to be retained.

The early eighteenth century saw an almost universal acceptance of a belief in a plurality of worlds. Writers, from the obscure to the famous, revelled in it.[18]

> All these illustrious worlds, and many more,
> Which by the tube astronomers explore:
> And millions which the glass can ne'er descry,
> Lost in the wilds of vast immensity;
> Are suns, are centres, whose superior sway
> Planets of various magnitudes obey.[19]

Hand in hand with this belief, there was a general emphasis on the infinite extent of the universe. Such an emphasis was a necessary part of Newtonianism. According to Newton, gravitation was a universal property of matter (this was, of course, an assumption: observational confirmation of its plausibility only gradually accumulated). It followed that every piece of matter in the universe was attracted by every other piece. Newton pointed out that in a finite universe all the matter present would therefore eventually clump together; stability was only possible in an infinite universe.[20] In any case, as telescopes delved deeper and deeper into space, it became increasingly difficult to see how the universe could have a boundary.

> Where, ends this mighty building? Where begin
> The suburbs of Creation? Where, the wall
> Whose battlements look o'er into the vale
> Of non-existence? Nothing's strange abode![21]

Not everyone was happy with the current interest in the plurality of worlds. Some writers counselled caution, pointing out that it was all guess work.

> Whether those stars, that twinkling lustre send,
> Are suns, and rolling worlds those suns attend,
> Man may conjecture, and new schemes declare;
> Yet all his systems but conjectures are.[22]

Others suggested that whether the concept was right or wrong it was more important to concentrate on things close at hand. 'Though we see the greatness and wisdom of the Deity in all the seeming worlds that surround us, it is our chief concern to trace him in that which we inhabit.'[23] (This was, of course, also Pope's attitude.) Despite these objections, the belief that innumerable other inhabited worlds existed in the universe became a commonplace of eighteenth-century theology. It can even be found in the verse paraphrases of the Bible which were popular at the time.[24]

As we have seen in the previous chapter, writers in the early seventeenth century were already exercised by the theological questions which followed from assuming a plurality of worlds. In the eighteenth century these questions became even more insistent. Were other planetary systems

> Form'd when the world at first existence gain'd?
> And to one final period all ordain'd?
> Or, since wide space they independent fill,
> Apart created, and creating still?
> Do scriptures clear, the aw'd assent oppose?
> They chiefly *our* original disclose
> Do they assert, ere we in being came,
> God ne'er was own'd by the Creator's name?
> Where then were Angels, elder race to man?
> Who fell seduc'd, perhaps, ere he began:
> Do they assert prolific pow'r at rest
> Shall in no future instance shine confest?[25]

But answers, too, were being formulated. For example, the Day of Judgement was presented as the end, not simply of the Earth, but of the whole, infinite, Newtonian universe.[26]

The major problem was who populated these other worlds. It had long been assumed that the plenitude of God would provide inhabitants wherever there was the opportunity. But the concept of a chain of being, as accepted in the seventeenth and early eighteenth centuries, assumed that each member of the chain had unique characteristics. Hence, although other worlds might be inhabited, it would be by creatures other than Man. So far as can be judged from the writings of the time, the inhabitants of other planets were generally considered to excel us. At least, these are the ones that generally receive mention.[27]

As the eighteenth century progressed, the idea of a stationary, immutable chain of being[28] began to give way to the concept of an evolutionary chain of being; that is, to the idea that a creature could change its position in the scheme of things— typically by progressing upwards. This emphasis on progress was not restricted in its application only to living things: it was also applied to stars, and led to a new interest in their evolution with time.

> The *stars*, from whence?—Ask *Chaos*—he can tell.
> These bright temptations to idolatry,
> From *darkness*, and *confusion*, took their birth;
> Sons of *deformity!* from fluid dregs
> Tartarean, first they rose to masses rude;
> And then, to spheres opaque; then dimly shone;
> Then brighten'd; then blaz'd out in *perfect day*.
> *Nature* delights in progress; in advance
> From worse to better.[29]

One factor which played an important part in the trend from a stationary to a progressive chain of being was the growing belief in the uniformity of nature. This, in turn, stemmed mainly from the emphasis (often Newtonian in inspiration) on the existence of universal laws. Thus, instead of arguing that creatures on other planets would differ from those on Earth because they filled different niches in the chain, it was now argued that they would be the same because they were subject to the same laws.

Of all the concepts introduced by Newton in the *Principia* his idea of gravitation proved to be the most controversial. In itself the word was not new: it had been used before Newton to describe the attractive power of the Earth. Nor was the idea of an attractive force between different bodies in the solar system new; as we have seen speculations on magnetic interaction had been circulating since the early years of the seventeenth century. ('Magnetic power' actually continued to be used during the early eighteenth century, as a synonym for gravitation.[30]) Where Newton deviated from his contemporaries was in refusing to discuss what he meant by gravitational force. So

long as the concept worked, he had no wish to publish speculations on its mode of operation. Continental scientists considered
this suspension of judgement as unscientific, and unhesi-
tatingly attacked it. Moreover, they objected very strongly to
one of the basic assumptions of Newtonian gravitation—that a
force could be transmitted between two bodies which were not
in direct contact. This they regarded as an unfortunate return
to the medieval belief in 'influences'. Newton, himself, was not unmoved by this fear, but he felt that his assumption must be right,
or the entire theory fell to pieces. If it was assumed that there was
material between the planets in a sufficient quantity to transmit
forces, then his calculations showed that the friction generated
would rapidly cause the planets to spiral into the Sun. Hence, he
was forced to assume the existence of action at a distance.

The *Principia*, like the *De Revolutionibus* of Copernicus, was a
difficult book to read and few people were able to follow the
original in detail. Its importance, however, was recognized to be
so great that numerous popularizations for non-mathematicians
appeared in quick succession. The first of these was the Boyle
lectures for 1692 (sermons on natural theology instituted in
memory of Robert Boyle[31] who died in 1691; John Evelyn
was one of the first Trustees). The series was given by Richard
Bentley, the great classical scholar, who became a few years later
a much detested (and long-lived) Master of Trinity, Cambridge.
Bentley's sermons were devoted to a repudiation of atheism in
general and of Epicurean philosophy in particular. To this
end he invoked Newtonian cosmology, and, in order to make
sure that he had understood the ideas correctly, he entered into
direct correspondence with Newton.

From these letters and other writings, we can see why Newton's work became so important for eighteenth-century natural
theology. There was, in the first place, the question of the transmission of the gravitational force referred to in the previous
paragraph. Newton, himself, seems to have visualized the forces
in the solar system as being transferred by a hypothetical medium—the aether—which did not impede motion (this concept
was elaborated considerably in the nineteenth century). But
he equally approved the view that the transmission of forces
required direct intervention by God. Moreover, he felt that the

gravitational interactions in the solar system were so varied that the system would be unstable over any long period of time. Hence, it required the constant presence of God to maintain its order. Newton also invoked an act of God for the initial placement of the planets in their orbits.

> With what an aweful world-revolving power
> Were first th' unwieldy planets launch'd along
> Th' illimitable void! Thus to remain,
> Amid the flux of many thousand years.[32]

Thus several different aspects of Newton's world system seemed to provide direct evidence for the existence of God.[33] (As a minor point, the word *attraction* had its own emotional overtones which fitted in well with the concept of a God of Love.[34])

There was, however, another side to Newtonianism: it represented the culminating triumph of the mechanical philosophy. This led in the early eighteenth century to the observation that gravitation could also be used in the completely opposite sense as a buttress for mechanical pictures of the world.[35] The mechanical aspect of Newtonianism grew in importance as the century progressed; by the mid-century, therefore, we find the limitations of science receiving increased emphasis (e.g. in Christopher Smart's *The Omniscience of the Supreme Being*).

Newton's introduction of God into the working of the solar system was regarded with less sympathy on the Continent than in this country. For example, it was derided as an odd opinion by Leibniz: he said it was as if God Almighty had to wind his clock up from time to time. (This analogy between the solar system and a clock was popular from the seventeenth to the nineteenth century.[36] The point was that a clock was owned to be the invention of a mind and therefore the far more complicated solar system must be the creation of a mind that much greater.)

In 1715 a quarrel of major importance flared up between Leibniz on the Continent and Samuel Clarke in this country over their respective views of the relationship between God and nature.[37] Leibniz argued that God had designed the world so well in the beginning that there had been no need to interfere with its operations since.[38] Clarke (writing on behalf of Newton) rejected this on the grounds that it led to a denial of revelation, and thence towards deism. The controversy echoed down the century: as late as the 1770's a poem appeared comparing the two sides of the argument (W. H. Roberts' *A Poetical Essay on the Providence of God*).

Despite the opposition to deism by Newton and his leading supporters, the general effect of Newtonianism on eighteenth century minds was to create sympathy precisely for that. The influential writings of John Locke (a leading Newtonian) seemed to point this way; for, although Locke accepted revelation as a way of discovering truth, he managed to give his readers the firm impression that revealed truth was less important that truth obtained from reasoning.[39] One obvious deistic trend in the eighteenth century was the appearance of innumerable effusions of praise for the Supreme Being and for the universe which so clearly delineated his attributes. Addison's *Ode*, the best-known of these (it still appears in hymn books), is a moderate example.

Young's *Night Thoughts* reveals how far this line of reasoning could lead away from traditional Christian thought. He refers to the heavens as 'Nature's system of divinity',[40] and remarks that the worship of celestial objects in times past was so logical as hardly to be idolatry.[41] Moreover, he observes, the heavens can be seen from all over the Earth; hence knowledge of God is available everywhere: not only in Christian or Jewish lands.[42*] These views were particularly common in the Church of England. Dissenters were less likely to accept such departures from traditional doctrine. Isaac Watts,† for example, frequently wrote in a contrary vein.

> Thy voice produc'd the seas and spheres,
> Bid the waves roar, and planets shine;
> But nothing like thy Self appears,
> Through all these spacious works of thine.[43]

* These ideas were, of course, particularly developed by the eighteenth-century deists. Thus Tom Paine argued, in *The Age of Reason*, that observations of the universe provide a true theology, unlike the false one provided by the Bible.

† Watts wrote a popular eighteenth-century astronomy text (*First Principles of Astronomy and Geography*) which was recommended to John Wesley by P. Doddridge and was also used by Priestley.

It is of some interest, however, that the replies to *Night Thoughts* which subsequently appeared implied rather that Young had made an insufficient use of science.

There was one further important result of the Newtonian idea that God was still at work in the solar system: it rapidly undermined the old belief that the Fall of Man had brought about the ruination of the physical world (as Burnet had accepted). It was argued instead—for example, in the series of Boyle lectures given by William Derham—that God's guiding action in the solar system implied that only Man had fallen.

At the beginning of the eighteenth century, Newton published a major work on *Opticks*. This was written in English and was much less mathematical than the *Principia*. Of especial interest was his description of experiments with prisms by means of which he broke up white light into a coloured spectrum. The aesthetic attraction of the results, and the relative ease of the style, made the book widely popular. Its influence can be traced in many eighteenth-, and even nineteenth-century writers. The questions he examined were, however, mainly terrestrial—such as the explanation of the rainbow—and not astronomical.[44]

One point which did have some astronomical bearing was Newton's discussion of the velocity of light. It had been realized long before, that light might have a finite velocity. Bacon had written on the subject, and Galileo had experimented, but the first reasonable results were not obtained until 1675 (by Rømer in Paris) from observations of the satellites of Jupiter. Newton later re-examined Rømer's results and obtained a slightly different value for the velocity of light. Since his discussion of the subject was widely read, the idea that light moved at a finite speed became generally accepted in this country.[45] Newtonians thus believed, on the one hand, in a finite velocity of light and a universe of infinite extent; on the other, they continued to accept a short time-span of a few thousand years since the creation of the world. This led to the speculation that some stars were too distant to be seen: the light from them not having had time to reach the Earth since the universe began.

> How distant some of these nocturnal suns!
> So distant (says the sage), 't were not absurd

> To doubt, if beams, set out at *Nature's* birth,
> Are yet arriv'd at this most foreign world[46]

The *Opticks* shows more clearly than the *Principia* the strong neo-Platonic streak that ran through Newton's thought. It can be seen, for example, in his attempts to link the visual spectrum with the musical octave. He seems to have been influenced by the Cambridge Platonists, particularly Henry More (who was a pupil at the same school as Newton, though not at the same time).

We have seen that besides its theological significance, astronomy was also important in medieval times for its practical value—in time-keeping and in astrology. Astrology fell into disfavour during the eighteenth century, and good time-keeping became routine with the introduction of pendulum clocks (first developed by Huyghens in the seventeenth century[47]). But astronomy continued to be of the greatest practical importance, for as its old uses disappeared they were replaced by the problem of determining the longitude. With the rise in importance of overseas commerce and of the British Navy it became an urgent necessity to devise methods for finding accurate positions at sea. (The significance of the problem was already recognised in the seventeenth century. When Dryden wrote: 'Instructed ships shall sail to quick Commerce,' he added a footnote saying it would be by a more exact knowledge of the longitude.[48]) Navigation was regarded as a part of astronomy, so the determination of longitude became a prime problem for astronomers[49]—Charles II set up the Greenwich Observatory specifically for this purpose.

Latitude determination was easy enough; not so longitude. In the middle of the seventeenth century even longitudes on land were poorly determined; although it was known that the longitudes given in classical writings—which had been used in medieval times—were considerably in error.[50] A determination of longitude is basically a determination of the difference in time between two places on the Earth's surface. It was recognized that, if clocks could be improved in accuracy, better longitudes would soon follow[51] as, indeed, they did when pendulum clocks became generally available. Except in a dead calm, however, pendulum clocks would not work on board ship, so the search for a universally applicable method continued. It had been noted earlier in the seventeenth century that the Earth's magnetic field varied in magnitude and direction at different longitudes. For a while, there was hope that this could be used to determine position on the Earth's surface. Such expectations were dashed when it was discovered that the magnetic field at any point varied irregularly with time. However, when at the beginning of the eighteenth century Parliament offered a prize of £20,000 for an accurate method of determining longitude at sea, many of the amateurs who were attracted to the problem tried to devise methods based on the geomagnetic field. One such was Zachariah Williams who felt so certain of winning the prize that he came to set up house in London with his daughter. His plan, needless to say, was rejected by the experts, but Samuel Johnson regarded it with favour and was responsible for a re-publication of Williams' ideas which appeared in 1755.

Johnson was probably acquainted with a member of the Board of Longitude—the body which officially judged applications for the prize money. When David Garrick came up with Johnson from the latter's academy near Lichfield he was entrusted to the care of John Colson. Colson was a member of the Board of Longitude, and is said to have been the model for Gelidus in the *Rambler* (No. 24).

Several very odd schemes were proposed for the prize—not all of them by cranks. For example, William Whiston suggested that ships should be stationed at known points in the ocean and that at fixed intervals of time they should fire shells. Other ships in the vicinity could determine their position by noting the difference in time between seeing the flash from the shell and hearing its explosion. His idea was greeted with considerable popular derision.[52] (It may be noted in passing that Dr Johnson also became acquainted with Whiston about the middle of the eighteenth century—he met him at Tunbridge Wells—but by that time Whiston was over eighty.)

There was, however, a fairly general agreement amongst the main competitors for the prize money that one of two methods would succeed in the race to determine the longitude. The first was by the accurate observation and calculation of the position of the Moon relative to the positions of background stars. The second was by the development of a clock which would keep time accurately at sea. As it turned out, both methods proved successful before the end of the century.* As early as 1775 Dr Johnson could record seeing a small spring-driven watch capable of determining the longitude at sea. In this country both methods remained, and remain today, related to the Greenwich Observatory: the first depended on the positions of the Moon and the stars which were tabulated in the *Nautical Almanac*, published from the Observatory; the second depended on the accurate running of chronometers and these were checked and regulated at Greenwich.

As has been mentioned, the original impulse for the Observatory at Greenwich came from a report on the longitude problem; this was presented to Charles II by a Royal Society committee. By the last quarter of the seventeenth century, however, the Royal Society was already in danger of fading out of existence. We have seen that attacks on the Society were very numerous during the latter part of the seventeenth century. Direct altercations—such as one between Joseph Glanvill and Henry Stubbe[53]—over the value of the new science were irritating, but the growing ridicule and contempt was a good deal more dangerous. Thomas Sprat, who later became Bishop of Rochester, wrote a history of the Royal Society only a few years after its formation. He was impelled to do this by his desire to explain the principles on which the Society was founded, and so show that it was not in any way ridiculous. Samuel Butler's poems were probably circulating freely at court during this period; as we have seen, they contained many gibes at the new Society.

Several plays about this time have a plot, or a sub-plot, based on the satirization of a virtuoso. The word *virtuoso* originally meant an amateur natural philosopher, and therefore covered almost all those who were then seriously interested in science. As such, it was used by Glanvill in his defence of the Royal Society. But it quickly acquired a humorous overtone,

---

* The lunar method was developed particularly by the German astronomer, Tobias Mayer; the first really accurate chronometer was constructed by John Harrison in England.

and came to mean someone who prized the useless, or the trivial, for its own sake; who delighted in polemics; and who never produced any results of value to the population at large. These were also the faults with which the Royal Society as a whole was taxed.[54]

> That those who greedily pursue
> Things wonderful instead of true,
>
> In vain strive Nature to suborn,
> And, for their pains, are paid with scorn[55]

These criticisms became muted after Newton's triumphs, but, instead, there was raised once again the fear that a study of science might lead to spiritual pride.

> Trace Science then, with Modesty thy guide;
> First strip off all her equipage of Pride[56]

The satirical attacks on the virtuosi, however, unlike those more seriously intended, did not usually emphasize irreligion as one of his major defects.

The Scriblerus Club, formed in the early eighteenth century with Pope, Swift, Arbuthnot, and Gay amongst its members, aimed to ridicule all the current false taste in learning. The *Memoirs of Martinus Scriblerus* were mainly written by Pope, but John Arbuthnot, who was a physician, supplied most of the scientific and medical ideas. One of the fields chosen for comment was the contemporary astronomy. The advances attributed to Scriblerus in this pursuit provide an interesting insight into which parts of the subject were currently claiming popular attention.

> To him we owe all the observations on the parallax of the Pole-star, and all the new theories of the Deluge.
> A mechanical explanation of the formation of the universe, according to the Epicurean hypothesis.
> A computation of the duration of the sun, and how long it will last before it be burned out.
> An answer to the question of a curious gentleman: How long a new star was lighted up before its appearance to the inhabitants of our earth? To which is subjoined a calculation,

how much the inhabitants of the moon eat for supper, considering that they pass a night equal to fifteen of our natural days.

A demonstration of the natural dominion of the inhabitants of the earth over those of the moon, if ever an intercourse should be opened between them, with a proposal of a partition-treaty among the earthly potentates, in case of such discovery.[57]

The first of these—the observation of stellar parallax—was a main theme of astronomy once the heliocentric theory was firmly established. As we have seen, motion of the Earth round the Sun implies an apparent small oscillation in the positions of the stars: the size of the oscillation depending on the distance of the star. The discovery of stellar parallax would therefore both confirm the heliocentric hypothesis and indicate the scale of the stellar system. In fact, despite the expenditure of a very great amount of energy, stellar parallax evaded detection until well into the nineteenth century.

Scriblerus' subsequent mention of 'the new theories of the Deluge' refers, as we have seen, to Burnet and his followers. We have similarly noted the attribution—vehemently denied—of Epicurean views to natural philosophers at this period. One further point may be noted about this. Although Newton accepted a low age for the solar system (indeed, he sought to confirm it from his own investigations into biblical chronology), Newtonianism produced a strong undercurrent of feeling that an infinite universe might also demand an eternity of time.

> The boundless *space*, through which these rovers take
> Their restless roam, suggests the sister thought
> Of boundless *time*.[58]

This ties in with Scriblerus' third point—the duration of the Sun—for whatever might be supposed about the universe as a whole, Newton's work seemed to show that the solar system at any rate could not possibly endure for ever. Newton had envisaged light as consisting of streams of very small corpuscles. It was naturally supposed that these corpuscles had a definite, if minute, mass. Hence, it was argued that no star could radiate light for ever since, sooner or later, all of its mass would be dissipated.

> in a year the golden torrents, sent
> From the bright source, its losses scarce augment:
> Yet without end, if you the waste repeat,
> Th' eternal loss grows infinitely great.
> Then, should the Sun of finite bulk sustain,
> In every age, the loss but of a grain;
> If we suppose those ages infinite,
> Could there remain one particle of light?[59]

It was also felt that there must be a small amount of material in between the planets and that this, acting over long enough periods of time, would always make the planets spiral into the Sun.[60]

Although there was some discussion in the eighteenth century of whence the Sun derived its energy, this did not become a problem of vital concern in astronomy until Victorian times. Most people were willing to dismiss questions of astronomical evolution as Dr Johnson did: 'Many philosophers imagine that the elements themselves may be in time exhausted; that the sun, by shining long, will effuse all its light; and that, by the continual waste of aqueous particles, the whole earth will at last become a sandy desert. I would not advise any readers to disturb themselves by contriving how they should live without light and water. For the days of universal thirst and perpetual darkness are at a great distance. The ocean and the sun will last our time, and we may leave posterity to shift for themselves.'[61]

The discussion by Scriblerus of new stars continued a topic already well over a century old. But the question of how long it took the light from such a star to reach the Earth was evoked by the contemporary interest in the finite speed of light. The question of inhabitants of the Moon and of mutual commerce with them came originally, as we have seen, from Kepler's speculations at the beginning of the seventeenth century.

Later on in the adventures of Scriblerus we read of a sort of Mohole project*: 'a proposal, by a general contribution of

---

* A recent American proposal—now abandoned—to drill through the surface layers of the Earth.

all princes, to pierce the first crust or nucleus of this our earth quite through, to the next concentrical sphere. The advantage he proposed from it was, to find the parallax of the fixed stars; but chiefly to refute Sir Isaac Newton's theory of gravity, and Mr Halley's of the variations.'[62] The possibility of testing Newton's theory by descending into the Earth had been recognized from the beginning, although experiments were not made until much later. We have already remarked that Halley's theory of the magnetic variations required the Earth to have an inner core rotating independently of the outer shell. Hence it could be tested by piercing through the crust.

There was also a second proposal: 'to build two poles to the meridian, with immense lighthouses on the top of them, to supply the defect of nature, and to make the longitude as easy to be calculated as the latitude.'[63] which was hardly more eccentric than some of the actual suggestions put forward at the time.

The world in the Moon still figured largely in popular thought of the period: many of the satires on virtuosi refer to it. Thus the virtuoso in Shadwell's play of that title is asked

'Do you believe the Moon is an Earth, as you told us? SIR NICHOLAS GIMCRACK: Believe it! I know it; I shall shortly publish a Book of Geography for it. Why, 'tis as big as our Earth; I can see all the mountainous parts, and Vallies, and Seas, and Lakes in it; nay, the larger sort of Animals, as Elephants and Camels; but publick Buildings and Ships very easily. I have seen several Battles fought there. They have great Guns, and have the use of Gun-powder. At Land they fight with Elephants and Castles. I have seen them.'[64]

The similarity of this to Butler's poem, *The Elephant in the Moon*, (which circulated at about the same time) is too obvious to need stressing.

In the same year that the *Principia* was published, a new play called *The Emperor in the Moon* was produced. It portrays a character who was so interested in the possibility of another world in the Moon, that he neglected the world in which he lived. In the text appear such familiar names as Godwin and Wilkins. The authoress, Mrs Aphra Behn, like several other of the

satirists, had a competent acquaintance with the ideas she paro-
died. Indeed, she translated into English one of the most popular
astronomical books of the seventeenth century: Fontenelle's
Conversations on the Plurality of Worlds.

Fontenelle was more a popularizer of science than an original
researcher, but his position as secretary of the French Academy
of Sciences throughout almost the whole of the first half of the
eighteenth century made him a figure of considerable influence.
The Plurality of Worlds was published the year before the *Principia* (the exposition was naturally based on the Cartesian system). It consists of a dialogue between a Marchioness and a
Philosopher. The talk ranges over a variety of topics, but, as the
title would imply, there is particular emphasis on the number of
other planetary systems like our own, the possibility of life on the
Moon, and related subjects. (Fontenelle was considerably influenced by John Wilkins' book about the Moon.)

The number of satires on virtuosi declined in the eighteenth
century, perhaps because, for the first quarter of the century,
Newton was President of the Royal Society, which thereby
gained tremendously in prestige. However, conventionally
satirical comments can still be found in the *Rambler*, and Peter
Pindar's sketches appeared in the latter half of the century.
One eighteenth-century satire of this type, entitled the *Humours
of Oxford*, provides a corrective to the view that Newtonian
cosmology was immediately and universally accepted in this
country. The major humour of the play is, predictably enough
pedantry, an excess of which is possessed by Lady Science, one
of the characters. (She is nicknamed Lady Gimcrack: a reference
back to Shadwell's play.) At one stage she questions a prospective
suitor for her daughter's hand and, to test his worth, asks three
vital questions. The first of these is an inquiry whether he
prefers the Ptolemaic, or the Copernican, system. (Glanvill
recorded that in 1665 general belief still favoured Ptolemy. In
the mid-eighteenth century John Wesley could still oppose
Copernicanism.) Lady Science then asks the candidate two
further questions, which are: Has he any skill in Judicial
Astrology? Will it ever be possible to find out the longitude?

The increasing importance of the new science at the end of the
seventeenth century was paralleled by the surprising growth of

interest shown in it by women. This was perhaps stimulated by the example of the charming Marchioness in Fontenelle, who helped to remove the stigma of unfeminine eccentricity from such pursuits. The extensive scientific writings of the distinctly eccentric Duchess of Newcastle during the seventeenth century have been remarked on. The early eighteenth century gave rise to several female intellectuals (who, after the mid-century, came to be called blue-stockings).

One factor in this increased interest in science was the large number of itinerant lecturers—many of them excellent scientists—who described the elements of Newtonian theory in popular terms. They were an important influence leading to the better dissemination of scientific knowledge in the eighteenth century as compared with the seventeenth.

In the mid-seventeenth century Pepys had complained more than once of the difficulties he encountered in obtaining answers to even elementary scientific questions. 'Spong* and I had also several fine discourses upon the globes this afternoon, particularly why the fixed stars do not rise and set at the same hours all the yeare long, which he could not demonstrate.'[65] But by the early eighteenth century a resident in London would have had no problem in finding someone to answer his questions.

The lecturers usually advertised a series of talks on a specific topic which could be attended by subscription. A considerable proportion of their audiences was female.

> Some nymphs prefer *astronomy* to *love*:
> Elope from mortal man, and range above.
> The fair philosopher to Rowley flies,
> Where, in a *box*, the whole creation lies:
> She sees the planets in their turns advance,
> And scorns, Poitier, thy sublunary dance:
> Of Desaguliers she bespeaks fresh air;
> And Whiston has engagements with the fair.[66]

Whiston we have encountered before. His Boyle lectures, given in 1707, attracted much criticism (from Pope amongst others), and three years later he was deprived of his Chair at Cambridge for holding unorthodox theological views. He then

* A well-known London instrument maker.

moved to London where he earned a living by giving courses of lectures on science (he was supported in this by both Addison and Steele). Pope seems to have been interested in Whiston's writings and attended his lectures in 1713. Many of the lecturers used their talks as a method of publicizing their books and *vice versa*. One of the most popular astronomy texts of the eighteenth century was written by James Ferguson, another of the London lecturers. Unlike Whiston, Ferguson was not a university teacher: when he met Dr Johnson in 1769, Boswell referred to him as the 'self-taught philosopher'. Ferguson was, however, a Fellow of the Royal Society, as also was Desaguliers. The latter, another freelance lecturer, was a friend of Newton's and a leading popularizer of his ideas in this country.

A common characteristic of these lecturers was their extensive use of experimental apparatus for demonstration purposes, much of it often devised by themselves. Thus Desaguliers invented the planetarium: an instrument rather similar in intent to the medieval equatorium, but based on the Newtonian system. 'Rowley's box' in the previous quotation is the orrery which Rowley invented. The orrery—a small-scale working model of the solar system—was a popular demonstration instrument during the eighteenth century (see, for example, Henry Jones' *Philosophy: a Poem address'd to the Ladies who attended Mr Booth's Lectures* which was published in 1746). Rowley, who was a native of Lichfield, received an honourable mention for his work from two later residents—Samuel Johnson and Erasmus Darwin. The instrument was named after Charles Boyle, fourth Earl of Cork and Orrery (and a distant relative of Robert Boyle), for whom, according to Sir Richard Steele, one of the first models was built.

Charles Boyle, it may be noted, was linked, in an indirect way, with Swift's entry into the field of satire on science, for he was involved in defending the authenticity of a series of letters, known as the *Epistles of Phalaris*, which were supposed to date from the sixth century B.C. These were shown to be spurious by Richard Bentley, but only after they had been praised by Sir William Temple, who was Swift's patron. The subsequent dispute rapidly developed into another episode in the long struggle between the Ancients and the Moderns. Swift was thus involved

on the side of the Ancients, and published his somewhat equiv-
ocal support in the *Battle of the Books* (1704). In the same year he
published *A Tale of a Tub*, which also mentions the controversy.
(Both of these books were actually written some years before
publication.) As would be expected, the new philosophy was
one of the topics touched upon. Swift's major attack on science—
in Gulliver's voyage to Laputa—did not appear, however,
until some twenty years later.

Mathematics and astronomy played a large part in the life
of the Laputans. For them, mathematics—with geometrical
figures particularly emphasized—went hand in hand with music.
(This may be an oblique reference to the Pythagorean origin
generally attributed to contemporary science.) The main preoccupation of the Laputans is a little unusual: they are continually terrified that there will be changes in the celestial bodies,
for instance 'that the Earth by the continual Approaches of the
Sun towards it, must in Course of Time be absorbed or swallowed
up. That the Face of the Sun will by Degrees be encrusted with
its own Effluvia, and give no more Light to the World. That, the
Earth very narrowly escaped a Brush from the Tail of the last
Comet, which would have infallibly reduced it to Ashes; and
that the next, which they have calculated for One and Thirty
Years hence, will probably destroy us.'[67]

The reputed decrease in the Sun-Earth distance had, as we
have seen, long been a standard proof of the decay of the solar
system. The possibility that the Sun might become encrusted
with its own effluvia depended on the belief, common at the
time, that sunspots were similar to terrestrial volcanoes. It
was assumed by analogy that the lava thrown out might, on
cooling, produce an opaque layer on the solar surface. Descartes
had suggested that the sudden appearance of 'new' stars might
be explicable in terms of spots. He thought that the spots on
these stars had accumulated until the whole surface was dark-
ened, when the original fire broke through again. This belief
seems to have had some currency at the end of the seventeenth
century, for we find John Ray specifically denying that the end
of the world would come when the Sun was overwhelmed by
spots.

Shortly after the passage quoted above, Swift also cites the efflux of light from the Sun as a further indication of its ultimate death. As we have seen, this was, indeed, accepted as evidence by Newtonians. Finally, the end of the world due to the close passage of a comet was a commonplace at this time, mainly as a result of Whiston's advocacy. Swift actually mentions Whiston's interest in comets elsewhere: 'on Wednesday morning (I believe to the exact Calculation of Mr Whiston) the Comet appear'd'.[68]

In describing the Laputans, Swift remarked that their disquiet came from causes which very little affected ordinary mortals; however, the end of the world was, in fact, a topic of considerable interest in this country during the early eighteenth century. Some of this derived from the attraction of describing the physical events involved. We have already mentioned the prose accounts of Burnet and Whiston, but similar attempts also appear in the poetry of the period (e.g. Aaron Hill: *The Judgement Day*). Interest in the Last Judgement and the physical events connected with it then diminished somewhat, only to revive again about the mid-century as a result, particularly, of the disastrous Lisbon earthquake.

According to Swift, the Laputan astronomers had instruments excelling any available in Europe. With these instruments they had discovered

> ...two lesser Stars, or *Satellites*, which revolve about *Mars*; whereof the innermost is distant from the Center of the primary Planet exactly three of his Diameters, and the outermost five; the former revolves in the Space of ten Hours, and the latter in Twenty-one and an Half; so that the Squares of their periodical Times, are very near in the same Proportion with the Cubes of their Distance from the Center of *Mars**; which evidently shews them to be governed by the same Law of Gravitation, that influences the other heavenly Bodies.[69]

The two moons of Mars were, in fact, first discovered in the United States some century and half after the publication of

* This relationship is known as Kepler's third law: it was derived empirically by Kepler in the early seventeenth century, and theoretically by Newton in the *Principia*.

Gulliver's Travels, having escaped detection before owing to their extremely small size (both are less than ten miles in diameter). They are actually situated at two and threequarters and seven Martian diameters from the centre of the planet, with periods of about seven and a half, and thirty and a quarter, hours respectively. The question which has attracted much discussion is: how was Swift's prediction made? The reason for the number of Martian satellites is obvious enough. After Galileo's early work had shown that there were four moons of Jupiter, it was realized that there existed a sequence from Venus with no moons, through the Earth with one moon, to Jupiter with four. In order to complete this run Mars should logically have two moons, and this became a fairly common seventeenth-century assumption. There was no obvious compulsion, however, to choose the periods that he did.

The reference to the Laputan telescopes is of some further interest, for Swift may have had in mind the reflecting telescope* that Newton introduced in the last quarter of the seventeenth century. (John Evelyn records seeing it at the Royal Society in February 1672.) It was much shorter that the comparable refractor,* and as there was no chromatic aberration,† the stellar images were much clearer. For these reasons, reflectors became popular in the eighteenth century, and many of the instrument-makers in this country turned them out to order. In 1762 Dr Johnson stayed at Plymouth with John Mudge who was awarded a medal by the Royal Society for his investigations into the manufacture of telescope mirrors.

At a later point in *Gulliver's Travels*, Swift makes a direct attack on Newton and on the *Principia*. Gulliver is visting Glubbdubdrib, the Island of Sorcerers. The governor of the island has the ability to summon the spirits of the dead.

> I then desired the Governor to call up *Descartes* and *Gassendi*, with whom I prevailed to explain their systems to *Aristotle*. This great Philosopher freely acknowledged his own Mistakes

* A reflecting telescope (or a reflector) is one which has a mirror as the main light-gathering element. This compares with a refracting telescope (or refractor) which uses a lens, or system of lens.

† Chromatic aberration is the inherent defect of a telescope lens (but not a mirror) whereby the stellar images are seen to be multi-coloured.

in Natural Philosophy, because he proceeded in many things upon Conjecture, as all Men must do; and he found, that *Gassendi** who had made the Doctrine of *Epicurus* as palatable as he could, and the *Vortices of Descartes*, were equally exploded. He predicted the same Fate to Attraction, whereof the present Learned are such zealous Asserters. He said, that new Systems of Nature were but new Fashions, which would vary in every Age; and even those who pretended to demonstrate them from Mathematical Principles, would flourish but a short Period of Time, and be out of Vogue when that was determined.[70]

Besides his major objections to astronomy, Swift seems to have had a rather odd minor dislike: he objected to the excessive use of astronomical imagery in contemporary writing.

> No simile shall be begun
> With *rising* or with *setting sun*,
> . . . .
> No son of mine shall dare to say,
> *Aurora usher'd in the day*,
> Or ever name the *Milky Way*.[71]

His contemporaries, however, were trying hard to come to terms with Newtonianism; the poets were finding this particularly difficult. Newton had a low opinion of poetry; Locke agreed with him, comparing poetry with gaming and remarking that neither were of much advantage except for those who had nothing else to live on. Even before the advent of Newtonianism, the Royal Society's attack on the use of ornate language had been seen as a questioning of poetic convention. Certainly the spread of Newtonian concepts seems to have been a major influence in the growth of the typically didactic poetry of the early eighteenth century. Many poets welcomed Newtonian science. James Thomson, who may well have been introduced to Newtonian ideas early on whilst he was at Edinburgh University, was one of these.

---

* Gassendi, a French astronomer and Roman Catholic priest of the seventeenth century, was a leading advocate of atomism, and was frequently classified with Hobbes as an Epicurean.

With thee, serene Philosophy, with thee,
And thy bright garland, let me crown my song!
Effusive source of evidence, and truth![72]

Thomson's main poem *The Seasons* underwent constant revision during the years 1726–46, with a considerable increase in the amount of science it contained. His writings were highly influential: quite a lot of eighteenth-century poetry had its Newtonianism mediated via Thomson. The emphasis, however, was transferred rather to a contemplation of the landscape than to astronomy, and this tendency was further increased by the growth of popular interest in natural history, as compared with astronomy, after the middle of the century. It should be added, however, that occasional voices were raised against the infiltration of Newtonian ideas into poetry throughout the eighteenth century.

Before leaving the theme of Newtonianism in the eighteenth century, some brief mention should be made of its extension into the sphere of morals, and of its application to thinking about the social order. The subject is assigned a small part of this chapter not because it is unimportant, but because there is only a tenuous connection with Newtonian astronomy.

The idea of order in the eighteenth century was frequently linked with the old belief in a chain of being. Initially, the concept of a fixed chain of being was linked with a static social order. As a result, although the universe that Pope knew differed considerably from Shakespeare's, their conclusions concerning the necessity for order and stability in social relationships were much the same.

The least confusion but in one, not all
That system only, but the whole must fall.
Let Earth unbalanc'd from her orbit fly,
Planets and suns run lawless through the sky.[73]

(The Day of Judgement was regarded as a time when the order of the universe failed; hence this extract from Pope may be found echoed in many contemporary accounts of the end of the world.)

This emphasis on order was used in natural theology as the major argument for the existence of God: it revealed God's wisdom in nature. The idea was often extended further into an argument for the general benevolence of God and, hence, to a belief that evil in the universe was a necessary adjunct to the overall good. This, in turn, buttressed the arguments for a static social order. Later in the eighteenth century, as we have seen, the concept of a static chain of being gave way to the idea of an evolving chain, so that this particular support for a non-changing order became less convincing; the argument from the order of the universe remained, however. Because the order of the heavens and the laws governing it were of theological as well as scientific interest, astronomical investigations were the preserve of the pious man. It was, indeed, argued that, even if an astronomer was not pious to begin with, his investigations would make him so. One aspect of this belief is the frequent suggestion that Newton was able to derive the laws governing the universe only because he was a highly religious man.

We have noted that the word *attraction* tended to retain its other connotations as well as its strictly scientific meaning in eighteenth-century Newtonianism. Thus it was used to express the relationship between man and God, and also between man and man. Newtonian mechanics could, indeed, be taken over as a whole into the discussion of completely different fields, e.g. as a support for the principle of limited monarchy.

> Like Ministers attending ev'ry Glance,
> Six worlds sweep round his Throne in Mystick Dance.
> He turns their Motion from its devious Course,
> And bends their Orbits by Attractive Force:
> His pow'r coerc'd by Laws, still leaves them free,
> Directs, but not Destroys, their Liberty;
> Tho' fast and slow, yet regular they move,
> (Projectile Force restrain'd by mutual Love,)
> And reigning thus with limited Command,
> He holds a lasting Sceptre in his Hand.[74]*

The analogy between Newtonian mechanics and government by means of a system of checks and balances was highly popular in the eighteenth century. We can, perhaps, see its logical culmination in the Constitution of the United States.

* Compare the use of this Newtonian image with the image of the cosmic dance in Elizabethan writings.

CHAPTER VII

The Victorian Reaction

UP to this point in our survey, astronomy has been the most important science. The situation changed, however, during the eighteenth century. By the end of that century both physics and chemistry had begun their development into soundly based and significant sciences, and in the nineteenth century, geology and biology followed suit. These last two fields were highly popular among non-scientists: more so than physics and chemistry. Partly as a result of this, the relative decline of public interest in astronomy became more marked in Victorian times. Nevertheless, astronomy was not deprived of its high prestige: thus it seems likely that the significance in astronomy of observations accumulated over long periods of time led to this aspect of the subject being copied in other fields of study (e.g. political economy) which developed during the nineteenth century.

For many years astronomy had been the only state aided science in Britain (through the Greenwich Observatory), and it had held a major position in what science teaching there was at Oxford and Cambridge. This, too, changed during the nineteenth century: teaching appointments in other sciences slowly became available and state aid was occasionally extended (e.g. the Geological Survey was set up in 1835). There was, however, a more important reason for the declining influence of astronomy. In all previous centuries it had been a subject with practical applications: first in astrology and the determination of time, then in the determination of position at sea. With the final solution of this latter problem, astronomy became for the first time of no practical importance. This was already becoming evident in the latter half of the eighteenth century. Thus Dr Johnson wrote to Susannah Thrale concerning a possible meeting with William Herschel (this was some three years after

Herschel became world-famous for his discovery of the planet Uranus).

> With Mr. Herschel it will certainly be right to cultivate an aquaintance; for he can show you in the sky what no man before him has ever seen, by some wonderful improvements which he has made in the telescope. What he has to show is indeed a long way off, and perhaps concerns us little, but all truth is valuable and all knowledge is pleasing in its first effects, and may be subsequently useful. Of whatever we see we always wish to know; always congratulate ourselves when we know that of which we perceive another to be ignorant. Take therefore all opportunities of learning that offer themselves, however remote the matter may be from common life or common conversation.[1]

This is damning with faint praise; the astronomer in *Rasselas* will not even go that far—he confesses that he has chosen the wrong subject for study having spent his time in the attainment of knowledge which is only remotely useful to mankind.

Whereas, up to the middle of the eighteenth century, almost all major writers referred naturally to astronomy as an integral part of their culture, this now ceased to be true. Burns, although he seems to have had a surprising interest in natural theology (he read Derham and Ray) revealed little of this in his poetry. Dickens' voluminous writings contain little beyond passing references, e.g. to a maker of navigational instruments in *Dombey and Son*. Perhaps this is only an aspect of the general fragmentation of knowledge in Victorian times; as Dean Inge remarked, the number of great subjects in which Dickens took no interest whatever is amazing—and Dickens was by no means unique in this respect. The general decline of interest in astronomy does mean, however, that a writer who has little to say about the current astronomy, may have very definite views on some other branch of science (as, for example, Browning on evolution*).

During the first half of the eighteenth century, adherence to some form of deism or, at least, a distaste for revelation and

---

* Browning made an extensive use of star imagery in his writings, but few, if any, of his images refer to contemporary astronomical ideas.

miracles increased. Later in the century this evolved towards a growing agnosticism. But the latter part of the century also saw a spirited evangelical counter-attack, more particularly by the Methodists. The deistic trend led to considerable deviations from the biblical description of the origin of the world; most significantly the short time-scale of the universe which had bothered some earlier writers was now often extended. There was, moreover, an increasing number of suggestions that the age of the Earth was not necessarily the age of the universe: the latter could be older, even eternal.[2] As we have seen, the concept of an eternal universe came originally from classical sources and, under the title of Epicureanism, had been condemned a century earlier. The growing eighteenth-century belief that God's creative activity was not limited to the traditional biblical period of six days also developed ultimately from an earlier source—this time the Christian idea of the plenitude of God. It was argued that the immeasurable power of God could not have been exhausted by only a week's work: rather the period must have been much longer and might still be continuing.[3]

In the eighteenth and nineteenth centuries, an increased attention was paid to the possible evolution of celestial bodies: it was no longer generally assumed that they were unchanging throughout the lifetime of the universe. This interest had been stimulated initially by Newton's comments on the part played by comets but, during the nineteenth century, it was greatly encouraged by the emphasis on evolution in geology and biology. The question of change was also linked with the assumed age of the universe: an explanation of how and why the stars continued to shine only became urgent when a long period of time was involved.

Towards the end of the eighteenth century, William Herschel thought that he had detected evolution not of stars, but of groups of stars. The great reflecting telescopes which he built enabled him to examine the heavens in greater detail than anyone had before. He noted very many clusters of stars: some with the stars far apart, others with them closer together, and was led to conclude that, although stars started their lives separately, they gradually congregated together owing to their mutual gravitational attraction.

Star after star from Heaven's high arch shall rush,
Suns sink on suns, and systems systems crush,
Headlong, extinct, to one dark centre fall,
And Death and Night and Chaos mingle all![4]

The similarity of this to the numerous descriptions of the Day of
Judgement in the first half of the eighteenth century is evident;
the difference comes in the next few lines, where Erasmus
Darwin tells us that after this catastrophe, nature will start
again to build another set of systems like the original.

The increased interest in geology at the end of the eighteenth
and during the nineteenth century led to an overwhelming
conviction—at least amongst geologists—not only that the short
time-scale for the Earth was quite inadmissible, but that the
times required were, in fact, immensely long—a hundred
million years, or more. Later in the nineteenth century, astronomy came to oppose geology (and biology) on this issue. Not
that astronomers were any more prepared to accept six thousand
years than geologists, but the period of time that they did require
could be measured rather in terms of a few million years. This
difference was closely tied up with the question of stellar evolution. Thus Lord Kelvin estimated that the Sun only had enough
energy supplies to last for some ten million years: after that it
would be finished. The clash of opinion was only resolved finally
(in favour of the geologists) in the twentieth century. In the latter
half of the nineteenth century, the relatively short time-scale
favoured by the astronomers was quoted as support by opponents
of biological evolution (which evidently depended on the longer,
geological time-scale being correct). Charles Darwin admitted
that he was highly perturbed by the discrepancy.

When speaking of the time-scale we must remember that
many Victorian Evangelicals continued to insist on a strict six-
day period for the creation of the world. So far as they were
concerned geology and astronomy were equally blameworthy
for disregarding this part of scripture. Early echoes of this
condemnation can be found, for example, in Cowper.[5]

The moderate Evangelical viewpoint in the later eighteenth
century was in some respects rather similar to that expressed by
Milton in the mid-seventeenth century. There was, for example,

the same emphasis on the need to remember that God is always more than science.[6] There was also, however, a growing undercurrent of feeling not only that human reason was less important than the quest for God, but also that it might be contrary to this quest.

> While Science bloom'd, and lib'ral Arts improv'd
> And fancy o'er the fields of Nature rov'd
> While nat'ral Knowledge to perfection grew,
> How few once thought of being *born anew*![7]

An examination of Cowper's criticisms in *The Task* shows that his attack was not directed against science itself but rather against scientists who approached the universe with arrogance instead of humility. He specifically commends Newton as the type example of a pious scientist.[8] This attitude was typical of the eighteenth century: in the nineteenth century the basis of attack changed; it came to be against science as such, and not merely against its misrepresentation. One major force behind this change was developments on the Continent.

During the first half of the eighteenth century, Newtonian ideas—championed particularly by Voltaire—gradually displaced Cartesian philosophy on the Continent. The subsequent development of theoretical astronomy there—more especially by the French mathematicians—was much more sophisticated than anything occurring in England, with the result that, towards the end of the century, a more highly developed Newtonian astronomy started to filter back across the Channel. This elaborated Newtonianism differed from the earlier form in one particularly important respect: several of the features which had formerly made Newtonianism valuable to natural theology had disappeared. For example, according to Newton the gravitational interactions of the planets were so complicated as to require God's assistance if the solar system were to retain its order. The continental mathematicians now showed, on the contrary, that the solar system could remain stable over long periods of time without any need for external interference. This increased emphasis on the mechanical nature of the universe at the same time that the churches were increasingly emphasizing the personal was an important factor in the disruption of the eighteenth-century harmony between astronomy and religion. We may note, for example, Charles Kingsley's words—which would have seemed absurd a century before. 'Tell us not that the world is governed by universal law; the news is not comfortable, but simply horrible.'[9]

William Blake cannot be considered as in any way a typical commentator on this division; nevertheless his writings do foreshadow several of the nineteenth-century preoccupations with science. Blake believed that the cult of reason which had grown up during the eighteenth century was undermining both religion and poetry.

> To cast off Rational Demonstration by Faith in the Saviour,
> To cast off the rotten rags of Memory by Inspiration,
> To cast off Bacon, Locke & Newton from Albion's covering,
> To take off his filthy garments & clothe him with Imagination,
> To cast aside from Poetry all that is not Inspiration.[10]

He detested the scientific emphasis on solid, tangible matter[11], and was violently opposed to the whole idea of the scientific method with its questioning and experimenting.[12] As in the previous quotation, this dislike was generally personified; he used certain names almost as an abbreviation for particular attitudes: Bacon—the originator of the scientific method; Newton—who mechanized the universe; Locke—who tried to do the same to Man; Voltaire and Rousseau—prototypes of the atheist.

Blake believed that Newtonian science had been in opposition to religion from the beginning.[13] Whereas Newton's contemporaries extolled him for having finally cleared the new science from the charge of Epicureanism, Blake now identified the two. 'Such is the end of Epicurean or Newtonian Philosophy; it is Atheism.'[14]

As might be expected, Blake disagreed entirely with the general eighteenth-century emphasis on natural theology (though, interestingly, he devised illustrations for Young's *Night Thoughts*)

> how is this thing, this Newtonian Phantasm,
> This Voltaire & Rousseau, this Hume & Gibbon &
> Bolingbroke,
> This Natural Religion, this impossible absurdity?[15]

Hume enters here particularly for his denigration of miracles; yet in a sense, Hume was on Blake's side. He, too, had opposed natural theology, arguing that, although the design of the universe might show intelligence, it did not indicate goodness. Arguments similar to this increased suspicion of science amongst the Evangelicals.

Blake is unusual amongst his contemporaries in his disregard for, and indeed denial of, elementary scientific results; for example, his assertion that the Earth is flat.

> The Sky is an immortal Tent built by the sons of Los...
> And on its verge the Sun rises & sets, the Clouds bow
> To meet the flat Earth & the Sea in such an order'd Space:
> The Starry heavens reach no further...
> ...As to that false appearance which appears to the reasoner
> As of a Globe rolling thro' Voidness, it is a delusion of Ulro.[16]

In the nineteenth century, indifference to the results of science was, perhaps, commoner. Rossetti, for example, was not at all sure that the Earth moved round the Sun, and was only prepared to agree that it might matter scientifically because Galileo (a fellow countryman of Dante's) had thought so.

One result of this indifference (or antagonism) to science was a yearning for the old stability, which occasionally gave rise to an interest in older ideas—Yeats' use of astrology, at the end of the nineteenth century, for example. This may be compared with Scott's modification of the plot of *Guy Mannering* at the beginning of the century because he did not think that his audience would stomach too much emphasis on astrology. Scott was, incidently, considered by contemporary astrologers to be most sympathetic to their cause. A translation of Ptolemy's *Tetrabiblos* which appeared in 1822 bears the inscription

> To the Author of 'Waverley'. This translation of a work containing the best accredited principles of Astrology is dedicated; with the most profound admiration of his unrivalled Talents, which could alone have restored interest to the speculations of an antiquated science.[17]

Opposition to science was, however, still unusual at the end of the eighteenth century. Much of the linkage between science and religion still remained. As we have seen, Cowper related Newton's greatness to his piety in the traditional manner. We find a similar sort of praise for William Herschel at the turn of the century. 'I wish you had been with me the day before yesterday, when you would have joined me, I am sure, deeply, in admiring a great, simple, good old man—Dr. Herschel.'[18]

Some years before, Herschel had met Napoleon, and Thomas Campbell—the writer of this letter—was eager to question him about the meeting.

'I was anxious to get from him as many particulars as I could about his interview with Buonaparte, The latter, it was reported, had astonished him by his astronomical knowledge. "No" he said; "The First Consul did surprise me by his quickness and versatility on all subjects; but in science he seemed to know little more than any well-educated gentlemen; and of astronomy much less, for instance, than our own king." ... "I remarked," said the Astronomer, "his hypocrisy in concluding the conversation on astronomy by observing how all these glorious views gave proofs of an Almighty wisdom". I asked him if he thought the system of Laplace to be quite certain, with regard to the total security of the planetary system, from the effects of gravitation losing its present balance? He said, No: he thought by no means that the universe was secured from the chance of sudden losses of parts.'

Wiliam Herschel was knighted some four years after this visit by Thomas Campbell. His son, Sir John Herschel, later succeeded to his father's position as the leading British astronomer, and was highly influential in the advancement both of astronomy and of science in general during the nineteenth century.

Herschel genuinely seems to have had a high opinion of George III. When he leapt from obscurity to fame by discovering a new planet—the first to be found in historic times—he wished to call it *Georgium Sidus* after the King, and this name was, in fact, used for some time in Britain. Erasmus Darwin, ten years after the discovery of the planet, queried, in *The Economy of Vegetation*, whether the new star of 1572 could have been the *Georgium Sidus*. At the end of the 1820s we find William Hazlitt still using it as the common name for the planet.[19] Elsewhere, it was rejected; the discovery was made in 1781: the American War of Independence was only just over, and George III was not generally popular abroad. After a period during which the name *Herschel* had some currency, a classical name, *Uranus*, came into general use: so as to keep in line with the other planets. (There was another, similar, naming controversy when the next planet, *Neptune*, was discovered in the mid-nineteenth century.)

The totally unexpected discovery of Uranus captured the popular imagination

> Then felt I like some watcher of the skies
> When a new planet swims into his ken.[20]

(Keats may conceivably have obtained his knowledge of Herschel's work from a prize book he received at school— Bonnycastle's *Introduction to Astronomy*.) Herschel was received in audience by the king, and was ultimately appointed by him to the post of Royal Astronomer (not Astronomer Royal, who was at that time Maskelyne). This post carried with it a small salary, though Herschel did not become completely independent financially until after his marriage to a widow who possessed extensive private means. Fanny Burney met the Herschels shortly after their marriage in 1788 and recorded in her diary: 'His wife seems good-natured: she was rich, too! And astronomers are as able as other men to discern that gold can glitter as well as stars.'[21]

It is noticeable in Campbell's interview with Herschel that one of the major questions he asks concerns the stability of the solar system. We have noted the theological significance of this. Herschel's reasons for doubting the stability differed, however, from those of traditional Newtonianism. He was much more concerned with the possibility of sudden changes such as explosions (catastrophism was popular in the scientific thought of the period). Laplace was the leading contemporary French theoretical astronomer whose major work, the *Mécanique Céleste*, summarized the eighteenth-century developments of Newtonian astronomy. In jumping directly from Napoleon's comments on natural theology to Laplace's theory of the solar system, Campbell seems to have had in mind the well-known story about the two. According to the most detailed account, Napoleon remarked to Laplace that there was no reference to a Creator anywhere in the *Mécanique Céleste*. Laplace replied: 'Je n'avais pas besoin de cette hypothèse-là.' Napoleon later passed on this reply to Lagrange (who was almost Laplace's equal as a theoretical astronomer). Lagrange observed: 'Ah! c'est une belle hypothèse; ça explique beaucoup de choses.'

The *Mécanique Céleste* came to symbolize in the nineteenth century the entire view of the universe as a mechanical system which replaced the God-permeated universe of the earlier Newtonianism. It was used in this sense by Clough

> And as of old from Sinai's top
> God said that God is one,
> By Science strict so speaks He now
> To tell us, There is None!
> Earth goes by chemic forces; Heaven's
> A Mecanique Celeste!
> And heart and mind of human kind
> A watch-work as the rest![22]

Notice here that the watch analogy, which had formerly been used to represent the design of the universe, is now being used to indicate the mechanization of Man.

At the turn of the eighteenth century, Erasmus Darwin was a poet of considerable popularity. His epics, although devoted mainly to animate creation, also dealt incidentally with the astronomy of the day. (It is indicative of the rapid change in taste that Byron, the most popular poet of the early nineteenth century, hardly mentions astronomy; although he did summon up the interest to visit Herschel and peer through his telescope.) Darwin is mainly remembered now as a link in the development of thought from the evolutionary chain of being of the eighteenth century to the progressive evolution of Victorian times. He also, however, supported contemporary ideas of evolution in astronomy—particularly those put forward by William Herschel.

> 'LET THERE BE LIGHT!' proclaim'd the ALMIGHTY LORD,
> Astonish'd Chaos heard the potent word:—
> Through all his realms the kindly Ether runs,

And the mass starts into a million suns;
Earths round each sun with quick explosions burst,
And second planets issue from the first;
Bend, as they journey with projectile force,
In bright ellipses their reluctant course;
Orbs wheel in orbs, round centres centres roll,
And form, self-balanced, one revolving Whole.
—Onward they move amid their bright abode,
Space without bound, THE BOSOM OF THEIR GOD![23]

These dozen lines actually contain references to two of Herschel's ideas—according to Darwin's notes. The first few refer to his work on nebulae*; only a handful of these were known prior to Herschel: he showed that they were common. The last lines concerning 'projectile force', although they sound rather like earlier eighteenth-century verse on the origin of the solar system, actually refer here to the hypothesis that, just as the planets move round the Sun, so the stars all move round some other centre.

Herschel originally thought that the nebulae were 'island universes'—systems of stars like our own Milky Way galaxy. Later he came to accept that at least some of them were made rather of a kind of 'shining fluid' (as Halley had originally suggested). The distinction was important, for whereas the first concept indicated that stars were scattered throughout infinite space, the latter view led to the widely held nineteenth-century belief that the Milky Way comprised all the visible matter in the universe. This concept held predominance until only a few decades ago, but, despite this, the island-universe theory never completely lapsed. One of Tennyson's later poems possibly refers to it.

The fires that arch this dusky dot—
Yon myriad-worlded way—

* *Nebula* was the name applied to any body outside the solar system whose image appeared blurred through the telescope (a star has a sharp image). Use of the word led to endless confusion throughout the nineteenth century since, in fact, the bodies it described fell into two distinct groups: on the one hand there were the clouds of gas or clusters of stars within our own Galaxy, on the other, the external galaxies—vast clusterings of stars like our own Milky Way.

The vast sun-clusters' gather'd blaze,
World-isles in lonely skies,
Whole heavens within themselves, amaze
Our brief humanities.[24]

The question of the size of the universe provoked most controversy in the twentieth century, however; in the nineteenth century the main centre of interest was the time-scale of the universe. As has been mentioned, the important argument here hinged mainly on geology—in the debate between uniformitarian and catastrophist ideas. The former suggested that the observed surface features of the Earth were generally explicable as the results of prolonged action by forces still at work. The latter insisted that the major features could only be explained by postulating occasional catastrophic alterations in the conditions. There was, in fact, a rather similar debate going on at the same time in astronomy over the origin of the solar system. On the one hand there was the nebular hypothesis proposed particularly by Laplace; this supposed that the Sun and the planets had formed from a contracting cloud of material, and may be thought of as the uniformitarian theory. On the other hand, there was the catastrophist idea (of which Erasmus Darwin was very fond[25]) that the planets were formed by explosive ejection from the Sun.

Eventually, the uniformitarian concept won out in both astronomy and geology. In astronomy this had no immediate bearing on the time-scale, but in geology it meant that the Earth must have existed over a long period of time (whereas the catastrophist theory could make do with a much shorter period). During the first quarter of the nineteenth century, however, a majority of British geologists were catastrophists and it was this concept which had the greater public favour. Of Byron's infrequent scientific references, two (in *Cain* and *Don Juan*) concern the French palaeontologist, Cuvier, and his catastrophist ideas. Catastrophist theories gradually disappeared—at least among professional geologists—after the publication of Lyell's *Principles of Geology*, the first volume of which appeared in 1830.

The scientific developments of the early nineteenth century

led some clergymen to a quite modern concept of the interpretation of scripture. For example, the Reverend Baden Powell was already saying in the 1830s that the Old Testament contained the religious system given to the Israelites, not astronomical and geological knowledge for Christians.[26] Although this radical attitude was unusual, advocates of the new uniformitarian ideas were, in fact, subject to relatively little clerical attack. This can be attributed in part to the fact that they were prepared, at least initially, to preserve the belief in a recent origin for Man. Whereas formerly it had been supposed that the span of six thousand years applied to the lifetime of the Earth, it could now be supposed that this measured the time since Man appeared on Earth. However, although this central emphasis on the uniqueness of Man eased the adoption of new geological (and astronomical) ideas, it equally made the adoption of new ideas on the evolution of animals more difficult. In 1844 a great furore was caused by the publication of the *Vestiges of the Natural History of Creation*, which contained the suggestion that higher forms of life had evolved from more primitive. (The anonymous appearance of the book—actually written by a Scotsman, Robert Chambers—caused widespread speculation as to its author: Thackeray was one suggested contender.) From our point of view, the interesting thing about the book is that it saw astronomical evolution as a first stage on the road to biological evolution. Thus, the *Vestiges* actually starts with a discussion of the nebular hypothesis of Laplace.

When Disraeli wrote *Tancred*, a year or two later, he introduced a parody of the *Vestiges* under the title of *The Revelations of Chaos*. Tancred is told that 'everything is explained by geology and astronomy, and in that way. It shows you exactly how a star is formed; nothing can be so pretty! A cluster of vapour, the cream of the milky way, a sort of celestial cheese, churned into light, you must read it, 'tis charming.'[27]

The nebular hypothesis (which this is describing), although normally associated with Laplace, had actually been put forward in a rather similar form by Immanuel Kant several years before. Kant had also propounded the concept of 'island universes' some time before it was suggested by Herschel. His work had little influence in Britain, however, for few people were acquainted with it; a major exception being Coleridge. There are frequent references to Kant in Coleridge's notes and lectures, and some of these, are to his astronomical ideas: for example, to his 'island universe' theory. 'With somewhat greater confidence I dare acknowledge, that this representation of the Starry Universe fails to impress my mind with that super-superlative Sublimity, which Kant and many other great Men consider it so calculated to inspire. To me it appears an endless repetition of the same Image: nor can I conceive, how the Thought of a blind Mare going round and round in a Mill can derive Sublimity from the assurance, that there are a million of such Mills, each with a dozen or more blind Mares pacing round and round.'[28] This passage follows immediately after a discussion of the 'grindstone' theory of the Milky Way (hence, perhaps, his reference to mills). This 'grindstone' theory was the idea—which Kant attributed to Thomas Wright of Durham —that the Milky Way galaxy was flattened in shape so that, looked at from outside, it would, indeed, resemble a grindstone. Coleridge complained (not without reason) that the Milky Way did not seem to him to have the uniform appearance of a cross-section through a grindstone.

Coleridge enjoyed looking at the stars. He had been a fascinated watcher of the planet Venus at school, and one of his first poems was addressed to the evening star. He seems to have accepted the idea that every star possessed its own planetary system, but not the hitherto typical belief that each planetary system was inhabited. He questioned:

But why, of necessity, any? Must all possible Planets be lousy? None exempt from the *Morbus pedicularis* of our verminous man-becrawled Earth?[29]

He warmly admired Bruno's speculations, and toyed for a time with the idea of writing his biography. His approval of neo-Platonism naturally led him also to appreciate Kepler, whom he preferred to Bacon.[30] Nevertheless, Coleridge had a high opinion of Bacon, and considered that he stood in the Platonic tradition. He was much less warmly inclined towards Newton, though he was prepared to admit that Newton was a genius.

My opinion is this—that deep Thinking is attainable only by a man of deep Feeling, and that all Truth is a species of Revelation. The more I understand of Sir Isaac Newton's works, the more boldly I dare utter to my own mind, & therefore to *you*, that I believe the Souls of 500 Sir Isaac Newtons' would go to the making up of a Shakespeare or a Milton. But if it please the Almighty to grant me health, hope, and a steady mind, (always the 3 clauses of my hourly prayers) before my 30th year I will thoroughly understand the whole of Newton's Works—at present, I must content myself with endeavouring to make myself entire master of his easier work, that on Optics. I am exceedingly delighted with the beauty and newness of his experiments, & with the accuracy of his *immediate* Deductions from them—but the opinions founded on these Deductions, and indeed his whole theory is, I am persuaded, so exceedingly superficial as without impropriety to be deemed false. Newton was a mere materialist—*mind*, in his system is always passive,—a lazy Looker-on on an external World.[31]

His attitude in this respect was much closer to Blake's. Like Blake, he stressed the essential connection between Newton and Locke and subsequent developments, and like Blake he complained that science limited vision. Here the resemblance ends. Coleridge was an interested reader of scientific matters. This is most evident in his prose jottings, but can occasionally be distinguished in his poetry too. It will be remembered that his prescription for writing an epic poem included ten years devoted mainly to the study of science (astronomy being one of the subjects specifically mentioned).[32]

In actual fact, Coleridge's best-known scientific reference is in a lyric:

> The horned Moon, with one bright star
> Within the nether tip[33]

This is believed to refer to an intriguing astronomical problem of the late eighteenth, and early nineteenth, centuries. A few years before the *Ancient Mariner* was written, Maskelyne, the Astronomer Royal, had communicated to the Royal Society *An*

Account of an Appearance of Light, like a Star, seen in the dark Part of the Moon, on Friday the 7th March, 1794. The phenomenon had been noted previously by William Herschel*, who had determined that the point of light corresponded to the position of the lunar crater *Aristarchus.* Similar appearances were seen at intervals during the nineteenth century by other observers. Herschel, himself, believed that he had witnessed a lunar volcano in eruption. However, astronomers in the last century gradually became convinced that the Moon was a completely dead world; so the observations came to be interpreted rather as due to some difference in the light reflected from the crater and from its surroundings. In the last few years, there have been some indications that eruptive volcanoes may occur on the Moon; so, perhaps, Herschel's guess was correct after all.

There is one other reference in the *Ancient Mariner* which may directly reflect Coleridge's astronomical reading:

> The upper air burst into life!
> And a hundred fire-flags sheen,
> To and fro they were hurried about![34]

This is rather reminiscent of Thomson's description of an aurora, and it is known that Coleridge, like Thomson, read the book by Maupertuis which describes such a display. It is, of course, also possible that Coleridge was simply describing something he had seen.

Some of Coleridge's interest in science may have been transmitted to Wordsworth, but Wordsworth's ideas on science were being formed long before he met Coleridge. One of his earliest poems, written as a school exercise, spoke of science in glowing terms.[35] At university, science continued to evoke his interest. He described the fascination that astronomy had for him at this time in some famous lines of *The Prelude* (addressed to Coleridge).[36] He speaks of astronomy in these as the 'geometric science': a reflection of the fact that, when he was at Cambridge, astronomy was still taught as a form of applied geometry—rather as it had been in medieval times.

It is possible that his contacts with the scientific Fellows of Trinity helped him to understand the scientists themselves. He

---

* Fanny Burney mentions this in her diary for 30 December 1786.

was, moreover, on terms of closest acquaintance with at least two outstanding scientists. The friendship between himself, Coleridge and Sir Humphry Davy is well known. Davy was esteemed by his friends as a poet: his taste was sufficiently highly regarded for him to be entrusted with the task of correcting the second edition of the *Lyrical Ballads*. Wordsworth was also, however, a firm friend of the Royal Astronomer for Ireland, Sir William Rowan Hamilton. He visited Hamilton at Dunsink Observatory in 1829. Whilst there, Hamilton chided him for showing a lack of reverence for science in the *Excursion*. Wordsworth replied that he venerated science that raised the mind to the contemplation of God; his opposition was simply to science that put this end out of view—an attitude which reminds us of Cowper. It was his friendship with Hamilton which led Wordsworth to add the famous lines on Newton to his second version of the *Prelude*.[37]

It is evident that Wordsworth was not basically antagonistic to Newton, nor was he opposed to Newtonian science as such. (Indeed, at one stage, Coleridge feared that Newtonian ideas were depersonalizing Wordsworth's image of God, and that *Tintern Abbey* reflected this.) Where Wordsworth expresses a disdain it is for book-learning as compared with a direct apprehension of nature; for analysis as compared with synthesis. When he says: 'Enough of Science and of Art'[38]—science here has its old connotation (still customary in the earlier nineteenth century) of knowledge as a whole. Of course, scientific work did come under this general ban. For example, in one of his lesser-known poems, Wordsworth describes a showman who has set up a telescope and is using it to provide people with sights of the various astronomical bodies. Wordsworth concludes

> Whatever be the cause, 'tis sure that they who pry and pore
> Seem to meet with little gain, seem less happy than before:
> One after one they take their turn, nor I have one espied
> That doth not slackly go away, as if dissatisfied.[39]

Scientific investigation apart, Wordsworth enjoyed looking at the heavens; but whereas Coleridge favoured Venus, Wordsworth looked first for Jupiter.[40] Apparently his sister, too, got into the habit of looking for the planet—not always successfully.

'When we returned many stars were out, the clouds were moveless, and the sky soft purple, the lake of Rydale calm, Jupiter behind. Jupiter at least *we* call him but William says we always call the largest star Jupiter.'[41]

The fifth book of the *Prelude* contains a clear account of the comparative importance of science and poetry, as Wordsworth saw it. He relates it as a dream in which he sees an Arab carrying two objects—a stone and a shell. The Arab told him that the stone

> Was 'Euclid's Elements:' and 'This', said he,
> 'Is something of more worth'; and at the word
> Stretched forth the shell[42]

The shell represents the arts (specifically poetry), the stone—the sciences. Wordsworth is again using geometry (i.e. Euclid's *Elements*) as the equivalent of astronomy. Despite its lower place, it is evident from subsequent lines that astronomy is not being assigned an ignoble place.

Wordsworth's major qualms about science—as distinct from other fields of the intellect—were religious. As he grew older, and his religious views became increasingly orthodox, these doubts increased. His remarks in the *Excursion* have overtones both of Pope, and of Milton.[43] In his sonnet of 1838 *To the Planet Venus* he sadly comments

> True is it Nature hides
> Her treasures less and less.—Man now presides
> In power, where once he trembled in his weakness;
> Science advances with gigantic strides;
> But are we aught enriched in love and meekness?

At the same time, Wordsworth insisted that he was not blind to the

> worlds unthought of till the searching mind
> Of Science laid them open to mankind.[44]

It must be remembered, too, that the *Prelude* was revised periodically throughout his life; the opinions which he expressed there may thus be taken to represent his mature judgement.

It is related that Wordsworth once attended a dinner at which Lamb and Keats were also present. During the course of it, Lamb incited his fellow guests to drink a toast to 'Newton's health and confusion to mathematics.' He argued, and Keats agreed with him, that Newton's work on light had destroyed the poetry of the rainbow.[45] Keats, despite his study of medicine (which he considered quite useful, and not detrimental to his poetic activity), referred little to science: such comment as there was seems antagonistic. In this he was diametrically opposed to Shelley.

Shelley was enthusiastically in favour of science. Unlike almost all his fellow-writers of the nineteenth century, he actually tried to do experiments himself (particularly chemical ones), encouraged, it seems, partly by Erasmus Darwin's example. (He apparently discussed Darwin's experiments with Byron.) It is, in fact, possible to trace a rather tenuous link between Darwin and Shelley. James Lind, who was acquainted with the members of the Lunar Society (to which Darwin belonged) came down to the south of England to be George III's physician at Windsor. He was an amateur astronomer himself, and was soon on friendly terms with William Herschel (who, as Royal Astronomer, lived nearby). Lind befriended the young Shelley, and it is quite possible that Shelley received some instruction in astronomy from him. Shelley's main source of scientific knowledge, however, apart from private reading, was Adam Walker, an itinerant lecturer in the eighteenth-century tradition, who gave instruction to schools. These lectures were later published by Walker as *A System of Familiar Philosophy*, and reflections of them may be found in Shelley's writings. For example, the idea that meteors derive from rising bubbles of marsh gas.[46]

'Tis said, she first was changed into a vapour,
And then into a cloud, such clouds as flit,
Like splendour-winged moths about a taper,
Round the red west when the sun dies in it:
And then into a meteor, such as caper
On hill-tops when the moon is in a fit:
Then, into one of those mysterious stars
Which hide themselves between the Earth and Mars.[47]

As can be seen from this, the word *meteor* was still a ragbag including several diverse phenomena—much as it had been in medieval times. Shelley was confusing the will-o'-the-wisp effect seen over marshes with the meteors of the upper atmosphere. According to Cowper, even these latter remained 'Portentous, unexampled, unexplain'd'.[48] The correct explanation of meteors (that they are particles from interplanetary space which burn up in the Earth's atmosphere) was in fact put forward at about the time Shelley was born. Its acceptance, not surprisingly, was rather slow: in 1790 the Paris Academy had refused to consider any more reports of stones falling from the sky, for, they said, scientists were now too enlightened to believe such superstition.

It will be noted that Shelley goes on to speak of mysterious stars between the Earth and Mars. He was almost certainly thinking of the minor planets, or asteroids. The first of these small bodies (whose paths actually lie mainly between Mars and Jupiter) was discovered in 1801, three more were found in the next six years (no more were then detected until 1845). It was suggested early on that the asteroids were the remnants of a planet that had exploded: an idea that fitted in satisfactorily with the current emphasis on astronomical catastrophes.

Some of Shelley's most interesting references to astronomy occur in his early poem *Queen Mab*, for here he also provides an extensive battery of notes. The initial theme of the poem shows the fairy, Queen Mab, taking the spirit soul of the sleeping Ianthe into her chariot, and carrying her away through the heavens

> Whilst round the chariot's way
> Innumerable systems rolled.[49]

Shelley appended a long note to the words 'innumerable systems'. The first paragraph of this declared that the concepts of astronomy and especially the plurality of worlds were incompatible with Christianity. He followed this up elsewhere in the notes by declaring that 'the consistent Newtonian is necessarily an atheist'. It is evident that Shelley, at least in this poem, was in basic agreement with Blake: both believed that Newtonian science was necessarily irreligious, but where Blake deplored,

Shelley gloried in it*. (How great a difference, in either case, from poets of a century before.)

In the second paragraph of his note on the plurality of worlds, Shelley wrote: 'The nearest of the fixed stars is inconceivably distant from the Earth, and they are probably proportionably distant from each other. By a calculation of the velocity of light, Sirius is supposed to be at least 54,224,000,000,000 miles from the Earth.' Direct measurement of stellar distances was not achieved until almost twenty years after Shelley's death. Prior to that all estimates depended primarily on guesswork, such as Shelley quotes here. These were normally based on the assumption that all stars were like the Sun and that, on the average, all were an equal distance apart.

Another of Shelley's notes to *Queen Mab* dealt with a point which, unlike stellar distances, had just been cleared up. This was the problem of the obliquity of the ecliptic. It had long been known that the obliquity was decreasing (we have seen that the Elizabethans took this as one of the signs of decay in the universe), but there was no way of knowing whether the angle would continue to decrease, or whether it would increase again at some time in the future. The French astronomer, Laplace, showed that the latter was the case (i.e. the obliquity oscillated very slowly about some mean value). Shelley explicitly rejected Laplace's solution on the grounds of 'the strong evidence afforded by the history of mythology, and geological researches'. By this he meant, presumably, that it did not fit in with his own ideas of the working of the world. These were, in a sense, the converse of Milton's: whereas Milton had believed that the tilt of the Earth's axis was a consequence of the Fall, Shelley suggested that the gradual decrease in the obliquity was related to the perfecting of the human race. Man would finally become regenerate, both physically and morally, when the poles of the Earth

> no longer point
> To the red and baleful sun
> That faintly twinkles there.[50]

* Neither Blake nor Shelley, however, accepted the Newtonian idea of time passing at an unalterable rate. Shelley insisted that our sensation of the passage of time depended rather on the succession and intensity of our thoughts.

'The red and baleful sun' is the pole star. Shelley's description of it as 'red' is distinctly surprising, but it may be that he was envisaging it as it would be at some distant date in the future, when the Earth's equator ultimately coincided with the ecliptic.

Shelley's interest in science has received prominent notice during the present century. Whitehead, for example, claimed that science was a main element in Shelley's thought, and one which thoroughly permeated his poetry. He gave as an instance of this the stanza from *Prometheus Unbound* in which the Earth declares to the Moon 'I spin beneath my pyramid of night'[51]. Whitehead comments 'This stanza could only have been written by someone with a definite geometrical diagram before his inward eye—a diagram which it has often been my business to demonstrate to mathematical classes.'[52] Without denying Whitehead's thesis, it is important not to over-emphasize Shelley's scientific notions. To take the example of the Earth's shadow that Whitehead cites; this was really a poetic common-place—it can be found both before Shelley (e.g. in Milton[53]) and after (e.g. Housman[54]). Milton and Housman refer to the shadow more aptly as a cone rather than a pyramid.

If, in fact, it became necessary to choose the nineteenth-century poet who had the greatest knowledge of science, and the greatest interest in it, the award would undoubtedly go not to Shelley, but to Tennyson. (As a demonstration of the professional touch that Tennyson brought to his astronomical comments, it is enlightening to compare his description of the Earth's shadow[55] with Shelley's.) It is evident from the statements of Tennyson's numerous scientific acquaintances—even allowing for their exaggeration—that they held him in considerable respect.[56] Tennyson was especially fascinated by astronomy. Sir Norman Lockyer—one of the leading British astronomers in the latter half of the nineteenth century—has left a short description of Tennyson's astronomical interests which is worth quoting in detail.

I soon found that he was an enthusiastic astronomer and that few points in the descriptive part of the subject had escaped him. He was therefore often in the observatory. Some of his remarks linger fresh in my memory. One night when the moon's terminator swept across the broken ground round Tycho* he said, 'What a splendid Hell that would make'. Again after showing him the clusters in Hercules and Perseus he remarked musingly, 'I cannot think much of the county families after that'. In 1866 my wife was translating Guillemin's *Le Ciel* and I was editing and considerably expanding it; he read many of the proof sheets and indeed suggested the title of the English edition, *The Heavens*.

In the seventies, less so in the eighties, he rarely came to London without discussing some points with me, and in these discussions he showed himself to be full of knowledge of the discoveries then being made.

Once I met him accidentally in Paris; he was most anxious to see Leverrier† and the Observatory. Leverrier had the reputation of being *difficile*; I never found him so, but I certainly never saw him so happy as when we three were together, and he told me afterwards how delighted he had been that Tennyson should have wished to pay him a visit. I visited Tennyson at Aldworth [Tennyson's home] in 1890 when he was in his 82nd year. I was then writing the 'Meteoritic Hypothesis' and he had asked for proof sheets. When I arrived there I was touched to find that he had had them bound together for convenience in reading, and from the conversation we had I formed the impression that he had read every line. It was a subject after his own heart, as will be shown further on. One of the nights during my stay was very fine, and he said to me, 'Now, Lockyer, let us look at the double stars again', and we did. There was a 2-inch telescope at Aldworth. His interest in Astronomy was persistent until his death.

The last time I met him (July 1892), he would talk of nothing but the possible ages of the sun and earth, and was eager to know to which estimates scientific opinion was then veering.[57]

Lockyer was not the only leading astronomer with whom Tennyson was on terms of close acquaintanceship. He was also,

---

* A large lunar crater named after Tycho Brahe.

† Leverrier was the leading French theoretical astronomer about the mid-nineteenth century. He was best known for his prediction of the existence of the new planet, Neptune, which was discovered in 1846.

for example, a friend and neighbour of Charles Pritchard, who subsequently became Savilian Professor of Astronomy at Oxford. At Cambridge, Tennyson had been one of William Whewell's favourite pupils; echoes of Whewell's book, *Astronomy and General Physics* have been detected in *In Memoriam.*

It was his keen amateur interest in astronomy and in looking through telescopes* which add a particularly authoritative note to Tennyson's descriptions of the heavens. Take, for example

> Many a night from yonder ivied casement, ere I went to rest,
> Did I look on great Orion sloping slowly to the West.
>
> Many a night I saw the Pleiads, rising thro' the mellow shade,
> Glitter like a swarm of fire-flies tangled in a silver braid.[58]

Orion slopes towards the horizon, when rising or setting, because it appears at such times to be lying on one side. (We may compare the very similar image by Robert Frost in this century

> You know Orion always comes up sideways
> Throwing a leg up over our fence of mountains.[59])

Tennyson's description of the Pleiades as 'tangled in a silver braid' is even more interesting. The brighter stars in the Pleiades have faint nebulosities associated with them, and it might reasonably be assumed that he was referring to these. However, the first certain evidence for the existence of such nebulae in the Pleiades was not forthcoming until nearly twenty years after these lines were written. (The nebulae are difficult to see with the naked eye, but relatively easy to photograph. Their existence was, therefore, not finally established until towards the end of the nineteenth century, when celestial photography became common.)

Tennyson mentions elsewhere the somewhat similar nebula in Orion, which is a good deal easier to see through a telescope.[60] Orion, together with the Great and Small Bears were Tennyson's favourite constellations; he often speaks of them.[61]

Although William Herschel's work had opened the way to a

---

* For example, Tennyson volunteered to join one of the parties visiting the Mediterranean in 1870 to observe a total eclipse of the Sun.

new interest in the stars, astronomical attention in the nineteenth century was still predominantly centred on the solar system. This was especially true for those amateurs—like Tennyson—who only possessed small telescopes. It is not surprising therefore that his poetry is particularly rich in references to the planets,[62] and to the minor bodies of the solar system— such as meteors.[63] (By the latter half of the century, the confusion over the word *meteor* was more or less cleared up: it possessed much the same connotation for Tennyson that it does for us.) He was especially fond of the planet Venus, and its dual role as morning and evening star.[64]

Tennyson was able to compress much of astronomical interest into very few words. Consider, for example, his reference to

> the snowy poles and moons of Mars,
> That mystic field of drifted light
> In mid Orion and the married stars.[65]

Mars was (and is) a popular object for amateur astronomers: it is the most interesting of the planets to look at owing to its variety of surface markings. The most obvious of these are the white polar caps. Although they had been noticed before, William Herschel was the first to provide reasonable evidence that they consisted of snow and ice—like the polar caps on the Earth—by showing that their extent varied with the Martian season. As has been mentioned previously (when discussing Jonathan Swift), the moons of Mars were not discovered until 1877. The 'drifted light in mid Orion' is, once again, the Orion nebula. The 'married stars' is a distinctively Tennysonian phrase for double stars: that is stars which revolve round each other. Herschel's researches had brought double stars into prominence; they became popular objects for observation during the nineteenth century.

Tennyson was hampered in his own efforts at astronomical observing by bad eyesight. Lockyer recorded 'He told me that without spectacles the two stars of the Great Bear forming the pointers appeared to him as two intersecting circular discs.'[66] This was of minor importance, however, for Tennyson's main pleasure lay in studying the new results obtained by others, particularly in the field of cosmology. He was always abreast of current ideas, and frequently incorporated them into his writ-ings. For example, the discovery of the new planet, Neptune, was soon incorporated into his poetry.[67] The events surrounding the discovery of the planet, in particular the controversy over the true discoverer—Leverrier in France, or Adams in England —were widely reported, and must have been known to any educated man of the time. Tennyson's references, however, were often much more erudite. For example:

> As tho' a star, in inmost heaven set,
> Ev'n while we gaze on it,
> Should slowly round his orb, and slowly grow
> To a full face, there like a sun remain
> Fix'd—then as slowly fade again,
> And draw itself to what it was before.[68]

He probably had in mind here one current explanation of why some stars varied in brightness. This had been advocated more especially by William Herschel, and suggested that if stars had spots like the Sun, and these spots were preferentially concen-trated on one side of the star, then rotation of the star would produce a regular variation in its brightness.

Again, Tennyson wrote of:

> A planet equal to the Sun
> Which cast it.[69]

Despite the use of the words 'planet' and 'Sun', this is probably a reference to the idea that the Moon was a fragment which broke away from the Earth. Erasmus Darwin had earlier men-tioned the belief, current at the end of the eighteenth century, that the division was due to an explosion whose scar remained as the Pacific ocean.[70] Towards the end of the nineteenth century, the idea was taken up in another form by G. H. Darwin (one of Erasmus Darwin's descendants), who suggested that the Earth and the Moon originally formed a single body which split into two components owing to a too rapid rate of rotation. This fission was supposed to have occurred early on in the history of the solar system, when the Earth was still a fluid mass. (It was generally accepted at that time that the earth had started off as a hot body which gradually cooled and solidified.[71] This was, indeed, thought to be a necessary consequence of the nebular hypothesis for the origin of the solar system.[72])

The main fascination of astronomy for Tennyson, as for most of his contemporaries, was what it had to say concerning the extent and duration of space and time. It was here that it trod in regions of religious thought, where reconciliation seemed difficult. In this regard Tennyson, like Cowper years before, linked astronomy with geology.

> Poet, that evergreen laurel is blasted with more than
>   lightning!
>
> These are Astronomy and Geology, terrible Muses![73]

Much of the trouble in Victorian eyes was that scientific progress seemed to be inexorably leading in the same direction as the old Epicurean tradition which had been so strongly repudiated in the seventeenth century. Tennyson's description of the ideas of Lucretius was too close an echo of the nineteenth-century reality for comfort.[74] (Thomas Huxley, it may be noted, once compared Tennyson with Lucretius as a poet.) Indeed, some of Tennyson's writings which sound almost as if they are describing Epicurean ideas are, in fact, solidly based on hypotheses advanced by his contemporaries.

> Must my day be dark by reason, O ye Heavens, of your
>   boundless nights.
> Rush of Suns, and roll of systems, and your fiery clash
>   of meteorites?[75]

The 'clash of meteorites' in this passage derives from Lockyer, who believed that all space was pervaded by streams of meteoritic particles. If two streams collided, they could agglomerate to produce one of the various celestial bodies.

The younger Tennyson was fairly optimistic about the progress of science[76]; as he grew older this optimism decreased. He was envious of Horace's good fortune, who

> scarce could see, as now we see,
> The man in Space and Time,
> So drew perchance a happier lot
> Than ours, who rhyme to-day.[77]

The very titles which appear amongst his poems—*Vastness, Despair*, etc.—indicate this preoccupation with space and time. It must be remembered, however, that Tennyson's cosmic gloom was due to a general contemplation of Man's place in the universe; that is, he was affected as much by the impact of Darwinian evolution as by the results of astronomy and geology. Nevertheless, he was more prepared for the growth of evolutionary ideas than most of his fellow writers. Thus, when the *Vestiges of Creation* came out he commented that it followed a line of reasoning with which he was already acquainted. This was certainly true. Whilst still an undergraduate at Cambridge, he had opposed the proposition that an intelligent first cause could be deduced from the phenomena of the universe. He was also almost certainly affected early on by Lyell's *Principles of Geology* —the great text of uniformitarianism—which appeared not long before his friend, Arthur Hallam, died. *In Memoriam* specifically repudiates the argument from design.[78]

It is interesting to compare Tennyson's reaction to the new scientific ideas on Man's place in the universe with those of his younger contemporary, Hardy. Like Tennyson, Hardy was harrowed by the vastness and hostility of the universe, and the littleness of Man.[79] The *Dynasts*, of course, embodies this theme, but of more direct interest from the astronomical point of view is one of his less well-known novels—*Two on a Tower*.* Hardy explains in the preface that

> This slightly-built romance was the outcome of a wish to set the emotional history of two infinitesimal lives against the stupendous background of the stellar universe.

The hero, an astronomer, emphasizes the terrors of astronomical time and space. Thus at one point he discusses the blank places in the Milky Way where no stars can be seen.

> Until a person has thought out the stars and their inter-spaces, he has hardly learnt that there are things much more terrible than monsters of shape, namely, monsters of

---

* *Two on a Tower* should be compared with *Miriam's Schooling* by Hale White. In the former, a marriage is disrupted by telescope-gazing; in the latter, it is saved.

magnitude without known shape. Such monsters are the voids and waste places of the sky.[80]

The idea that these dark places in the sky were actually holes between the stars had been suggested a good deal earlier by William Herschel, but was accepted throughout the nineteenth century. (They are now known to be regions where the background stars are blotted out by clouds of obscuring matter.)

Whereas Hardy's speculations led him to a thorough pessimism, Tennyson's turned him instead increasingly to the mystical side of religion. In this, he typified the reaction of a significant section of the Victorian intelligentsia: it can be seen, in part, as their reaction to the extreme mechanistic outlook of later nineteenth-century science.

Although many Victorian scientists remained Christians—sometimes exceedingly devout ones—the scientific writers most widely read by the public often were not; Thomas Huxley, for example, or Tyndall, to whom Gladstone once said, 'Professor Tyndall, leave God to the Poets and Philosophers, and attend to your own business.' (Benjamin Jowett limited the investigation of the ultimate mysteries even further. Speaking of Tennyson, he remarked that, 'Poetry may solve the riddle of the universe. Philosophy and science never can.') Gladstone at least felt the need to justify his position. Towards the end of his life, he made what was, perhaps, the last major attempt to reconcile the fossil record with the account of Creation given in *Genesis*. As his knowledge of geology was extremely limited, his reconstruction, not too surprisingly, failed. Gladstone was also opposed to the nebular hypothesis, but in this case he eventually agreed that it might be true.

The development of evolutionary ideas during the nineteenth century spelt the end of the traditional arguments for God from the design of the world. Between the beginning and the end of the nineteenth century, there was a very noticeable decrease in the belief that the hand of the Creator could be traced in the universe.[81] It was recognized fairly early on that the new ideas in astronomy cast some doubt on the arguments in this field. As a result, Paley's *Natural Theology* (published in 1802) was devoted almost entirely to evidences for God drawn from the biological sciences. (The short section devoted to astronomy propounded much the same arguments as had been given by Derham in his *Astro-Theology* a century before. There was one interesting addition: Paley suggested that the stability of the solar system, which Laplace had demonstrated, was itself evidence in favour of design.) Darwinian evolution, however, cast doubt on the biological arguments as well.

The downfall of the traditional arguments from design led to two main attitudes amongst Christians. The first discarded natural theology altogether, preferring to rely solely on personal faith. The second contended that evidence for God could be found from a contemplation of his works, but only by those who were already convinced Christians. (This is the approach reflected in John Keble's hymn: 'There is a book who runs may read'.) In either case, the old relationship between science and religion had disappeared.

Nineteenth-century writers, in complete opposition to their predecessors a century before, generally agreed that the developments in science then occurring, and their apparent conflict with traditional religion, could be traced back to Newton. So Swinburne could claim joyfully that the supernatural had now been driven out from both the inanimate and the animate.

> What Newton's might could not make clear
> Hath Darwin's might not made?[82]

Not all Victorian writers were oppressed by the results of science. Meredith, for example, found the vast size of the universe quite cheering.[83] Again, many in that age were not interested in science, or kept their interest in a separate compartment from their religion, or simply could not see that any conflict existed. Thus Gerard Manley Hopkins never seems to have felt any tension between his vocation as a priest, and his intense interest in nature. This may have been because his interest was essentially descriptive rather than scientific. (There is perhaps a parallel case in Matthew Arnold's dabbling in botany despite his general dislike of science.) On the other hand, Hopkins' interest in the heavens was most prominent when he was at Stonyhurst, which possessed an observatory. (He recorded in 1872 that he 'was at the Observatory to see an eclipse of the moon'.[84]) Hopkins' equanimity seems to have come at least partly from the fact that God was for him still visible in nature. This belief derived not from some argument of natural theology, but from his own imaginative intuition.[85] To this extent he falls into the same group as Keble, although as a Roman Catholic he was still expected to accept traditional natural theology.

It is possible, incidentally, that Hopkins had the rare experience of being present at the fall of a meteorite. This, too, occurred at Stonyhurst.

> Great fall of stars, identified with Biela's comet. They radiated from Perseus or Andromeda and in falling, at least I noticed it of those falling at all southwards, took a pitch to the left halfway through their flight. The kitchen boys came running with a great to do to say something red hot had struck the meatsafe over the scullery door with a great noise and falling into the yard gone into several pieces. No authentic fragment was found but Br. Hostage saw marks of burning on the safe and the slightest of dints as if made by a soft body, so that if anything fell it was probably a body of gas, Fr. Perry thought. It did not appear easy to give any other explanation than a meteoric one.[86]

The fact that comets can have streams of meteors associated with them was discovered in 1862—only ten years before Hopkins wrote this passage. The identification of the shower of meteors at the end of November with Biela's comet (named after its discoverer) was even more recent. It has never, in fact, been demonstrated that meteor showers are accompanied by meteorite falls: current thinking tends to suppose that meteors and meteorites may be distinct types of bodies. Hopkins presumably acquired his information from Perry who was then in charge of the Stonyhurst Observatory. He was a well-known astronomer of the day, whose death Francis Thompson commemorated in a short poem.[87]

As the nineteenth century progressed, the opinion developed amongst more thoughtful Christians that science was neutral, although it might help, or at least supplement, religious feelings that already existed. This may be called the moderate view of the relationship between science and religion. On one side of it stood

13

Huxley, claiming that science disproved the Christian religion (he actually asserted that it was astronomy more than any other branch of science which had made it impossible for people to accept the beliefs of their fathers).[88] On the other side stood Carlyle, claiming that science without religion was worthless.[89] (Carlyle was, it may be noted, proud of his mathematical abilities. He applied at one stage for the Chair of Astronomy at Edinburgh, and was highly annoyed when his candidature was rejected.)

The overall effect of nineteenth-century science was, however, indisputably obvious by the end of the century: it had led away from religion rather than towards it. Wilfred Blunt, for example, originally thought of becoming a Roman Catholic priest, but his study of science turned him into a sceptic. Yeats expressed a hatred of science because it robbed him of his boyhood religion.

> seek then,
> No learning from the starry men
> Who follow with the optic glass
> The whirling ways of stars that pass
> Seek, then, for this is also sooth,
> No word of theirs—the cold star-bane
> Has cloven and rent their hearts in twain,
> And dead is all their human truth.[90]

If we have been emphasizing the effect of nineteenth-century science in producing doubt, it is necessary to balance against this the support which science appeared to provide for the Victorian belief in progress. So far as astronomy, specifically, is concerned, this appears as a revived interest in Man's conquest of the universe.

> Disease will be extirpated; the causes of decay will be removed; immortality will be invented. And then, the earth being small, mankind will migrate into space, and will cross the airless Saharas which separate planet from planet, and sun from sun. The earth will become a Holy Land which will be visited by pilgrims from all the quarters of the universe. Finally, men will master the forces of Nature; they will become themselves architects of systems, manufacturers of worlds.[91]

In a similar vein, evolution could be seen as a mechanism which led not only to higher creatures elsewhere in the universe (a commonplace of the chain-of-being concept in the eighteenth century), but also to the possibility—perhaps even the certainty—that Man himself would become a higher creature.[92]

This more optimistic view of science was reflected towards the end of the nineteenth century in the growing popular interest in science fiction. We left the space fiction novel in the mid-seventeenth century, when accounts of voyages to the Moon were attracting considerable attention. In the latter half of that century, Cyrano de Bergerac wrote a popular fantasy on space travel which ran through several French editions from 1650 onwards, and appeared in an English translation in the same year that the *Principia* was published. Cyrano's main contribution to the genre was his first employment of rockets as a mode of propulsion to the Moon—albeit unintentional.

We have observed Samuel Butler's opinion of visits to the Moon. Wilkins' idea of a flying chariot was chosen for sardonic comment by Pope in the *Dunciad*.

> The head that turns at super-lunar things,
> Pois'd with a tail, may steer on Wilkins' wings.[93]

Defoe, too, found much material for satire in the Moon and its inhabitants. His major work in this field was *The Consolidator* (which contains a few rather off-hand comments about natural philosophers, particularly Bishop Wilkins, whom he seems to have disliked). The fascination of the tale is, however, the machine itself—the Consolidator of the title. This seems to have worked by some remarkable form of internal combustion. (There are, incidentally, arrangements for the operator to spend the voyage to the Moon in a state of suspended animation.)

The eighteenth century, as we have seen, came slowly to the conclusion that the Moon was a dead world, but the possibility that it harboured life was never entirely denied. Thomas Gray wrote (in Latin) of the Moon and its inhabitants during the eighteenth century. Byron remarked at the beginning of the nineteenth century that he supposed men would fly to the Moon some day despite the lack of atmosphere. In the middle of the century, we find Clough writing

> Of suns and stars, by hypothetic men
> Of other frame than ours inhabited,
> Of lunar seas and lunar craters huge
> And was there atmosphere, or was there not?
> And without oxygen could life subsist?[94]

From early in the eighteenth century until late in the nineteenth century, however, little of major significance was written in Britain on space travel. Even at the end of this period the new initiative came from outside—from the novels of Jules Verne in France. Verne's novels, which were translated into English almost as rapidly as they appeared, were remarkable for combining a passion for scientific verisimilitude with a visionary concept of the future. (As for the former, it may be noted that the numerical results in his early novels were carefully checked by a cousin who taught mathematics. This does not mean that all his results are accurate, nor that all his ideas are workable. For example, in *From the Earth to the Moon* his intrepid voyagers are shot off on the journey by a giant cannon. Although it is certainly possible, in theory, to put a satellite into orbit this way, the condition of the passengers after firing would hardly be very healthy.)

Verne had a good working knowledge of astronomy. In the novel just mentioned, and its sequel, *Round the Moon* he devoted some discussion to astronomy, including the history of lunar observation. He refers, for example, to Kepler's *Somnium*, and to the idea it contains that lunar craters are artificial creations. Many of Verne's astronomical suggestions, which may appear far-fetched today, were actually taken from speculations by quite reputable contemporary astronomers; his hypothesis, for example, that the far side of the Moon might have retained an atmosphere. This was probably adopted from his fellow-countryman, Camille Flammarion, a very effective popularizer of astronomy in the last century and a well-known astronomer.

Verne's most extensive discussion of astronomical history is to be found in one of his lesser-known novels, *Hector Servadoc*, in which he describes a collision between the Earth and a comet which results in a fragment of the former flying off into space.

There was still considerable interest in the possible consequences of such a collision in the nineteenth century. Flammarion forecast that a passage of the Earth through a comet's tail would produce mass poisoning of the population (from which, perhaps, Conan Doyle derived the inspiration for *The Poison Belt*). When, at the beginning of this century, such an encounter was actually predicted, the resulting distress was, in some places, Laputan in intensity. Wells, when he tackled the same theme, went to the other extreme. His book, *In the Days of the Comet*, describes a world which is temporarily gassed by a passing comet, but with the result that all the inhabitants become morally better and more benevolent. We may note in passing that several bright comets visible from Britain appeared during the nineteenth century. They aroused considerable popular interest: Thomas Lovell Bedoes' first poem—published in the *Morning Post* in 1819—described a comet which had recently appeared. Much of this interest stemmed back to the older astrological beliefs, even among educated people. In 1857, the Earl of Malmesbury noted in his diary: 'We are suffering under an extraordinary heat. People are really getting alarmed, for if it is occasioned by the comet, which is not yet visible, what must we expect when it reaches our Globe!'[95]

There was much discussion of possible world-wide catastrophes at the end of the century. Wells' short story *The Star* describes a physical catastrophe; a disaster of another sort is illustrated in *The War of the Worlds*. This latter story reflects a major controversy then raging amongst astronomers over the possibility of intelligent life on Mars. Wells, himself, favoured the existence of some form of life there.

The development of the science-fiction novel in Britain stems back in many ways to Wells, though he was undoubtedly encouraged to try his hand in this field by the success of Jules Verne. He always insisted, however, that his viewpoint was entirely different from the Frenchman's:

> These tales have been compared with the work of Jules Verne and there was a disposition on the part of literary journalists at one time to call me the English Jules Verne. As a matter of fact there is no literary resemblance whatever

between the anticipatory inventions of the great Frenchman and these fantasies... The interest he invoked was a practical one; he wrote and believed and told that this or that thing could be done, which was not at that time done... But these stories of mine collected here do not pretend to deal with possible things; they are exercises of the imagination in a quite different field.[96]

Wells' contemporaries took his protestations with a pinch of salt. For example, a parody of *The War of the Worlds* commented ' "I always mix you up with the man you admire so much—Jools Werne. And," he added with a sly look, "you *do* admire him, don't you?" In a flash I saw the man plain. He was a critic. I knew my duty at once: I must kill him.'[97]

Nevertheless, Wells' distinction was undoubtedly valid. The truth of his comments can, perhaps, be illustrated by the different ways in which the two writers tackled the problem of reaching the Moon. Verne, faced with the necessity for space travel, carefully extrapolated from known data, and produced the idea of an outsize shell projected from a gigantic gun.

Wells, faced with the same requirement, in *The First Men in the Moon*, circumvented it by introducing an unspecified, anti-gravitational substance. It should be remarked, however, that he was making no great innovation in this. An early American space voyager had used such a device (in a book actually written by one of Edgar Allan Poe's professors at the University of Virginia). Just one year before *The First Men in the Moon* was published, it was used again by another American, the astronomer, Simon Newcomb. Newcomb's novel, incidentally, was one of the forerunners of the type in which a scientist becomes the benevolent dictator of the world. Wells did, however, follow the basic rule of serious science fiction: that, once you have introduced an improbability, you follow out its consequences to the end. This was appreciated by his readers—the leading scientific journal, *Nature*, subsequently examined carefully his method of directing the sphere (by rolling shutters over the anti-gravitational substance), and argued whether it would work in the way he suggested.

As it happens, Verne's influence is most obvious in this novel.

Wells, himself, has remarked 'In *The First Men in the Moon* I tried an improvement on Jules Verne's shot, in order to look at mankind from a distance and burlesque the effects of specialization. Verne never landed on the moon because he never knew of radio and of the possibility of sending back a message. So it was his shot that came back. But equipped with radio, which had just come out then, I was able to land'.[98] It was in this book, too, that Wells revealed that he, like Verne, was acquainted with the *Somnium*. Cavor, after his capture by the Selenites, muses: 'Yes,' he said, 'Kepler with his *sub-volvani* was right after all'.[99]

Although Wells differed from Verne in his approach to science-fiction he was thus united with him in the attempt to provide logically constructed plots which did not contain obvious errors of fact. An example of this is his description in the *Time Machine* of how the heavens would appear several million years hence. (Not that he entirely avoided elementary mistakes: thus he tells us—also in the *Time Machine*—that 'the full moon rose, yellow and gibbous'.) This internal veracity may be seen as a common element of the two main traditions of science fiction: that of scientific realism (represented by Verne) on the one hand, and that of utopian, or satirical, commentary (represented by Wells) on the other. It distinguishes them both from the third possible strand of space fiction—pure fantasy; represented, for example, in the nineteenth century by the account of other worlds in *Sylvie and Bruno*. In this, Mein Herr (who appears to be a visitor from another planet, although he carefully refrains from saying so) asks the question: 'What is the smallest *world* you would care to inhabit?' He then goes on:

'...a scientific friend of mine, who has made several balloon-voyages, assures me he has visited a planet so small that he could walk right round it in twenty minutes! There had been a great battle, just before his visit, which had ended rather oddly: the vanquished army ran away at full speed, and in a very few minutes found themselves face-to-face with the victorious army, who were marching home again, and who were so frightened at finding themselves between *two* armies, that they surrendered at once!'[100]

References

If the work referred to is fairly readily available, only the essential bibliographical details have been given. Fuller references have been provided for works which are less easily obtainable, as also for works where a page number has to be specified. The line number cited refers to the first line of the quotation.

CHAPTER I

1 Aquinas, *Summa Theologica*, Part I, Question 68, Article 3, Burns Oates and Washbourne (1922) Vol. 3, p. 225
2 Milton, 'Paradise Lost', Book VII, l. 169
3 Vaughan, 'The World', l. 1
4 Donne, 'Obsequies to the Lord Harrington', l. 105
5 Gower, 'Confessio Amantis', Book VII, l. 673
6 Marlowe, *The Tragical History of Dr. Faustus*, Act II, Scene II, l. 39
7 *Ibid.* l. 63
8 *Ibid.* l. 51
9 Butler, 'Hudibras', Part II, Canto III, l. 877
10 Marlowe, *op. cit.*, Act II, Scene II, l. 43
11 Shakespeare, *Troilus and Cressida*, Act I, Scene III, l. 95
12 Donne, 'Good Friday, 1613. Riding Westward', l. 8; Drayton, 'Endimion and Phoebe', l. 674.
13 Gower, *op. cit.*, Book VII, l. 739
14 Caxton, *The Mirrour of the World*, Early English Text Society (Ed.) O. H. Prior (1913) p. 59
15 Dekker, *Old Fortunatus*, Chorus to Act II, l. 1 *The Dramatic Works of Thomas Dekker* (Ed.) F. Bowers (1953) Vol. I, p. 135
16 Butler, *op. cit.*, Part II, Canto III, l. 871
17 Bacon, *Novum Organum*, Book II, xlviii, *The Philosophical Works of Francis Bacon* (Ed.) J. M. Robertson (1905) p. 365 *et. seq.*
18 Butler, *op. cit.*, Part II, Canto III, l. 901
19 Milton, 'Paradise Lost', Book III, l. 481
20 Donne, 'A Valediction: forbidding mourning', l. 9
21 Marlowe, *op. cit.*, Act II, Scene II, l. 61
22 Donne, 'Good Friday, 1613. Riding Westward', l. 1
23 Donne, *ibid.*, l. 21
24 Milton, 'The Hymn', Stanza XIII, l. 131
25 Shakespeare, *The Merchant of Venice*, Act V, Scene I, l. 60
26 Caxton, *op. cit.*, p. 179
27 Donne, 'A Feaver', l. 21

28 Dryden, 'Absolom and Achitophel', l. 637
29 Shakespeare, *Romeo and Juliet*, Act III, Scene V, l. 13
30 Milton, 'Paradise Lost', Book IV, l. 556
31 Thomson, 'The Seasons: Autumn', l. 1108
32 Greene, 'Melicertus' Madrigal', l. 13, *The Plays and Poems of Robert Greene* (Ed.) J. C. Collins (1905) Vol. II. p. 254
33 Marlowe, *Tamburlaine the Great (Part I)*, Act IV, Scene II, l. 5
34 Greville, *Caelica*, VII, Stanza 3 (Ed.) U. Ellis-Fermor (1936)
35 Milton, *op. cit.*, Book V, l. 423
36 Caxton, *op. cit.*, p. 125
37 P. Fletcher, 'The Locusts', Canto V, Stanza 21, *The Poems of Phineas Fletcher* (Ed.) A. B. Grosart (1869) Vol. II
38 Gower, *op. cit.*, Book VII, l. 731
39 Milton, *op. cit.*, Book VII, l. 367
40 Bacon, *A Description of the Intellectual Globe*, Chapter 7, *op. cit.*, p. 697
41 Caxton, *op.cit.*, pp. 122–123
42 Chapman, 'The Teares of Peace', l. 1008
43 Donne, 'Epithalamion X,' l. 1
44 Spenser, 'Fairie Queen', Book III, Canto i, Stanza 16, l. 5
45 Marlowe, *Tamburlaine the Great (Part II)*, Act III, Scene II, l. 1
46 Chaucer, 'Hous of Fame', II, l. 730

CHAPTER II

1 Shakespeare, *As You Like it*, Act II, Scene VII, l. 20
2 Chaucer, *Canterbury Tales:* 'The Parson's Prologue', l. 5
3 Chaucer, *Canterbury Tales:* 'Introduction to the Man of Law's Prologue', l. 1
4 Shakespeare, *Henry the Fourth (Part I)*, Act II, Scene I, l. 1
5 Hardy, *Far from the Madding Crowd* (1889), Chapter II, pp. 11–12
6 Chaucer, 'Prologue' to the *Canterbury Tales*, l. 7
7 Spenser, 'Prosopopoia, or Mother Hubberd's Tale', l. 1
8 Lydgate, 'The Temple of Glas', l. 4, Early English Text Society (Ed.) J. Schick (1891)
9 Chaucer, 'Troilus and Criseyde', Book III, l. 624
10 Corbett, 'A letter sent from Doctor Corbet to Master Ailesbury, Decem. 9. 1618', l. 38; *The Poems of Richard Corbett* (Ed.) J. A. W. Bennett and H. R. Trevor-Roper (1955)
11 Herbert, 'The Agonie', l. 1
12 Chaucer, *A Treatise on the Astrolabe*, Part II, Section 3, l. 44
13 Donne, 'A Valediction: of the booke', l. 59
14 *Ibid.*, l. 61
15 Gorges, 'Poem No. 67', l. 3, *The Poems of Sir Arthur Gorges* (Ed.) H. E. Sandison (1953)
16 Shakespeare, *Midsummer Night's Dream*, Act III, Scene I, l. 44

17 Caxton, *The Mirrour of the World*, Early English Text Society (Ed.) O. H. Prior (1913) p. 40
18 e.g. Hawes, 'The Pastime of Pleasure', l. 2689, Early English Text Society (Ed.) W. E. Mead (1928)
19 Milton, 'Paradise Lost', Book IX, l. 679
20 II Peter, Chapter 3, verse 8
21 Psalm 90, verse 4
22 Shakespeare, *As You Like It*, Act IV, Scene I, l. 83
23 Donne, 'Sermon preached at Whitehall: April 18th, 1626', *The Sermons of John Donne* (Ed.) E. M. Simpson and G. R. Potter (1954) Vol VII, pp. 138–139
24 Browne, *Pseudodoxia Epidemica*, Book VI, Chapter 1
25 Psalm 102, verses 25–26
26 Donne, 'Sermon preached upon Whitsunday (?1625)', *op. cit.*, Vol VI, pp. 323–324
27 Spenser, 'Fairie Queen', Proem to Book V, Stanza 7
28 Butler, 'Hudibras', Part II, Canto III, l. 883
29 Spenser, *op. cit.*, Proem to Book V, Stanza 5
30 *Ibid.*, Stanza 8
31 Butler, *op. cit.*, Part II, Canto III, l. 865
32 Milton, *op. cit.*, Book X, l. 668

CHAPTER III

1 Gower, 'Confessio Amantis', Book VII, l. 679
2 Marlowe, *The Tragical History of Doctor Faustus*, Act II, Scene II, l. 33
3 Shakespeare, 'Sonnet No. 14'
4 Shakespeare, *Cymbeline*, Act III, Scene II, l. 27
5 e.g. Drayton, 'Endimion and Phoebe', l. 689
6 Coleridge, *The Death of Wallerstein*, Act V, Scene III, *The Dramatic Works of Samuel Taylor Coleridge* (Ed.) D. Coleridge (1852) p. 410
7 Browne, *Religio Medico*, Part II, Section 11, *The Works of Sir Thomas Browne* (Ed.) G. Keynes (1964) Vol. I, p. 88
8 Chaucer, *A Treatise on the Astrolabe*, Part II, Section 4, l. 14
9 Spenser, 'Fairie Queen', Book II, Canto ix, Stanza 52, l. 8
10 Chapman, 'Andromeda Liberata', l. 303
11 Spenser, *op. cit.*, Book III, Canto vi, Stanza 2, l. 1
12 Peele, *The Battle of Alcazar*, Act V, Scene I, l. 171, *The Works of George Peele* (Ed.) A. H. Bullen (1888) Vol. 1
13 Shakespeare, *The Winter's Tale*, Act II, Scene I, l. 105
14 Shakespeare, *Twelfth Night*, Act I, Scene III, l. 128
15 Drayton, *op. cit.*, l. 693
16 Gower, *op. cit.*, Book VII, l. 799
17 *Ibid.*, l. 750

18 Dekker, *The Shoemaker's Holiday*, Act V, Scene II, l. 103, *The Dramatic Works of Thomas Dekker* (Ed.) F. Bowers (1953) Vol. 1

19 Gower, *op. cit.*, Book VII, l. 781; l. 889 *et seq.*

20 Greene, *Menaphon*, in *Life and Complete Works of Robert Greene* (Ed.) A. B. Grosart (1964 reissue) Vol. VI, p. 46

21 Greene, *Mamillia*, (Part I), *op. cit.*, Vol. II, p. 35

22 Drayton, *op. cit.*, l. 419

23 Lyly, *The Woman in the Moone*, Act V, Scene I, l. 321, *Works of John Lyly* (Ed.) R. W. Bond (1902) Vol. III

24 Scott, *Guy Mannering*, Chapter IV, *The Waverley Novels* (1901) Vol. II, pp. 21–22

25 Chaucer, *Canterbury Tales:* 'The Wife of Bath's Prologue', l. 609

26 Peele, *Edward I*, Scene XVII, *The Works of George Peele* (Ed.) A. H. Bullen (1888) Vol. I, p. 188

27 Milton, 'Paradise Lost', Book VI, l. 313

28 Milton, 'Paradise Regained', Book IV, l. 383

29 Shakespeare, *King Richard the Third*, Act IV, Scene IV, l. 215

30 Chapman, *op. cit.*, l. 305

31 Dryden, 'Ode to the Pious Memory of the Accomplished Young Lady Mrs Anne Killigrew', l. 41

32 Heywood, *The Hierarchie of the blessed Angells*, (1635), Book III, p. 120

33 Raleigh, *The History of the World* (1736 edition), Vol. I, Chapter II, p. 20

34 *Ibid.*, p. 19

35 Donne, 'First Anniversary', l. 235

36 P. Fletcher, 'The Purple Island', Canto III, Stanza 9, l. 1, *The Poems of Phineas Fletcher* (Ed.) A. B. Grosart (1869) Vol. II

37 Drayton, 'The Owle', l. 581

38 P. Fletcher, 'The Locusts', Canto V, Stanza 20, *op. cit.*

39 Bacon, *Novum Organum*, Book II, xiii, *The Philosophical Works of Francis Bacon* (Ed.) J. M. Robertson (1905) p. 316

40 Chaucer, *Canterbury Tales:* 'The Chanoun Yemannes Tale', l. 826

41 Browne, *Religio Medico*, Part II, Section 11, *op. cit.*, Vol. I

42 Chaucer, *Canterbury Tales:* 'The Knight's Tale', l. 2271

43 Gower, *op. cit.*, Book VII, l. 1303 *et seq.*

44 Spenser, 'Prosopopoia: or Mother Hubberd's Tale', l. 1

45 Shakespeare, *Henry the Fourth (Part I)*, Act I, Scene II, l. 13

46 Milton, 'Paradise Lost', Book VII, l. 374

47 Milton, *op. cit.*, Book II, l. 709

48 Shakespeare, *Henry the Fourth (Part I)*, Act I, Scene I, l. 2

49 Shakespeare, *Julius Caesar*, Act II, Scene II, l. 30

50 Webster, *The White Devil*, Act V, Scene III, l. 30

51 Heywood, 'Prologue (spoken to the Palsgrave)', *The Dramatic Works of Thomas Heywood* (1964 reissue) Vol. VI, p. 354

52 Thomson 'The Seasons: Autumn', l. 1117
53 Milton, *op. cit.*, Book I, l. 597
54 Milton, 'Lycidas,' l. 100
55 Shakespeare, *King Lear*, Act I, Scene II, l. 100
56 Shakespeare, *Othello*, Act V, Scene II, l. 102
57 Bacon, *Novum Organum*, Book II, xii, *op. cit.* p. 311
58 Chaucer, *Canterbury Tales:* 'Prologue', l. 411
59 Donne, 'A Valediction of my Name in the Window', l. 33
60 Donne, 'First Anniversary', l. 391
61 Gower, *op. cit.*, Book VI, l. 1343
62 Milton, 'Paradise Lost', Book II, l. 898
63 Drayton, 'Endimion and Phoebe', l. 704
64 Greene, 'Melicertus' Madrigal', l. 13, *The Plays and Poems of Robert Greene* (Ed.) J. C. Collins (1905) Vol. II, p. 254
65 Greene, *Mamillia* (Part II), *Life and Complete Works of Robert Greene* (Ed.) A. B. Grosart (1964 reissue) Vol. II, p. 221
66 Ford, *The Sun's Darling*, Act V, Scene I, *Dramatic Works of John Ford* (Ed.) W. Gifford (1828) Vol. II, p. 432
67 Chaucer, *Canterbury Tales:* 'Prologue', l. 438
68 Browne, *Religio Medico*, Part I, Section 1, *op. cit.*, Vol. 1, p. 11
69 Chaucer, *Canterbury Tales:* 'The Tale of the Man of Lawe', l. 190
70 Gower, *op. cit.*, Book VII, l. 639 *et seq.*
71 Shakespeare, *All's Well That Ends Well*, Act I, Scene I, l. 1
72 Chapman, *The Conspiracy of Charles, Duke of Byron*, Act III, Scene I, *George Chapman* (Ed.) W. L. Phelps (1895) p. 368
73 Greene, See the 'Briefe Apologie' prefixed to *Planetomachia Works* (Ed.) Grosart, *op. cit.*, Vol. V, p. 15 *et seq.*
74 Chaucer, *A Treatise on the Astrolabe*, Part II, Section 4, l. 58
75 Webster, *The Duchess of Malfi*, Act V, Scene IV, l. 63
76 Middleton, *The Family of Love*, Act I, Scene I, l. 15, *The Works of Thomas Middleton* (Ed.) A. H. Bullen (1964 reissue) Vol. III, p. 12
77 Lyly, *Gallathea*, Act I, Scene I, l. 62; l. 69, *Works of John Lyly* (Ed.) R. W. Bond (1902) Vol. II, pp. 433–434
78 Bacon, *De Augmentis Scientiarum*, Book III, Chapter IV, *op. cit.*, p. 462
79 Raleigh, *History of the World*, *op. cit.*, Chapter I, p. 11
80 Browne, *Pseudodoxia Epidemica*, Book IV, Chapter 13, *op. cit.*, Vol. II, p. 336
81 Butler, 'Hudibras', Part II, Canto III, l. 235
82 Habington, 'Castara (Part III): Nox Nocti indicat Scientiam', *The Works of the English Poets from Chaucer to Cowper* (Ed.) A. Chalmers (1810) Vol. VI, p. 476
83 Butler, *op. cit.*, Part II, Canto III, l. 172
84 Shakespeare, *The Winter's Tale*, Act I, Scene II, l. 427

85 Heywood, *The Silver Age, op. cit.*, Vol. III, p. 163
86 Heywood, *King Edward IV (Part I)*, *op. cit.*, Vol. I, p. 64
87 Scott, *Guy Mannering*, Chapter III, *op. cit.*, p. 19
88 Lydgate, 'Seige of Thebes', Part III, l. 4052 Early English Text Society (Ed.) A. Erdmann (1911)

Chapter IV

1 R. Burton, *Anatomy of Melancholy :* 'Digression of Air' (Ed.) F. Dell and P. Jordan-Smith (1951) pp. 422–423
2 Shakespeare, *Henry the Sixth (Part I)*, Act I, Scene II, l. 1
3 Spenser, 'Fairie Queen', Book VII, Canto vii, Stanza 51, l. 3
4 Spenser, *op. cit.*, Proem to Book V, Stanza 8, l. 8
5 Browne, *Religio Medico*, Part II, Section 15 *The Works of Sir Thomas Browne* (Ed.) G. Keynes (1964) Vol. I, p. 93
6 Shakespeare, *Hamlet*, Act II, Scene II, l. 115
7 Donne, 'Devotions upon Emergent Occasions XXI'. See also: 'To the Countess of Bedford: T'have written then', l. 37
8 Davies, 'Orchestra', Stanza 51, *The Complete Poems* (Ed.) A. B. Grosart (1876) Vol. I, p. 180
9 More, 'Psychathanasia', Book III, Canto iii, Stanza 13, *The Complete Poems of Dr. Henry More* (Ed.) A. B. Grosart (1878)
10 Browne, *Pseudodoxia Epidemica*, Book VII, Chapter 18, *op. cit.*, Vol. II, pp. 541–542
11 Burton, *op. cit.*, p. 424
12 Milton, 'Paradise Lost', Book VIII, l. 130
13 Bacon, *A Description of the Intellectual Globe*, Chapter 6, *The Philosophical Works of Francis Bacon* (Ed.) J. M. Robertson (1905) p. 685
14 Wilkins, *A Discourse concerning a New Planet*, in *The Mathematical and Philosophical Works of John Wilkins* (1708) p. 223
15 Luther, *Tabletalk. See* A. D. White *A History of the Warfare of Science with Theology in Christendom* (1901) Vol. I., p. 126
16 Colossians, Chapter II, verse 8
17 Calvin, *Institutes of the Christian Religion*, Book I, Chapter 5, *The Library of Christian Classics* Vol. XX (Ed.) J. J. McNeill and F. L. Battles (1960) p. 53
18 Genesis, Chapter I, verse 7
19 Raleigh, *The History of the World* (1736) Vol. 1, Chapter I, p. 9
20 *Ibid.*
21 Ascham, *The Schoolmaster*, in *Ascham : English Works* (Ed.) W. A. Wright-Roger (1904) p. 190
22 Shakespeare, *All's Well That Ends Well*, Act II, Scene III, l. 1
23 Herbert, 'Vanitie (I)', l. 1
24 Herbert, 'Divinitie', l. 25
25 Milton, *op. cit.*, Book VIII, l. 70
26 Book of Wisdom, Chapter 11, Verse 20

27 Bacon, *Novum Organum*, Book I, xciii, *op. cit.*, p. 287
28 Corbett, 'A letter sent from Doctor Corbet to Master Ailesbury', l. 49, *The Poems of Richard Corbett* (Ed.) J. A. W. Bennett and H. R. Trevor-Roper (1955)
29 Aubrey, *Brief Lives*: 'Thomas Hariot'
30 Shakespeare, *Love's Labours Lost*, Act I, Scene I, l. 88
31 Burton, *op. cit.*, p. 425
32 Bacon, *A Description of the Intellectual Globe*, Chapter 6, *op. cit.*, p. 685
33 Burton, *op. cit.*, p. 426
34 Heywood, *The Hierarchie of the Blessed Angells* (1635) Book III, pp. 153–154
35 Spenser, *op. cit.*, Proem to Book II, Stanza 3, l. 6
36 Milton, *op. cit.*, Book VII, l. 621; *op. cit.*, Book III, l. 566; *op. cit.*, l. 669
37 Bacon, *A description of the Intellectual Globe*, Chapter 6, *op. cit.*, p. 684
38 Burton, *op. cit.*, p. 423
39 Browne, *Pseudodoxia Epidemica*, Book II, Chapter 2, *op. cit.*, Vol. II, p. 88 *et seq.*
40 Milton, *op. cit.*, Book III, l. 582
41 Cowley, 'The 34. Chapter of the Prophet *Isaiah*', Note 1 to Stanza 3, *The Poems of Abraham Cowley* (Ed.) A. R. Waller (1905) p. 216
42 Bacon, *A Description of the Intellectual Globe*, Chapter 7, *op. cit.*, p. 692
43 Donne, 'To the Countess of Bedford: T'have written then', l. 68; 'An Epithalamion, Or marriage song on the Lady Elizabeth', l. 39
44 Dryden, 'Upon the death of the Lord Hastings', l. 43. *See also* 'Ode to Mrs Anne Killigrew, l. 174
45 Jonson, *The Speeches at Prince Henry's Barriers*, l. 66, *Ben Jonson* (Ed.) C. H. Herford, P. and E. Simpson Vol. VII, p. 325
46 Corbett, 'Letter sent from Doctor Corbet to Master Ailesbury', l. 33, *op. cit.*
47 Cowley, 'To the Royal Society', Stanza 8, l. 13
48 Aubrey, *Brief Lives*: 'Thomas Allen'
49 Greene, *Mamillia* (Part II), *Life and Complete Works of Robert Greene* (Ed.) A. B. Grosart (1964 reissue) Vol. II, p. 150
50 Butler, 'Hudibras', Part II, Canto III, l. 413 *et seq.*
51 Nashe, *Pierce Penilesse, His Supplication to the Divell* (Ed.) S. Wells (1964)
52 Browne, *Pseudodoxia Epidemica*, Book VI, Chapter 14, *op. cit.*, Vol II, p. 484
53 Glanvill, *Scepsis Scientifica* (Ed.) J. Owen (1885) Chapter XX, p. 150

Chapter V

1 Bacon, *Novum Organum*, Book I, cxxii, *Philosophical Works of Francis Bacon* (Ed.) J. M. Robertson (1905) p. 297
2 Browne, *Pseudodoxia Epidemica*, Book I, Chapter 6, Glanvill, *Scepsis Scientifica* (Ed.) J. Owen (1885) Chapter xvii
3 Butler, 'Hudibras', Part II, Canto III, l. 663
4 Bacon, *The Advancement of Learning*, Book I, *op. cit.*, p. 55
5 Cf. Wilkins, *The Discovery of a New World* (The Epistle to the Reader), *Mathematical and Philosophical Works of John Wilkins* (1708)
6 e.g. Bacon, *Novum Organum*, Book I, xcviii, *op. cit.*, p. 289
7 Bacon, *De Augmentis Scientiarum*, Book III, Chapter 4, *op. cit.*, p. 461
8 Bacon, *A Description of the Intellectual Globe*, Chapter 5, *op. cit.*, p. 681
9 Bacon, *Novum Organum*, Book II, xxxvi., *op. cit.*, p. 345
10 *Ibid.*
11 Bacon, *Preparative towards a Natural and Experimental History:* Introduction, *op. cit.*, p. 402
12 Bacon, *A Description of the Intellectual Globe*, Chapter 5, *op. cit.*, p. 682
13 Bacon, *Novum Organum*, Book II, xxxix, *op. cit.*, p. 352
14 Wotton, Letter to the Earl of Salisbury, 13th March, 1610, *The Life and Letters of Sir Henry Wotton*. Logan Pearsall Smith (1907) Vol. I, p. 486
15 e.g. J. Fletcher, *The Lover's Progress*, Act III, Scene I, *The Works of Beaumont and Fletcher* (Ed.) A. R. Waller (1907) Vol. V, p. 117; J. Fletcher, *The Honest Man's Fortune*, Act IV, Scene I, *op. cit.*, Vol. X, p. 254
16 e.g. Bacon, *Novum Organum*, Book II, xxxix, *op. cit.*, p. 351; Milton, 'Paradise Lost', Book V, l. 261
17 e.g. Milton, *op. cit.*, Book III, l. 590; Davenant 'Gondibert', Book II, Canto V, Stanza 17, *The Works of the English Poets* (Ed.) A. Chalmers (1810) Vol. VI, p. 402
18 e.g. Jonson, *News from the New World in the Moon*, in *Works of Ben Jonson* (Ed.) W. Gifford (1816) Vol. VII, p. 354
19 Pepys, *Diary*: 8th August, 1666
20 Glanvill, *Scepsis Scientifica*, *op. cit.*, Chapter xx, p. 150
21 Bacon, *Novum Organum*, Book II, xxxix, *op. cit.*, p. 352
22 Browne, *Pseudodoxia Epidemica*, Book IV, Chapter 12, *The Works of Sir Thomas Browne* (Ed.) G. Keynes (1964) Vol. II, p. 309
23 Browne, *Pseudodoxia Epidemica*, Book VI, Chapter 5, *op. cit.*, Vol. II, p. 424
24 Bacon, *A Description of the Intellectual Globe*, Chapter 6, *op. cit.*, p. 688

25 e.g. Milton, 'Paradise Lost', Book VII, l. 579
26 e.g. Donne, 'The Primrose', l. 6
27 Browne, *Pseudodoxia Epidemica*, Book IV, Chapter 12, *op. cit.*, Vol. II, p. 309
28 Wilkins, *A Discourse concerning a New Planet*, *op. cit.*, p. 211
29 Margaret Cavendish, Duchess of Newcastle, *The Description of a New World called The Blazing-World* (1668) p. 26
30 Jonson, *News from the New World in the Moon*, *op. cit.*, p. 356
31 Butler, *op. cit.*, Part II, Canto III, l. 733
32 Wilkins, *The Discovery of a New World*, *op. cit.*, pp. 10–11
33 Evelyn, *Diary*: 4th October, 1641
34 Wilkins, *The Discovery of a New World*, *op. cit.*, pp. 68–69
35 Butler, 'The Elephant in the Moon', l. 53
36 Browne, *Pseudodoxia Epidemica*, Book VII, Chapter 13, *op. cit.*, Vol. II, p. 520
37 Hobbes, Letter to the Duke of Newcastle: 26th January, 1633/4, *The Manuscripts of his Grace the Duke of Portland preserved at Welbeck Abbey*. (1893) Vol. II, p. 124
38 Milton, *Areopagitica*, in *The Works of John Milton* (General Editor) F. A. Patterson (1931) Vol. IV, p. 330
39 Heywood, *The Hierarchie of the Blessed Angells*. (1635) *See* the 'Argument' of Book IX (p. 563)
40 Jonson, *News from the New World in the Moon*, *op. cit.*, p. 358
41 Wilkins, *The Discovery of a New World*, *op. cit.*, p. 115
42 Butler, 'The Elephant in the Moon', l. 13
43 Dryden, 'Annus Mirabilis', Stanza 164
44 Butler, 'Hudibras', Part II, Canto III, l. 782
45 *See* e.g. Dryden, 'The Hind and the Panther', Part III, l. 450; Pope, 'Moral Essays (Epistle I to Richard Temple, Viscount Cobham)', l. 156; Gay, 'Shepherd's Week (Saturday)', l. 63
46 Browne, *Pseudodoxia Epidemica*, Book VI, Chapter 14, *op. cit.*, Vol. II, p. 483
47 Browne, *Religio Medico*, Part I, Section 45, *op. cit.*, Vol. I, p. 56
48 Newton, Letter to Hooke: 5th February, 1675/6, *The Correspondence of Isaac Newton* (Ed.) H. W. Turnbull (1959) Vol. I, p. 416
49 Evelyn, *Diary*: 10th September, 1676
50 Dryden, 'To My Honour'd Friend Dr. Charleton', l. 23
51 Cowley, 'To the Royal Society', Stanza 5
52 Glanvill, *Scepsis Scientifica*, *op. cit.*, Chapter xi, p. 66
53 Aubrey, *Brief Lives*: 'Hobbes' (Ed.) A. Powell (1949) p. 260
54 Glanvill, *Scepsis Scientifica*, *op. cit.*, Chapter xx
55 e.g. Dryden, 'Annus Mirabilis' Stanza 166, *An Essay of Dramatic Poesy*, *Essays of Dryden* (Ed.) W. P. Ker (1900) pp. 36–37
56 Butler, *op. cit.*, Part II, Canto III, l. 179
57 Cowley, 'Ode upon His Majesties Restoration and Return', Stanza 1, l. 11

58 Evelyn, *Diary*: 29th March, 1652
59 Evelyn, *Ibid*: 12th December, 1680
60 Johnson, *Life of Samuel Butler*, in *Lives of the English Poets* (Ed.) G. B. Hill (1905) Vol. I, p. 216

Chapter VI

1 e.g. Thomson, 'A Poem Sacred to the Memory of Sir Isaac Newton'; Hughes, 'The Ecstacy', *The Works of the English Poets* (Ed.) A. Chalmers (1810) Vol. X, p. 61
2 Thomson, 'The Seasons: Summer', l. 1560
3 Bowden, 'A Poem Sacred to the Memory of Sir Isaac Newton', *Poetical Essays, on Several Occasions* (1735) Vol. II, p. 16
4 Pope, 'Essay on Man', Epistle II, l. 35
5 Pope, 'The Dunciad', Book IV, l. 453
6 Thomson, 'A Poem Sacred to the Memory of Sir Isaac Newton', l. 40
7 Thomson, 'Liberty', Part III, l. 45
8 Desaguliers, 'The Newtonian System of the World' (1728) p. 2 (footnote)
9 Thomson, 'A Poem Sacred to the Memory of Sir Isaac Newton', l. 82
10 Goldsmith, *An History of the Earth* (1774) Vol. I, p. 3
11 Thomson, 'The Seasons: Winter', l. 859
12 Thomson, 'A Poem Sacred to the Memory of Sir Isaac Newton', l. 76
13 Aubrey, *Brief Lives*: 'Thomas Hariot'
14 Pepys, *Diary*: 1st March, 1665
15 Savage, 'The Wanderer', Canto I, *The Works of the English Poets* (Ed.) A. Chalmers (1810) Vol. XI, p. 302
16 Thomson, 'The Seasons: Summer', l. 1725
17 e.g. Gay, Pope and Arbuthnot, *Three Hours after Marriage*(Ed.) R. Morton and W. M. Peterson (1961)
18 e.g. Thomson, 'A Poem Sacred to the Memory of Sir Isaac Newton'; Prior, 'Solomon', Book I, l. 520; Young, 'Night Thoughts: Night IX', l. 778, *Young's Night Thoughts* (Ed.) G. Gilfillan (1853)
19 Blackmore, 'The Creation', Book II, *The Works of the English Poets* (Ed.) A. Chalmers (1810) Vol. X, p. 349
20 Thomson, 'The Seasons: Autumn', l. 1354
21 Young, 'Night Thoughts: Night IX, *op. cit.*, l. 1519
22 Gay, 'A Contemplation on Night', l. 27
23 Goldsmith, *op. cit.*, Vol. I, pp. 6–7
24 Broome, 'The XLIII Chapter of Eccelesiasticus: A Paraphrase', *The Works of the English Poets* (Ed.) A. Chalmers (1810) Vol. XII, p. 31

25 M. Browne, 'Essay on the Universe', Book III, l. 171, *Poems on Various Subjects* (1739)
26 Hill, 'Judgement Day': Preface (1721)
27 e.g. Young, 'Night Thoughts: Night IX', *op. cit.*, l. 657; Blackmore, 'The Creation', Book III, *op. cit.*, p. 353
28 Pope, 'Essay on Man', Epistle I, l. 241
29 Young, 'Night Thoughts: Night IX', *op. cit.*, l. 1953
30 Blackmore, 'The Creation', Book II, *op. cit.*, p. 349
31 Thomson, 'The Seasons: Summer', l. 1556
32 Thomson, *op. cit.*, l. 32
33 Blackmore, 'The Creation', Book II, *op. cit.*
34 Thomson, *op. cit.*, l. 94
35 Prior, 'Alma', Canto II, l. 245
36 e.g. Blackmore, 'The Creation', Book III, *op. cit.*, p. 353
37 Prior, *op. cit.*, Canto III, l. 335
38 Young, 'Night Thoughts: Night IX', *op. cit.*, l. 1275
39 Locke, *Essay concerning Human Understanding*, Book IV, Chapter 18
40 Young, 'Night Thoughts: Night IX', *op. cit.*, l. 644
41 *Ibid.*, l. 805
42 *Ibid.*, l. 1663
43 Watts, 'The Creator and Creatures', Stanza 3, *Horae Lyricae* (1709) p. 15
44 Thomson, 'The Seasons: Spring', l. 208
45 Hughes, 'The Ecstasy', *op. cit.*, p. 62
46 Young, 'Night Thoughts: Night IX', *op. cit.*, l. 1226
47 Arbuthnot, *An Essay on the Usefulness of Mathematical Learning*, in *Life and Works of John Arbuthnot* (Ed.) G. A. Aitken (1892) p. 424
48 Dryden, 'Annus Mirabilis', Stanza 163
49 Arbuthnot, *op. cit.*, p. 427
50 Browne, *Pseudodoxia Epidemica*, Book VI, Chapter 14, *The Works of Sir Thomas Browne* (Ed.) G. Keynes (1964) Vol. II, p. 483
51 Wotton, Letter to Sir Edmund Bacon, 5th December, 1638(?) *Life and Letters of Sir Henry Wotton* Logan Pearsall Smith (1907) Vol. II., p. 396
52 Prior, *op. cit.*, Canto III, l. 368
53 Butler, 'The Elephant in the Moon', l. 431
54 *See* Shadwell, *The Virtuoso* (Ed.) M. H. Nicolson and D. S. Rodes (1966)
55 Butler, *op. cit.*, l. 509; l. 519
56 Pope, 'Essay on Man', Epistle II, l. 43
57 *Memoirs of Martinus Scriblerus*, Chapter XVII (Ed.) C. Kerby-Miller (1950) pp. 166–167
58 Young, 'Night Thoughts: Night IX', *op. cit.*, l. 1174
59 Blackmore, 'The Creation', Book V, *op. cit.*, p. 365

60 *Ibid.*
61 Johnson, *The Idler*, No. 3, *Works of Samuel Johnson* (Ed.) W. J. Bate, J. M. Bullitt and L. F. Powell (1963) Vol. II, p. 10
62 *Memoirs of Martinus Scriblerus, op. cit.*, p. 168
63 *Ibid.*
64 Shadwell, *The Virtuoso*, Act. V, Scene II, l. 80
65 Pepys, *Diary* : 19th August, 1666
66 Young, 'Satire V: On Women', *The Works of the English Poets* (Ed.) A. Chalmers (1810) Vol. XIII, p. 393
67 Swift, *Gulliver's Travels: Voyage to Laputa, etc.*, Chapter II (Ed.) L. A. Landa (1965) p. 132
68 Swift, *A True and Faithful Narrative of What passed in London*, in *Prose Works of Jonathan Swift* (Ed.) T. Scott (1910) Vol. IV, p. 278
69 Swift, *Gulliver's Travels: Voyage to Laputa, etc.*, Chapter III, *op. cit.*, p. 137
70 Swift, *ibid.*, Chapter VIII, *op. cit.*, p. 160
71 Swift, 'Apollo's Edict', l. 12; l. 20, *Collected Poems of Jonathan Swift* (Ed.) J. Horrell (1958) Vol. II, pp. 592–593
72 Thomson, 'The Seasons: Summer', l. 1730
73 Pope, 'Essay on Man', Epistle I, l. 249
74 Desaguliers, 'The Newtonian System of the World', *op. cit.*, pp. 23–26 (See also the 'Introduction')

Chapter VII

1 Johnson, Letter to Susannah Thrale: 25th March, 1784, *The Letters of Samuel Johnson* (Ed.) R. W. Chapman (1952) Vol. III, p. 144
2 Armstrong, 'The Art of Preserving Health', Book II, l. 550, *The Potential Works of Armstrong, Dyer and Green* (Ed.) G. Gilfillan (1858) pp. 29–30
3 Smart, 'On the Eternity of the Supreme Being', *The Collected Poems of Christopher Smart* (Ed.) N. Callan (1949) Vol. I, pp. 223–224
4 Darwin, 'The Botanic Garden (Part I): The Economy of Vegetation', Canto IV, l. 385
5 Cowper, 'The Task', Book III, l. 150
6 Steele, 'The Elevation', Stanza 1, *Hymns, Psalms and Poems* (1882)
7 Kershaw, 'The Methodist', *See* H. N. Fairchild, *Religious Trends in English Poetry* (1942) Vol. II, p. 93
8 Cowper, *op. cit.*, Book III, l. 252
9 Kingsley, *The Meteor Shower*, in *The Water of Life and Other Sermons* (1890) p. 180
10 Blake, 'Milton', Book II (43), l. 3
11 Blake, 'The Everlasting Gospel', l. 35

12 e.g. *Ibid.*, l. 45
13 Blake, 'Europe: A Prophecy (11)', l. 4
14 Blake, Annotation to Reynold's Discourse VII, *Poetry and Prose of William Blake* (Ed.) G. Keynes (1927) p. 1010
15 Blake, 'Milton', Book II (42), l. 11
16 Blake, 'Milton', Book II (28), l. 4; l. 8; l. 15
17 Ashmand, *Ptolemy's Tetrabiblos* (1822)
18 Campbell, Letter of September 15, 1813, *Life and Letters of Thomas Campbell* (Ed.) W. Beattie (1849) Vol. II, pp. 234–235
19 Hazlitt, *Flaxman's Lectures on Sculpture*, in *Complete Works of William Hazlitt* (Ed.) P. P. Howe (1933) Vol. 16, pp. 339–340
20 Keats, 'On First Looking into Chapman's Homer', l. 9
21 Burney, *Diary*: 3rd October, 1788, *Diary and Letters of Madame D'Arblay* (Ed.) C. Barrett (1892) Vol. III, p. 45
22 Clough, 'The New Sinai', Stanza 5
23 Darwin, *op. cit.*, Canto I, l. 103
24 Tennyson, 'Epilogue', *Poetical Works of Tennyson* (1953) p. 530
25 Darwin, *op. cit.*, Canto I, l. 107
26 Powell, *See* C. C. Gillispie *Genesis and Geology* (1959) p. 182
27 Disraeli, *Tancred*, Chapter IX (Bradenham Edition: 1927) Vol. X, p. 112
28 Coleridge, *Inquiring Spirit* (Ed.) K. Coburn (1951) Note 113, p. 139
29 Coleridge, *op. cit.*, Note 200, p. 257
30 Coleridge, In: *Coleridge on the Seventeenth Century* (Ed.) R. F. Brinkley (1955) p. 46
31 Coleridge, Letter to Poole: 23rd March, 1801, *Collected Letters of Samuel Taylor Coleridge* (Ed.) E. L. Griggs (1956) Vol. II, p. 709
32 Coleridge, *Biographia Epistolaris* (Ed.) A. Turnbull (1911) Vol. I, pp. 130–131
33 Coleridge, 'The Ancient Mariner'*, l. 210
34 *Ibid.*, l. 313
35 Wordsworth 'Lines written as a School Exercise at Hawkshead'
36 Wordsworth, 'The Prelude'†, Book VI, l. 115
37 Wordsworth, 'The Prelude', Book III, l. 61
38 Wordsworth, 'The Tables Turned', l. 29
39 Wordsworth, 'Star-Gazers', l. 29
40 Wordsworth, 'The Prelude', Book IV, l. 247
41 Dorothy Wordsworth, *Journal*: 29th January, 1802, *Journals of Dorothy Wordsworth* (Ed.) E. de Selincourt (1941) Vol. I, p. 104
42 Wordsworth, 'The Prelude', Book V, l. 88
43 Wordsworth, 'The Excursion', Book IV, l. 947
44 Wordsworth, 'To the Moon (Rydal)', l. 40

* 1834 version
† 1850 version

45 Keats, 'Lamia', Book II, l. 229
46 Shelley, 'Prometheus Unbound', Act II, Scene II, l. 71
47 Shelley, 'The Witch of Atlas', Stanza III, l. 65
48 Cowper, 'The Task', Book II, l. 58
49 Shelley, 'Queen Mab', Part I, l. 252
50 Shelley, 'Queen Mab', Part VI, l. 44
51 Shelley, 'Prometheus Unbound', Act IV, l. 444
52 Whitehead, *Science and the Modern World* (1925) Chapter V,
    p. 105
53 Milton, 'Paradise Lost', Book IV, l. 776
54 Housman, 'Revolution'
55 Tennyson, 'The Ancient Sage', *op. cit.*, p. 511
56 Lodge, In: *Tennyson and his Friends* (Ed.) Hallam Tennyson
    (1911) pp. 280–284
57 Sir Norman Lockyer and W. L. Lockyer, *Tennyson as a Student and
    Poet of Nature* (1910) p. 2
58 Tennyson, 'Locksley Hall', *op. cit.*, p. 91
59 Frost, 'The Star-Splitter', l. 1
60 Tennyson, 'Merlin and Vivien', *op. cit.*, p. 361
61 Tennyson, e.g. 'Maud', Part I, iii, *op. cit.*, p. 269; 'In Mem-
    oriam', CI, *op. cit.*, p. 256; 'The Princess; A Medley', Part IV,
    op. cit., p. 175
62 Tennyson, e.g. 'The Palace of Art', *op. cit.*, p. 42; 'Locksley
    Hall Sixty Years After', *op. cit.*, p. 525
63 Tennyson, 'The Lady of Shalott', Part III, *op. cit.*, p. 27
64 Tennyson, 'Locksley Hall Sixty Years After', *op. cit.*, p. 525
65 Tennyson, *See*: Sir Norman Lockyer and W. L. Lockyer, *op. cit.*,
    p. 78
66 Sir Norman Lockyer and W. L. Lockyer, *op. cit.*, p. 31 (footnote)
67 Tennyson, 'In Memoriam', XXI, *op. cit.*, p. 235
68 Tennyson, 'Eleanore', Stanza VI, *op. cit.*, p. 22
69 Tennyson, 'To E. Fitzgerald', *op. cit.*, p. 499
70 Darwin, *op. cit.*, Canto II, l. 76
71 Tennyson, 'In Memoriam', CVXIII, *op. cit.*, p. 261
72 Tennyson, 'The Princess; A Medley', Part II, *op. cit.*, p. 162
73 Tennyson, 'Parnassus', Stanza II, *op. cit.*, pp. 810–811
74 Tennyson, 'Lucretius', *op. cit.*, p. 150
75 Tennyson, 'God and the Universe', Stanza I, *op. cit.*, p. 830
76 Tennyson, 'Locksley Hall', *op. cit.*, p. 91 *et seq.*
77 Tennyson, 'Epilogue', *op. cit.*, p. 530
78 Tennyson, 'In Memoriam', CXXIV, *op. cit.*
79 Hardy, 'At a Lunar Eclipse'
80 Hardy, *Two on a Tower*, Chapter IV (1952 Edition) p. 33
81 Compare: Montgomery, 'Satan', in: H. N. Fairchild, *Religious
    Trends in English Poetry* (1957) Vol. IV, p. 35; Dowden 'A
    Child's Noonday Sleep', *Ibid.*, p. 94
82 Swinburne' 'The Commonweal', Stanza XXV

83 Meredith, 'Meditation Under Stars'
84 Hopkins, *Journal*: 22nd May, 1872, *The Journals and Papers of Gerard Manley Hopkins* (Ed.) H. House and G. Storey (1959) p. 220
85 Hopkins, *Journal*: 24th September, 1870, *op. cit.*, p. 200
86 Hopkins, *Journal*: 27th November, 1872, *op. cit.*, pp. 227–228
87 Thompson, 'A Dead Astronomer'
88 Huxley, *On the Advisableness of Improving Natural Knowledge. Lay Sermons* (1883) pp. 13–14
89 Carlyle, *Sartor Resartus*, Chapter X
90 Yeats, 'Song of the Happy Shepherd'
91 Reade, *The Martyrdom of Man*, Chapter IV (1924 edition) p. 423
92 Tennyson, 'In Memoriam', CXVIII, *op. cit.*, p. 261
93 Pope, 'The Dunciad', Book IV, l. 451
94 Clough, 'Uranus'
95 Earl of Malmesbury, *Memoirs of an Ex-minister* (1885) p. 399
96 Wells, *The Scientific Romances of H. G. Wells* Preface (1933)
97 Graves and Lucas, *The War of the Wenuses* (1898) pp. 91–92
98 Wells, *op. cit.*, Preface
99 Wells, *The First Men in the Moon* (1901) Chapter XIII, p. 142
100 Carroll, *Sylvie and Bruno Concluded*, Chapter XIII, *The Complete Works of Lewis Carroll* (1939) p. 557

INDEX